DUST in the ROAD

RECOLLECTIONS OF A DELTA BOY

*"Come in, sit down and close the do'…
let me tell you some of
everything I know."*

– Duff Dorrough

A Collection of Stories from *Delta Magazine*

HANK BURDINE

Dust in the Road: Recollections of a Delta Boy

For information contact:

Coopwood Publishing Group, Inc.

P. O. Box 117, 125 South Court Street

Cleveland, Mississippi 38732

662.843.2700

deltamagazine.com

ISBN: 978-0-692-17918-5

Printed in Canada

FIRST EDITION

COVER PHOTO: Taken on the front porch at Gum Grove Plantation, Pluto, Mississippi by Micaela Cianci
Photo on page 4 and 5 by John Monfort Jones

Acknowledgement

A very special thanks and gratitude to my publisher and editors at *Delta Magazine* for believing in me and providing the platform and the opportunity for me to write these stories down for posterity. This magical, mystical, and magnificent place we call the Delta is a lure and a place held dear by all of us who have ever called it home. And many thanks to my readers who have hopefully never been bored with my scribbles. There are many more Delta stories out there. We have just begun.

– Hank Burdine

TO MY SALLIE

Who moved to the Mississippi Delta after I said to her,
"Stick around, kid, I'll teach you a trick or two..."
Guess who taught whom?

Foreword

A couple of years ago at Howard Brent's Panther Tract, a 4400-acre wilderness paradise near the Yazoo River, Hank Burdine staged a re-enactment of the fateful Mississippi Delta bear hunt at which President Theodore Roosevelt famously did not shoot a tethered bear. Though Hank's hunt was held more than a century after the original, he pulled off an event that was both a faithful homage and a contemporary celebration. He laid an enormous bonfire, erected tents, and planned a festive opening night feast. He assembled the direct descendants of the original hunters—including Simon Roosevelt, Teddy's great-great grandson, and Huger Foote, whose great grandfather and namesake had been with Roosevelt back at camp enjoying a sandwich and libation when the bear came tearing through their blind (thus leading to his captivity). He also made the rules: like their predecessors, the hunters were on horseback and allowed to use only knives on their quarry (which in this case were the feral hogs currently even more populous than the black bear was in the early days of the 20th century).

From start to finish the event was pure Hank. It spoke to his deep love and knowledge of history and of the Delta itself. Of his abiding respect for our forbears as well as the land and all its creatures. Of his good taste (the tent in which the governor slept was outfitted with an Oriental rug) and his prowess at pretty much everything from making the perfect bloody mary to building a spectacular and seemingly endless bonfire. And like all events organized by Hank—from impromptu road trips to a Bluegrass and Barbecue Festival—it was enormous fun. To borrow a phrase from Larry Pryor, one of the great Delta characters profiled in this book, Hank can *always*, always be counted on to "keep up the hurrah." He is both prodigious Master of the Hunt and beloved Master of the Hurrah.

While he has long been a marvelous ambassador of the region we both love so much, he has lately—blessedly—become its historian. It turns out that Hank can write as well as he can talk a story. Whether charting the invention of that immortal gourmet treat, the fried dill pickle, or reminding us of the greatness of the artists and musicians we've been lucky enough to have among us, he is preserving our serious history and chronicling some of our highest times (the pieces on the late great One Block East and Mink's Supper Club come immediately to mind).

Like Hank, I grew up in Greenville, but I learned a hell of a lot from his dispatches—about everything from Larry Pryor's "seasonal rituals" and raucous mule races to how much Henry Johnson paid a river pirate for the three thousand acres of prime cotton land that became Chatham, Mississippi ($50 and a keg of whiskey). He writes fondly of singer and pianist Muriel Wilkins (who inspired the Marc Cohn hit "Walking in Memphis") and the celebrated restaurateur Mary Mahoney (of course, he was great friends with both). He takes deep dives into the careers of Matsy Wynn Richards, the groundbreaking photographer, and Leon Koury the brilliant Greenville sculptor who studied under Malvina Hoffman. He writes not just of Holt Collier, the legendary African American hunting guide who wrestled and subdued Roosevelt's lucky bear, but also of his noble dog Jocko. His pieces are important reminders of the Delta's arduous beginnings and cultural richness. But there are frivolities too. Now, we all can relive the night Hank lost his britches at a Debutante party in Beulah.

So, with this volume, Hank has added to his titles. A million years ago, I knew him as Uncle Red, host of multitudes of memorable parties in his houses both downtown and on Lake Ferguson, the friend who got me out of countless teenage scrapes and who, occasionally, set me on the right path. Since then, far more importantly, he has been a devoted husband and super supportive single father. But no matter what his role, he has never lost his enthusiasm for life its own self. Everybody who is lucky enough to know him knows that joy is in the offing whenever Hank turns up with his truck or his boat, his grill, and his succulent supply of duck poppers. He is the inventor of the now-fabled Sandbar Boombox and enabler of countless good times, whether in a duck hole or at Doe's Eat Place (where he is a member of the family). But he is also a profound poet of place. And we are all better for it.

– Julia Reed

Introduction

My mama, Baby Jane Rule, always said that it was the people that made the Delta so special and unique. I agree, as I did on most things with her however, I believe that it was the inimitable circumstances that made those very people so special and unique. By the turn of the twentieth century, only a small percentage of what we call the Delta, not the actual crow's foot delta of the Mississippi River below New Orleans but our Delta, had been cleared and was habitable. This almond shaped wedge of land began at the base of the Chickasaw Bluffs below Memphis and carved its way southward along the Loess Hills, following the hill-born streambeds of the Coldwater, Yocona, Yalabousha, Tallahatchie, and Yazoo Rivers. (Damn, don't you love those names!) And when the frothy waters hit Walnut Ridge just north of Vicksburg, they spilled out into and were gobbled up by the Mississippi River. Between the hills and the big river were interior streams called the Sunflower, Big Sunflower, Little Sunflower, Quiver River, Fighting Bayou, Deer Creek, Black Bayou, and numerous others. These streams and the Mississippi River knew no bounds, and they flooded annually, sometimes two or three times each year.

Because of the historic annual floods, the riparian banks of the rivers and streams were replenished during each high-water cycle with silt and humus accumulated from over 41 percent of the continental United States and two provinces of Canada. The excess rainwater from the Appalachian Mountains to the Rocky Mountains came right through our front door. In its path was left possibly the most fertile soil on earth. It has been said of Deer Creek, which at one time began on the east bank of the Mississippi River, "God could have made better dirt than Deer Creek, but He figured He just didn't need to." In some places the topsoil is almost 150 feet deep. And this fecund land grew trees, huge trees. White, red, and water oak, ash, gum, pecan, sycamore, black willow, hackberry, and bald cypress trees grew in unfettered abundance. Each year this bottomland was replenished and nourished with nutrients and moisture from the rise and fall of the rivers. And because of the meandering and shifting course of the Mississippi River and others, the Delta was flat, very flat and fertile. And in this jungle of enormous trees and almost impenetrable canebrakes, thickets and swamps lived black bear, panther, wild turkey, deer, monstrous alligators and alligator snapping turtles, cottonmouth water moccasins, and diamond backed rattlesnakes. In the bayous, lakes, and sloughs swam huge needle-nosed and alligator gar, flathead catfish, perch, bream, and bass. Every winter came 40 percent of all migrating North American waterfowl, blackening the skies as ducks and geese sought refuge amidst the smorgasbord of acorns, pecans, and wild grass seeds, floating on the rivers and sloughs and in the flooded bottomland hardwood forests.

And by the turn of the last century, the West had been won, belching and smoking steam locomotives on transcontinental railroads were carrying goods, products, and produce coast to coast, the gold had been dug out of California and Alaska, and the very last frontier in America was this mosquito ridden, almost uninhabitable, flood ravaged, and un-accessible swamp we call the Delta. Before the Civil War, Natchez had been known to harbor more millionaires per capita than anyplace else in our country. South Carolinians had ventured upriver from Natchez and accessed the beautiful Lake

Washington in the middle of the Delta, as had patriarchal Kentuckians coming downriver on flatboats. Settlers had crept upstream from Vicksburg into its heart at Rolling Fork on packet boats steaming up Steele Bayou, Deer Creek, and the Sunflower Rivers, clearing the canebrakes and cutting the huge trees to farm the lush ground that was waiting for the plow. Northern timber companies realized the immense wealth of hardwood and cypress that was waiting to be harvested. Railroad companies began nudging steam whistled and clanging locomotives ever deeper into the north Delta, hauling out the massive logs to screaming sawmills in Memphis. The railroads then began to sell to farmers the excess right-of-way that had been granted to them from the state. Protective and solidly designed well-built levees were being built in a coordinated effort to bring some sort of flood control to the Delta. The last frontier was being cleared as King Cotton took hold, and the wealth, culture, and societal ways of the aristocratic newcomers, along with the blues infused, back breaking labor force that allowed it all to happen, dug deep into this wonderful dirt, and soon it all began to blossom, eventually creating our beloved Mississippi Delta.

From aristocrats to peddlers and hardworking Chinese, Lebanese, Jewish, and Italian families, along with the myriads of African American hard working and dedicated legions, this Delta was wrought out of a steaming jungle. Literary, artistic, musical, and political greats emerged as the levees were built and the waters receded and were held at bay and the steel plows crept further and further into the heart of this "…land which man has deswamped and denuded and derivered in two generations," as William Faulkner described in his novel, *Big Woods*.

My granddaddy, James Rule, came with his brothers and their daddy from Kentucky to clear the trees and farm along Lehrton Landing on the Sunflower River. Once they built a sawmill, the Rules started planting cotton and then built a gin and a commissary and eventually started a bank, only to lose it all during the Great Depression by selling off what they had to keep the bank solvent, before closing the doors. My grandmother, Lida Word, came from the Black Belt Prairie region of east Mississippi and after losing her husband and all they had, bought some bulbs from Montgomery Ward in Chicago and opened Rule's Flower Shop in Ruleville, Mississippi. My daddy was from South Carolina yet worked his way here building concrete roads throughout the Delta, where only dirt roads previously existed. He always said, "I got Baby Jane out of Parchman" (Mississippi State Penitentiary at Parchman). Actually, she was the secretary to the warden at the time, and he was building the highway through the middle of the penitentiary when he met her. So, it is my belief, in agreement with my mama, that while the people of the Delta are what makes it so unique, it is the fact that in most cases it was our grandparents and great-grandparents that were the true pioneers of this region. And it was that pioneering spirit and blood and guts and tears and sweat that beat the Mississippi River back, felled the trees, and began to plow and mold the richest land imaginable in order to give to us today the Mississippi Delta.

– Hank Burdine

Contents

Early Delta

14   Bicentennial Plantation—Deep Dirt, Deep Roots, Deep Delta Legacies *(September/October 2016)*

18   Before Cotton was King—Timber Ruled *(January/February 2011)*

22   Heathman Plantation—When Cotton was King *(September/October 2010)*

27   The Paradox of Parchman Farm *(July/August 2013)*

32   Hopson Plantation—Model for Mechanization *(September/October 2013)*

36   The Great Bear Hunters of the Mississippi Delta *(November/December 2007)*

41   Holt's Feisty Friend *(November/December 2015)*

45   Bootlegging—The Oil of Conversation *(November/December 2008)*

49   Cotton in the Delta *(September/October 2017)*

52   Paving the Way *(November/December 2013)*

Indomitable Delta Characters

58   The Bride of Annandale *(January/February 2009)*

62   The Enigma of Willa Johnson *(March/April 2008)*

66   How Matsy Made History *(September/October 2008)*

70   The Life of a Delta General *(May/June 2009)*

74   Rosedale Moon and the Untouchable Perry Martin *(September/October 2007)*

78   Hot Moore—Super Cowman of the South *(November/December 2011)*

82   Larry Pryor—Delta Bon Vivant *(May/June 2008)*

86   The Birth of an Industry *(May/June 2010)*

89   Joe's Calling *(March/April 2014)*

93   Viva, La King Silky! *(May/June 2007)*

97   Buckwheat Wade—The Blond Bomber *(July/August 2014)*

100   The Lady Behind the Levee Who Wouldn't Leave *(March/April 2013)*

104   Muddy Water Ruskey *(January/February 2015)*

108   The Duck Doctor *(November/December 2014)*

112   Lil' Buck's First River Hunt *(November/December 2010)*

114   Matt's Journey *(May/June 2017)*

Delta Artists

120   A Remnant of a Wall *(March/April 2018)*

124   From the Hands of a Master *(July/August 2018)*

128   For the Love of Franke *(July/August 2008)*

132   The French Canadian Duo of the Delta *(November/December 2012)*

136   The Coffee House Blues of Leon Koury *(September/October 2008)*

140   As His World Turned *(January/February 2012)*

144   Casting Call *(September/October 2009)*

Delta Musicians

150 Sittin' on Top of the World *(May/June 2012)*

153 The Gentle Giant *(July/August 2016)*

157 True Blues *(July/August 2010)*

159 White House Blues *(January/February 2007)*

160 Nothing but the Blues *(September/October 2015)*

164 Walkin' in Memphis with Muriel and Marc *(March/April 2007)*

168 Muddy Water in His Blood *(March/April 2010)*

172 From Hellhole, Mississippi, to Carnegie Hall *(March/April 2016)*

176 Muddy Waters—Mannish Boy *(March/April 2017)*

179 Gentle Jerry—The Killer's Softer Side *(July/August 2011)*

A Bite to Eat and Drink in the Delta

184 5 O'clock in the Delta *(September/October 2014)*

189 Doe's Eat Place—A Cut Above *(September/October 2006)*

192 Meet Me at Mink's *(July/August 2007)*

195 Dinty Moore's Shady Nook Café *(March/April 2006)*

197 The Delta Deep Fried *(July/August 2013)*

199 Delta Hospitality on the Mississippi Gulf Coast *(May/June 2016)*

203 The Legacy of Lillo's *(March/April 2015)*

206 One Block East *(May/June 2013)*

210 Doe's Walls *(January/February 2014)*

A Few Places to Go in the Delta

216 The Legacy of Beaver Dam Lake *(January/February 2010)*

220 Croquet, Anyone? *(May/June 2014)*

223 Navigating the Delta Mystique *(January/February 2016)*

And Then Some

228 Alligator Hunting in the Delta *(September/October 2017)*

231 Fall is Festival Time in the Delta *(November/December 2017)*

234 Forsaking Finlay *(July/August 2015)*

238 Teddy's Return *(May/June 2015)*

241 The "Britchesless" Bachelor *(November/December 2008)*

Early Delta

Bicentennial Plantation—Deep Dirt, Deep Roots, Deep Delta Legacies

About the time of the Treaty of Dancing Rabbit Creek in 1830, the Treaty of Pontotoc, 1832, and after the Indian Removal Act of 1828, removing the Five Civilized Tribes of Native Americans, the Choctaws, Chickasaws, Cherokees, Seminoles, and Creeks, to the west, the Mississippi Delta, as we know it, was being defined. Land then could be bought from the state or from Native Americans that had acquired title to their ancestral lands through terms and conditions of the respective treaties. The young country was on the move. There were dense bottomland hardwood forests to be cleared and cotton to be planted and civilization to be brought to the deep and fecund swamplands of the South. However, for thousands of years, it had been inhabited by indigenous native people; yet, it was soon to be known as our Mississippi Delta.

It is believed, according to Spanish records, that in May of 1541, Hernando Desoto first viewed the Mississippi River from atop an Indian mound south of Memphis. This mound is located due east of what was to become a major shipping point on the Mississippi River at a bend known as Commerce Landing. By 1841, Commerce Landing was the county seat of Tunica County, had a population of five thousand people, and was known to rival neighboring Memphis as a trading center. Vicksburg and Natchez shared top billings with Commerce Landing as river towns with the highest tonnage of shipped cotton. But Memphis, Vicksburg, and Natchez sat atop bluffs, and Commerce was nestled on the flat high bank of the great Mississippi River.

According to a decades-old article in *Delta Review,* a steam powered packet boat named *Desoto* operated a busy schedule up and down the river with Commerce as its home port. However, by 1844 the river began eating away at its banks, and in Commerce, building after building fell into the swift current. The Western Bank of Commerce, which printed its own bills regionally known as "solid money," soon closed their doors. By 1848 the county seat was moved fifteen miles south to Austin, but that location was also threatened by the ever-changing river. Finally, the town of Tunica became the county seat and remains as such today.

In 1832, identical twin brothers Richard and Anthony Abbay came from Nashville and bought land from the state and also from Chickasaw Indians that had received lands according to the treaty of Pontotoc, paying fifty cents an acre for the Indian lands. A sizable place was put together by the brothers, and homes were built that later would also fall into the river. The Abbay brothers married the Compton sisters, and when Anthony's wife became disillusioned with the harsh, almost frontier Delta life and begged to return to the hills of Nashville, Anthony abided in her wishes and sold his land to his brother and moved away.

Richard Abbay had three sons and one daughter. One son died as a youth and another moved away. When Richard's wife Mary died in childbirth with his one daughter, he bade his remaining son Richard Felix to never marry, and he remained a bachelor his entire life. After the Civil War, Richard's daughter, Mary Susan, met and married Dr. George Washington Leatherman from Woodville. Upon Dr. Leatherman's untimely and

KAREN PULFER FOCHT

early death, Mary Susan soon moved home to the plantation with her son, Samuel Richard Leatherman. When Richard Abbay died, his son Richard Felix entered into a partnership with his nephew S.R. Leatherman in 1893. The place came to be known, and is today, as the Abbay and Leatherman Plantation.

Additional acreage was added whenever the occasion arose until a sizable place had been put together. Never one to sell any land, Richard Abbay had the foresight to sell his cotton for gold instead of Confederate money when war broke out and buried it all in a rather large teapot on the place. After the war, and retrieving his loaded teapot, he was able to keep the farm together and even add more holdings. When one of his granddaughters died after receiving an early inheritance, Richard was forced to buy the family land back from her widower at an exorbitant price. Showing his dislike for his grandson-in-law, Richard Abbay left in his will for this particular man, "one dollar and my undying hatred."

When S.R. Leatherman II decided to build a house, he chose a location adjoining the Indian mound from which Desoto first saw the mighty Mississippi River. He built a rambling Tudor-style home on a mound of dirt brought in next to the original Indian mound. According to a poignant memoir by Carroll Seabrook Leatherman, *Goodbye, Ole Miss*, her great-grandmother-in-law, "an eccentric old lady who always dressed in black when not in bed with a migraine, refused to let her grandson build anything on the Indian mound, believing that the spirits of the Indian dead resided there." Currently the "Desoto" Mound is resplendent with huge oak and pecan trees and well-kept gardens adorning its sides.

The Abbay and Leatherman Plantation is still in the hands of the family with additional lands having been added throughout the years. Against the original Richard Abbay's intent of never selling any land, but surely with a consequential wink of a good business deal, a small parcel of the original plantation was sold. A part of the Chickasaw lands, close to the river and deeded by the mark of an X, sits underneath the elaborate Sam's Town Casino.

Treaty of Dancing Rabbit Creek, Seeds of Stovall Farms

Some remember a historical marker sign that used to stand at the intersection of Highways 61 and 450 south of Shaw and close by the small town of Choctaw. It marked the southern boundary of the Treaty of Dancing Rabbit Creek of 1830 that deeded away lands held by the Choctaw Indian Tribe. One farm that goes back to that treaty is Stovall Farms, northwest of Clarksdale along the Mississippi River.

William Oldham came to the Mississippi Delta from South Carolina to cut timber about 1830. According to Stovall family papers, he acquired several tracts of land for $1.25 an acre and began clearing the timber and farming cotton. He married Nancy Carver; however, she decided to move back to South Carolina, freeing her servants and giving each of them forty acres of land and building them a church. Some took her surname, and certain tracts of Carver land remain on the county tax rolls today. In 1866, their granddaughter married Confederate Colonel William Howard Stovall II, a Memphis lawyer who had served as adjutant to the 154th Tennessee Regiment, and they moved to Coahoma County to run the plantation.

The Stovall family has long served their country beginning with William Howard Stovall Sr. serving in the War of 1812. W.H. Stovall III graduated from Yale in 1918 and went on to serve as a lieutenant in the U.S. Army Air Corps, 13th Air Squadron during WWI. He is credited with six aerial victories and received the Distinguished Flying Cross, the Victory Medal, the Legion of Merit with Oak Leaf Cluster, the Bronze Star, the Order of the British Empire, European Theatre of Operations Ribbon with five battle stars, the French Legion d'Honneur, and the Croix de Guerre. As a decorated fighter pilot, Howard Stovall returned home to the Delta and became a well-respected plantation manager and businessman. He returned to active duty as a major after the bombing of Pearl Harbor, soon to become a colonel serving as deputy chief of staff for the U.S. Strategic Air Force during WWII in England with several of his prior WWI comrades. He retired as a brigadier general. His son William Howard Stovall IV followed in his daddy's footsteps but was killed in action after downing two enemy aircraft while engaging seven over Bergsteinfurt, Germany. He is buried in Margraten, Holland.

While not defending our country, Howard Stovall III was at home on the farm. His land stewardship and pre-imminence in conservation practices garnered him much recognition including the Delta Council Achievement Award for 1967-68. He served as president of Cotton Council International and was awarded the Fiftieth Anniversary Medal for Contributions to American Agriculture by the Federal Land

Bank Association. He was the inspiration for the character Colonel Harvey Stovall in the book and movie *Twelve O'Clock High* starring Gregory Peck.

Cotton, corn, and soybeans have not been the only thing raised on Stovall Farms; the blues have been known to raise a ruckus on weekends also. McKinley Morganfield, better known as Muddy Waters, spent most of his first thirty years living in a hand-hewn cypress log cabin and working on the farm. It was here in 1941 that Alan Lomax came south to the Delta and recorded field workers for the Library of Congress. Soon after being recorded, Muddy moved to Chicago and established himself as the King of Chicago Blues. The log cabin has been moved and now sits in the Delta Blues Museum in Clarksdale. Muddy's induction into the Blues Hall of Fame in 1981 and the Rock 'n' Roll Hall of Fame in 1987, share a stone monument along with a Mississippi Blues Trail marker on the site of his home at the edge of a pecan orchard and cotton field. Carrying on Muddy's tradition, William Howard Stovall V resides in Memphis where he has been deeply involved in blues revitalization and awareness as past head of the Blues Foundation and currently a partner in the Resource Entertainment Group.

Today, Stovall Farms continues under family ownership and management with Gil Stovall overseeing all operations of Stovall Farms. The almost two-hundred-year-old plantation stands out as a prime example of good stewardship and land supervision. Stovall Farms has hosted numerous distinguished field trips including conservation and innovative technological farm practice tours. Farm Bureau and conservation districts have cited Stovall Farms as a model for pioneering state-of-the art farm practices. Utilizing precision land leveling and conservative irrigation practices, modern drainage techniques have been implemented with on-farm tailwater recovery and irrigation water storage methods using filter strips and cover crops. Stovall Farms is indeed a model plantation and quite a beautiful place to behold. The Lonesome Dove Sporting Club hosts an annual dove hunt on well-appointed fields such as the Dancing Rabbit Creek Field adjacent to Stovall family relative's original homestead "Seven Chimneys Farm," circa 1840.

History, heritage, culture, and dirt run deep in the Delta. The rich land and founding families intertwine like the fast-reaching and far-roaming muscadine vines that ran rampant through the verdant swamps and ridges of our flat land. What an interesting time it is that we live in to be able to realize this history and legacy and to conserve it for future generations.

Before Cotton was King—Timber Ruled

The Mississippi Delta, as we know it, is the alluvial floodplain of the Mississippi and Yazoo Rivers—bounded on the north by the Chickasaw Bluffs below Memphis, the east by the Loess Hills and Yazoo River, and the west by the Mississippi River. For eons, annual floodwaters inundated the flat land with excess rainwater coming out of the hills from the Tallahatchie, Coldwater, Yocona, and Yalobusha Rivers and from the Mississippi, which drains 41 percent of the continental United States and parts of two provinces in Canada. This flood plain was an impenetrable virgin hardwood bottomland forest covered with towering oak, cypress, cottonwood, elm, pecan, sycamore, sweet, red, and tupelo gums, and hackberry trees, among others. Indians lived and thrived along the high riparian riverbanks of the waterways growing maize (corn) and gathering nuts and berries and wild game from the forest and fish, turtles, and mussels from its many lakes and streams.

Because of its impenetrability and the annual flooding, not to mention yellow fever, malaria, oppressive heat, mosquitoes, bears, panthers, poisonous snakes, alligators, and other hardships of the region, the Mississippi Delta was one of the last frontiers in the nation to be settled. Following the Civil War, only a few areas had been cleared for cultivation along the Mississippi River and some interior streams. Ninety percent of the hardwood bottomlands in the Delta were yet to be cleared. In order to raise a crop, the timber had to first be cut and used for building purposes or burned. Some of the timber was marketed downriver by building log rafts and floating the logs to a mill far away. There was no transportation system in the Delta as roads were too hard to build in the yet to be drained and leveed swamp, and railroads had at this time no reason to nudge into the deep woods. Yet several things happened that would forever change the face and character of our Delta homeland.

The invention of the cotton gin enabled the widespread production of short staple cotton and thus made the fertile ridges of the Delta a prime location for planting cotton. Sharecropping and tenant farming made the clearing and cultivation of this land very profitable. The two-handled crosscut saw replaced the ax in felling the huge trees. Railroad companies saw the opportunity to buy great tracts of land and right-of-way from the state for their railroads and to re-sell surplus lands to timber investors and farmers wanting to move into the Delta and clear that land to farm. (At that time, cotton, timber, and other products could be hauled out on the new railroads.) And by the mid 1880s, timber reserves in the North and Northeast had become depleted by extensive logging. The major lumber companies of the North, not realizing the generous reproductive capacity of natural forests and following a policy of "cut out and get out," turned their forces to the great softwood forests of the Pacific Northwest, the southern pine and cypress stands of the lower South, and to the hardwood bottomlands of the Arkansas, Louisiana, and Mississippi Deltas. The nation was on a march and growing rapidly with its need for wood products a major part of the growth. In *Origins of the New South,* C. Vann Woodward states, "As for the investment of Northern capital, the South is glad to have it come. We welcome the skilled lumberman with the noisy mill." High ground, with its well-drained and profusely fertile soils was

PHOTO COURTESY OF GOOCH BROTHERS COLLECTION

W.E. Houser, first registered professional full-time forester for Anderson Tully in the 1950s, and a stack of red gum veneer logs. The log he stands by has marked 1,936 board feet of lumber in it.

sold to farmers by the timber companies, and the lower, often waterlogged heavier ground not suitable for farming before the extensive protective levee system was in place, was often turned back over to the state for non-payment of taxes after the timber was cut.

Lumber for houses, veneers, boxes, containers, and furniture was in great demand. The integrated railroad system began to allow the transportation of these products to markets all over America and the world. It was during this time that the South became the nation's most productive lumber manufacturing region. The timber industry was the South's leading industry regarding employees, payroll, revenue, and the geographical spread attributed to its sprawling forests. From 1904 to 1915, Mississippi was ranked third in timber producing states behind Washington and Louisiana.

Because of transportation avenues on the Mississippi River and interconnecting railroads, growing commercial opportunities and banking facilities and proximity to fertile bottomlands with twenty-one varieties of hardwoods from Arkansas, Missouri, and the Mississippi Delta, Memphis became a substantial center for shipment of logs and outsourcing of finished lumber products. Memphis soon became known not only as the "largest spot cotton market in the world" but also proclaimed itself as the "hardwood capital of the world."

Originally logs cut for market had to be transported to a navigable stream by either skidding behind mules or using an ancient caralog, a heavy two-wheeled wagon pulled by oxen. In 1905, the Lindsey brothers from Laurel invented the Lindsey Eight Wheel Log Wagon to replace the caralog. Soon skidders, huge winches attached to long cables,

19

skidded the logs to a rail head where steam log loaders loaded the heavy logs on railcars pulled by small steam locomotives on dummy lines that ended at primitive steam driven "peckerwood" or "ground hog" sawmills erected deep in the woods. These lines connected to other larger railroad lines able to market the processed lumber. As the tracts of land were cleared of marketable lumber, the dummy lines were simply removed and replaced in other areas that had not yet been cut. Because of the growth of the railroads, the number of sawmills in Mississippi grew from 295 in 1880 with a total investment of almost a million dollars to 608 mills in 1899 producing more than a billion board feet of lumber annually. (A board foot is one foot long, one foot wide, and one inch thick.) By 1910, Mississippi's timber industry represented a thirty-nine million dollar capital investment producing over forty-three million in annual revenues.

In 1889, a group of Lake States lumbermen from Benton Harbor, Michigan, decided to move their operations to Memphis and establish headquarters and a mill. The Anderson-Tully Company was formed and with its forward thinking ideas became a dominant force in the timber industry of the region. Anderson-Tully began buying timber land adjacent to the Mississippi River enabling the company to transport its logs to its own mills on the riverbank in Memphis adjacent to the railroad. The ever-growing need for shipping crates, barrels, kegs, boxes, furniture, flooring, veneers, plywood, and lumber allowed the Anderson-Tully Company to grow vertically and horizontally. Anderson-Tully began diversifying and re-investing its profits into more company-owned land, ensuring an economical source of good quality raw material. By utilizing an appreciating company owned investment, and by adhering to responsible forest management of the sustained growth aspect of regenerating forestland, Anderson-Tully was able to withstand many up and down cycles in the timber industry and evolve as a dominant force in the region. With several mills and diversified timber-related factories in Memphis, including its own river flotilla, the Patton-Tully Transportation Company formed in 1906; the company was well set to push forward into the twentieth century.

In 1881, a German immigrant named Herman Paepcke formed a company in Chicago and started a small lumber business and planing mill. As his business grew, he bought out his partners and formed the Chicago Packing Box Company, American Box Company, and later the Chicago Mill and Lumber Company. In 1893 Paepcke formed the Paepcke-Leicht Lumber Company and bought a sawmill in Greenville and twenty-five thousand acres of land on the Mississippi River. By 1909, the company owned over 125,000 acres of timberland in the Delta. Chicago had emerged as America's mail order capital with Montgomery Ward, Marshall Fields, Sears, Roebuck and Co., and Spiegel, among others, needing thousands of boxes and crates to ship products and merchandise into and out of Chicago. The marketing of the mail order catalog became a gold mine for Paepcke with much of the lumber for the boxes coming from his own timberland and mills in the Delta. By 1980, the Chicago Mill and Lumber Company operated three sawmills and two box factories in the Delta and owned over two hundred thousand acres of timberland in Mississippi and Louisiana.

In the interior of the Delta, many smaller mills were bought up by larger operations, and some families emerged as major players in the timber industry. Relocating to Yazoo City from Kentucky around 1900, four brothers of the Gooch family built a mill and began acquiring timberland. Specializing in hardwoods and cypress, the company produced lumber for housing, flooring, and the wooden container industry. The Gooch Brothers Lumber Company owned fifteen sawmills and over one hundred thousand acres of land by 1930.

The great demand for lumber to be used in barrel staves, boxes, crates, fruit, vegetable, and egg containers, kegs, tubs, pails, buckets, and baskets continued until around 1920 when the process for utilizing wood pulp for making strong and versatile corrugated boxes was perfected. Much hardwood was used in early automobile parts and frames until steel mills replaced wood. (One by-product of the excess hardwood used in the automobile industry was a technique developed and marketed as Kingsford Charcoal.) Houses were being built all over America, and hardwood flooring was in great demand. By the mid-'20s Memphis was called home to forty mills and numerous wood product plants. However, following the boom years of the '40s and '50s, with plastics, carpets, and other substitutions for wood products taking precedence, Memphis claimed only one mill by the early 1980s, yet it still had over 150 hardwood-using companies utilizing some sixteen thousand workers. During 1955, 1.2 billion feet of hardwood flooring was sold out of Memphis, yet only ninety-six million feet was sold in 1975. The city had become a marketing instead of a manufacturing mecca for hardwoods.

Anderson-Tully, in its ever-attentive desire to change with cycles and utilize modern technology and scientific regenerative timber management approaches, closed its Memphis operations and moved to Vicksburg in 1955. There it continues today in the hardwood business, supplying quality hardwoods worldwide from its almost three hundred thousand acres of timberland. Anderson-Tully has sawed more than 3.3 billion board feet of hardwood lumber since 1900. Today the Vicksburg operations ship carloads of mixed species of high-grade lumber to lumberyards in the United States and all over the world. Furniture manufacturers using Anderson-Tully lumber include Broyhill, Drexel Heritage, and Henredon Furniture, among others.

The Gooch Lumber Company legacy continues today with third-generation John Gooch Jr., along with Tully family member Kenny Hall, operating Cypress Depot in Ridgeland with a modern band sawmill supplying quality Delta cypress and hardwood products to homes all over the South.

And so the timber boom came in the 1890s and was gone by the 1930s, yet in its path was opened very possibly the most fertile farmland in the world. Over seventeen million acres of timberland had been cut in the lower Mississippi River floodplain with most of those acres going into very productive farmland. Many thousands of acres of the lesser productive and marginal land has been enrolled in WRP/CRP programs developed by Uncle Sam to put these lands back into hardwood trees and wildlife habitat. Will we ever again see the towering, massive forests that our Native American brothers and sisters lived in and depended on? It's doubtful, but we should visit and appreciate our state and national forests and plant an indigenous tree every chance we get.

Heathman Plantation—When Cotton Was King

My grandmother always said, "Nothing goes deeper than dirt." And in the Delta, dirt is DEEP. One of the oldest operating plantations in Sunflower County was known originally as Dogwood Ridge. Christopher Gillespie bought four tracts of land nestled around Indian Bayou west of Indianola totaling about eight thousand acres of cotton and timber in 1854. Land records show that in 1871, Gillespie sold his plantation to J.M. Heathman, and the name was changed to Heathman Plantation.

J.M. Heathman farmed the land for nearly fifteen years but died in 1885, and several years later, his widow Lillie married James A. Crawford, a DeKalb, Mississippi, native. Mr. Crawford was an able businessman who took over management of Heathman Plantation, turning it into a bustling community. The late Vernon Beard, son of longtime farm manager J.C. Beard, remembered being told that at one time four thousand people lived in and around the area. Mr. Crawford was not only responsible for numerous fellow Kemper County citizens relocating to the area as store and gin managers, clerks, and plantation riders but was also instrumental in bringing a large number of Italian families to farm as tenants on Heathman and a satellite farm closer to Shaw called Heathman's Deadening. Many of the successful Italian farming families living now around Shaw and Cleveland came originally to Heathman Plantation as tenant farmers. There is an abandoned cemetery at the old Heathman's Deadening site where many of these Italian immigrants were buried.

A regular stop on the Georgia Pacific Railroad, Heathman acquired a post office on August 13, 1888, and J. Holmes Baker, who had a law office in the depot, was named postmaster. The post office would remain in operation until 1956 when the mail was changed to a rural route of nearby Indianola, the county seat. Mr. Crawford built a store in 1889 along the road across from the railroad tracks. Because of the central location to so many people, Heathman had been made a voting precinct in 1895 and continued as such until 1974. In order that his tenants would have their medical needs met, Crawford brought in Dr. B.H. Campbell, also from Kemper County, and provided the plantation doctor with an office. His drugs arrived on the train in gallon jugs. Crawford paid his salary and gave him a car so he could tend to the needs of tenants that were unable to come to his office, located upstairs in the huge new brick commissary built in 1911. The store carried everything needed to live on the plantation. Boots, saddles, bridles, hoes, cloth, foodstuffs, and staples were all sold on credit to the tenants until harvest time when accounts were settled. The road to Indianola was dirt, as not many living in the Heathman area had transportation. Over time, Dr. Campbell meant so much to the community that thirty-four residents in the surrounding area presented Dr. Campbell with a new car in August of 1928 with a letter of gratitude expressing: "That may we do our small part in making your miles shorter, the bumpy roads smoother, the dark night brighter, we present this Ford with the hope that you and Mrs. Campbell will drive by our doors for many, many more and happy years."

PLANTATION PARTIES: Delta-style Soirees in the Society Pages

In 1894, Mr. Crawford built a big white plantation house described in the local newspaper, *The Sunflower Tocsin,* as "palatial." Upon opening their beautiful new home, the Crawfords gave a party the newspaper described as "one of the grandest entertainments ever given in Sunflower County." The Crawfords chartered a special train from Greenville, and about "thirty-five couples of young, careless, pleasure seeking people got off and made their way to the scene of the festivities." According to the society editor of *The Greenville Times,* "young friends from Washington and Sunflower Counties, and more distant places, arrived. Beauregard's Band furnished the music and the affair was probably the most elaborate and elegant ever given in Sunflower County. Dancing was the chief pleasure of the evening, and a most sumptuous supper was served at midnight." *The Sunflower Tocsin* added, "Ample justice was done in the gorgeous dining hall."

On September 6, 1919, the Crawfords sold Heathman Plantation to Herman Paepcke of Chicago and F. N. Robertshaw of Greenville for $1,100,000 with twenty-one notes at 6 percent interest. (The entire note was subsequently paid off four years later.) The place contained 6,775 acres of cotton, cattle, and timber. Herman Paepcke was a German immigrant who had started a small lumber planing and box manufacturing business in Chicago, which grew into a huge industrial conglomerate. His holdings included the Chicago Mill and Lumber Company in Greenville with a

COTTONLANDIA ARCHIVES

An image of forty tractors lined-up on Billups Plantation attest to the size of the operation in the mid-1950s

sawmill and twenty-five thousand acres of timberland. By 1909, the company owned over 125,000 acres of land.

Remembering growing up on Heathman in the '20s and '30s, the late Vernon Beard recalled memories of one of the first tennis courts to be built in Sunflower County, adjacent to the big house on the plantation. He said he spent many hours on Sundays sweeping the courts for the owners families and friends. As Vernon later became a SEC tennis champion on the Mississippi State team, he obviously found playing time for himself on the court too!

Herman Paepcke died in 1933. His son, Walter Paepcke, took over and grew the corporation, moving the headquarters from Chicago to Greenville in 1965. The Chicago Mill and Lumber Company operated three sawmills and two box factories and by 1980 owned over two hundred thousand acres of timberland in Mississippi and Louisiana. Meanwhile, Walter Paepcke and his wife had become well known in other circles, having gone to Aspen, Colorado, after World War II and formed the Aspen Institute and the Aspen Skiing Company. Their love of the arts and music and their involvement in civic affairs was instrumental in turning Aspen into an "American Salzburg," a reference to the city of culture and music in the Austrian Alps. After Walter Paepcke's death in 1960, his widow Elizabeth made Aspen her home and was known as the Grand Dame of Aspen until she died in 1994.

BECOMING BILLUPS: A Model of Mechanization and Gentleman Farming

Herman Paepcke had married Elizabeth Robertshaw Meade in 1912 and with her brother Frank N. Robertshaw operated Heathman as a model plantation using farm managers to oversee the operations. During this time the entire place was farmed with mules until farm mechanization began to take hold and the early tractors replaced the mules. During the time of transition from mule power to tractor power, farm manager J.C. Beard was dismissed and told to find another job. Beard moved to Greenwood and became a farm manager around Money. The Billups brothers, who were involved in the gas and oil business and had land holdings around Carrollton, became close friends with Beard. The Billups had an interest in acquiring Heathman Plantation, so, taking advantage of Beard's connection, they took him with them to Chicago to meet with Paepcke, who had three-fifths ownership of the plantation. Together, they were able to strike a deal for the Billups family to buy Heathman in December of 1946. It was a classic walk-out proposition, everything sold. Land, mules, implements, and all equipment, including a few early model tractors, buildings, houses, and cattle, all for ninety-two dollars an acre. Returning to Heathman, Beard was asked what he was doing on the place. Mr. Beard produced the signed contract of sale, and according to Tom Robertson replied, "Boys, I was fired as a farm manager of Heathman, but I am back now as general manager, and all of you are fired. So now you go find yourselves another job!" The name of the farm was changed to Billups Plantation, and the mules were soon replaced by modern and more efficient tractors. The beautiful white plantation house was used as a clubhouse for the Billups family until it was torn down in 1974. The big social event each year was a fall dove hunt replete with a sumptuous barbecue afterwards. In *Fevers, Floods and Faith,* a history of Sunflower County by Marie Hemphill, she states that, "On September 28, 1957, the Billups family were hosts for an old-fashioned barbecue for about 250 executives from the food distribution business from New York to California, who were attending the grand opening of the Lewis Grocer Company in Indianola. After the beautiful meal, the visitors were given a tour in air-conditioned buses of the farm operation, which is a model of mechanization."

Soon, Billups Plantation started growing certified seed under the Delta and Pine Land Company brand. While working at the Stoneville Experiment Station, J.C. Calhoun had developed a smooth leaf cotton plant making cotton easier to pick. He was hired in 1959 to move to Billups Plantation to manage the farm and work in the seed program. A graduate entomologist from LSU, Calhoun did not have a PhD but was called Dr. Calhoun anyway. A staunch advocate of "clean farming practices," he kept all ditches and fields as clean as possible and replaced the wooden tenant houses with modern brick homes. According to his daughter Suzanne Boone, "Daddy's rule was six days of work but never any work on Sundays. He never drove a truck, but instead rode up and down the dusty turnrows in his Chevrolet sedan dressed always in khaki pants, shirt, and his gentleman's hat."

Calhoun died in January of 1965 due to an untimely heart attack. J.W. Waldrup was moved to general farm manager upon Calhoun's death. Waldrup had been hired by Mr. Beard as store manager in 1952. "I had a wife and an automobile and I owed for both of them. I ran the store for a year before going out on the farm. I was just a boy that grew up in the cotton patch, but once on the farm, I got my college education from Dr. Calhoun!" When cattleman Joe Clements died, Waldrup told the Billups brothers, "You have 1,700 acres of lush grass and nine hundred head of cattle on the north end. You either need to get into the cattle business in a big way or get out." Soon, the cows were sold, the fences torn down, the pastures disced, and soybeans planted. Waldrup remained general manager until 1998. "Billups Plantation was the finest plantation in the Delta, no question about that," says Waldrup. "It was all in one block with everything right there. In all the years I was manager, we never had a season when we lost money—and that is saying something."

The W.T. Robertson and J.C. Robertson families of nearby Holly Ridge, who owned the adjoining Saint Rest Plantation, began leasing and farming the place in 1998, and in 2007 bought Billups Plantation containing 5,500 acres. The commissary still stands, yet with a new black and white bold painted facade on the red brick building, as its new owners have rechristened it "Heathman Plantation." Corn and rice now adorn the fields north of Highway 82 where the cattle operation had always been. The railroad depot had been torn down and the pit used to store coal for the steam locomotives had been filled with dirt in the 1970s. The cotton gin and loading dock that stood next to the railroad tracks had been demolished. A seed breeding facility where experimental seed research was done under the Bobshaw name is still standing.

Tom Robertson's wife Lois is especially interested in the restoration of the remaining buildings and the recording of the history of Heathman Plantation. Inside the old commissary is a big walk-in safe with two vault doors that contained boxes of records and deeds. Inside the two locked doors was another safe. One title opinion takes the ownership of the deeded land back to the original land grants from the U.S. Government to the State of Mississippi and forward. Tom Robertson remembers as a young man his daddy telling him, "Son, I wanted to buy that place in 1946, but I had just started farming and a hundred dollars an acre was a lot of money back then."

The Paradox of Parchman Farm
Hellhole to some, yet home to others, the story of Mississippi's infamous prison farm

Parchman Farm, long a dreaded name in the annals of the Mississippi Delta, began as a purchase of some twenty thousand acres of prime farmland by the state of Mississippi about 1900. The majority of the land was in Sunflower County consisting of over sixteen thousand acres of some of the richest bottomland in the world. Almost six miles across, the acreage covered forty-six square miles and was flat as a pool table. This desolate, faraway, and isolated place was to be the location of the new state penitentiary to replace the dilapidated stone-walled prison in Jackson. Located at the old Gordon Station, it was known as the Parchman Place, after the family that had owned it for years.

By 1904, Governor James K. Vardaman had cleared and drained most of the land and erected a sawmill to produce lumber for prison buildings. Cotton was planted on some of the several thousand acres and a profit of $185,000 was given to the state treasury in 1905. Huge vegetable gardens were planted, and chickens, turkeys, hogs, beef cattle, and a dairy herd were tended to in order to supply food for the convicts. A brickyard was built and wood-fired kilns made bricks from clay mined onsite. As the remaining timber was cleared, more and more camps were built, fifteen in all, stretching across the looming and foreboding horizon.

Because of the immense acreage to be tilled and the cost to fence in and patrol such a large place, there were no fences or walls at Parchman. The front gate was attached to nothing. Only administration buildings were close by and Camp Number One, also known as Front Camp, along with a railroad station, a cotton gin, and a warehouse. Further back on the farm was a canning factory, seamstress shop, dairy, a hospital, and carpentry shops. The prisoners slept and ate in long wooden barracks with barred windows known as "cages," located about a half mile apart. The mission of Parchman Farm was to turn a profit for the State of Mississippi and to provide a self-sufficient prison system for Mississippi's felons and murderers. And for a while it worked. And the prisoners worked, six days a week, from "can 'til can't."

After being convicted and sentenced to Parchman, a prisoner was met at the county jail and shackled by the penitentiary's traveling sergeant known as "Long Chain Charlie" and delivered to the prison. Once processed and given a physical exam, he or she was released for labor and issued prison attire. Males were issued ten-ounce duck pants and a seven-ounce duck shirt with horizontal black and white stripes known as "ring-a-rounds," and women were given heavy cotton dresses with vertical stripes called "up-n-downs." Identification numbers were stamped on the front and back of uniforms. Females were separated from male camps, and the entire population was housed in a segregated manner with blacks comprising the overwhelming majority of the prisoners.

Well I'm putting dat cotton in a 11 foot sack…
With a 12-gauge shotgun at my back.

The mission of the penitentiary was to produce as much money for the state treasury as possible with very little input from the state coffers, very similar to the free farming enterprises outside the gates. But the big difference was that the labor force at Parchman was rapists, murderers, and thieves. In order to maintain control over such a vast facility and almost 2,500 convicts, the "trusty system" was employed where prisoners were in charge of other prisoners in a manner that at first glance would seem impossible to work, but work it did for many years. A sergeant, state employee and white, was assigned to each camp. A pecking order evolves in any social group, and usually the "cage boss" was a lifetime prisoner well into his sentence. They accepted their plight and adapted to prison life. This was their home, and they ensured it ran smoothly. The sergeant or "Main Mos' Man" respected the cage boss, acknowledged his supremacy within the cage, and expected him to supply the necessary labor to meet the superintendent's quota of cotton each year. The cage boss respected the sergeant because he could demote him back into the ranks with hell to pay from his prior underlings. Of course the sergeants had snitches within the cages and were often assured that all was well, which oddly enough, it was, a great deal of the time. And when someone got out of line, the cage boss had his "drivers" who wielded black leather straps, three feet long and six inches wide. The smooth leather strap was used to whip the naked buttocks of men being held down by fellow inmates. The strap was called "black Annie."

Order was maintained by a hierarchy of "trustys," so called because of their willingness to abide by the rules and move up through the ranks. The cage boss, also called Cap'm, assigned duties to his drivers who were expected to directly supervise the convicts, called "gunmen" because they were always "under the gun" of "trusty shooters." Working in long tight files called the "long line," approximately one hundred men were overseen by six trusty shooters wielding 12-gauge shotguns. A "gun line" was drawn twenty feet in front of each shooter, and if anyone crossed that line, he was first warned and if he did it again in a threatening manner, he was shot in the lower limbs and crippled. If he broke and ran, there were 30-30 caliber Winchesters with which to shoot long distances in order to bring the "rabbit" down. As written in *Worse than Slavery* by David Oshinsky, the trusty shooters "formed a floating, flexible barrier between the gunmen and the free world. They were also the driver's protection as he rode among the gunmen giving orders or forcing them on to greater efforts." (Oftentimes, a trusty shooter was given a full pardon after stopping an escapee, which heightened the desire to be a trusty shooter while helping to discipline a gunman.) As one prisoner stated long ago, "Play by da shooters' rules, get along fine; turn rabbit in the row, be dead." At night, however, all prisoners were locked up in the cages with a long dining hall separating the gunmen from the trustys. It was up to the cage boss to maintain security, and no one ventured outside the cages at night. "Nightshooters," mostly salaried old white night watchmen, patrolled the cages outside and were authorized to shoot anything that moved.

During the long hot days of chopping cotton with hoes, or picking cotton by hand, the long line moved forward as one with their pace set by a "caller." Some say this practice had inspired the birth of the blues when a caller would chant a verse and one

MISSISSIPPI DEPARTMENT OF ARCHIVES AND HISTORY

hundred men would respond with a chorus, much like the cadence of a military march is set by a single member of the group and repeated by the rest. The caller in a long line had to be good and inventive, clever and sometimes funny. However, lost love and lonesomeness prevailed in many chants. According to *Down on Parchman Farm* by William Taylor, "Callers had to be clever: laughter was a necessity in the rows. They had to have soul, the power to uplift the spirit with rhythm: soul was the lifeblood of the long line; an uneven pace spoiled everything. A call too fast could wear a gunman down; one too slow would anger the Cap'm." One old prisoner recalled, "When you listenin' how the song run, the day just go by mo' faster and befo' you know it, the sergeant or the driver is hollerin' dinnertime!"

Many blues songs came from the long line. Some of the great Delta bluesmen spent time on Parchman, R.L. Burnside, Son House, and Bukka White, among others, including Elvis's daddy Vernon Presley. An especially well-known song spoke about the Midnight Special, the train that ran from Jackson to Parchman bringing loved ones on Sunday morning at dawn. It left Jackson at 12:05 a.m., and its huge piercing headlight could be seen for miles in the treeless expanse and its long mournful whistle heard as it wound its way through the little Delta towns on its way to Parchman.

"Yonder comes Miss Rosie, how in the worl' do I know
I can tell by her apron and da clothes she wo',
Umbrella on her shoulder, piece of paper in her hand,
She dun been to see da Guv'nor and come to free her man.
Let the Midnight Special shine its light on me
Let the Midnight Special shine her ever-lovin' light on me"

Almost 14 percent of the convict population was involved in the incentive program centered on the trusty system. Male trustys wore "up-n-downs," and the coveted position was the "trusty-servant." That elite cadre earned their position by good manners, docility, and superior domestic skills. Working in employees' homes or the superintendent's mansion, their duties involved cooking and janitorial work and other special duties within the penitentiary that lightened the paid staff workforce. Of course a position at the Mississippi Governor's Mansion in Jackson meant a certain pardon at the end of his term.

Well, I'm sittin' over here on Number Nine
And all I did was drink my wine...

Aside from the planting of cotton and vegetables on the great farm, there were many other working facets of prison life. Administration of the huge conglomerate was mostly performed by inmates, many learning managerial and vocational skills along the way. According to a press release in December of 1943, 5,700 bales of cotton had been ginned with a net profit of $358,000. Eighty thousand gallons of vegetables had been canned, and there was a large amount of stored food and livestock feed. The livestock inventory listed 3,800 hogs, 250 milk cows, 850 head of beef cattle, and 825 mules and horses. Between 1937 and 1941, 650,000 bricks and 1,350,000 board feet of lumber were produced to renovate existing buildings and build new ones. In 1941, Parchman was reportedly "the only profit-making prison in the country." But the profits of Parchman were delegated to the whims of the price of cotton, who was a fickle mistress, and the weather and bugs.

Of course, the prison was at the direction of the governor and the state legislature. Money was always of vital interest. Administrators were handpicked by the governor, and political infighting boiled like the noonday sun on the backs of the gunmen. Pardons could be granted, or bought sometimes, and if a prisoner obeyed the rules and worked his way up the ladder, an early release could soon be forthcoming. However, as stated in *Down on Parchman Farm*, some of the men who were offered clemency declined it, wanting to stay on. John Tabor rejected a pardon saying, "You can't beat this place for comfort." Murderer William Sullivan stated, "Better off than anywhere else," and he found his keepers "some of the finest people in the world." But we must realize at that time of the Great Depression, a large number of the free-world folk did well to feed and clothe themselves. "Quite clearly, life at Parchman Farm was a step up for many of its inmates."

Well, I'm gonna be here for the rest of my natural life,
And all I did was shoot my wife! – Mose Allison, "Parchman Farm"

Along with the decaying physical plant on the old Parchman Farm and the changing tide of the Civil Rights era in the '50s and '60s came sweeping declines in the cotton markets and political upheaval at the statehouse in Jackson. As a result of a federal lawsuit in 1971, presided over by Judge William Keady of Greenville, the once profitable farm was slowly turned into an integrated "constitutional prison," staffed by accredited penologists and civilian guards. Reforms were put into place and the old cages burned down as new concrete barracks surrounded by razor wire were built. The trusty system was abolished and black Annie forbidden. A prison law library was established and fifty square feet of living space was required for each new convict. A Department of Corrections was created by the state to oversee Parchman Farm, and thirteen thousand acres of fertile cotton ground was leased out to surrounding land holders. In the 1940s, the old system annually produced almost a million dollars profit to the state yet was now costing the state millions in infrastructure and operating costs each year.

Prison industries were opposed by competing private businesses, and the result was too many convicts with nothing to do. One inmate relayed, "You stay in these cages all day you build up a lot of hostility and it's got to get out somehow."

Author and previous warden Donald Cabana argues that the old penal farm was a "prison administrator's dream come true" and maybe Judge Keady "threw out the baby with the bath water" in an attempt to bring improvement. Yet one authority has stated, "It is safe to say that no other state has come such a long way with its prison, although, perhaps, no other state had such a long way to go."

Hopson Plantation—Model for Mechanization
How it made cotton-pickin' history

In 1852, the State of Mississippi deeded almost four thousand acres of some of the most fertile land in the world, nestled along the high banks of the Sunflower River and south of present day Clarksdale, to Howell Hopson. That deed is still in the Hopson family name today, passed down through generations of family members and operators of the farm. There are other Delta plantations of like size that remain in the original family circles, but none which has done more to change the face of agriculture worldwide and cause social change as has the Hopson Plantation.

Situated a mile south of the infamous Crossroads of Highways 61 and 49, where legend has it that bluesman Robert Johnson sold his soul to the devil for his world-renowned guitar abilities, the Hopson headquarters sits right across the railroad tracks from old Highway 49. The Hopson Commissary and the Shackup Inn now reside within the old buildings, warehouses, gin, grain bins, and tenant shacks. To visit there is to take a walk back in our history. The Hopson Commissary is chock-full of plantation and blues memorabilia and is a museum in itself, full of artifacts and farm implements and pictures of the way things used to be "down on the farm," before Hopson Plantation helped change the way farm operations were handled forever.

Prior to the days of mechanization, sharecroppers lived in cypress shacks scattered about the farm and surrounded by twenty-seven or so acres of ground for which the sharecropping family was responsible. On that land the cropper and his family tilled an acre vegetable garden and several acres of corn to feed his mule while the rest was to be planted in cotton. The sharecropper was furnished with a mule, his house, and all implements and seed to grow the crop. A credit account was set up at the plantation store where his various staples and sundry needs were supplied throughout the year. After the cotton had been picked and taken to the gin, settlement day arrived. The plantation's share of the crop was taken out first, and from the cropper's share came the indebtedness at the plantation store. Whatever was left over was given to the cropper. On plantations all across the Delta there was room for misuse of this system, but the Hopson Plantation was renowned for its honesty and fairness with its tenants, as were the great majority of the others.

Supervision of such a large operation was normally segregated into one thousand-acre units, each with an overseer or farm manager. It was his duty to look after all phases of the operation, the sharecroppers, farm productivity, mules, implements, and supervision of the headquarters, barns, and implement sheds relating to that particular unit. According to Dick Hopson, operating partner during the '40s, in a descriptive document written for family members, the overseer had to be "an agronomist, entomologist, agricultural engineer, animal husbandman, accountant, and human psychologist."

During the Great Depression, cotton was the main crop and cash income of the Delta. The sharecropping system depended heavily on mule power and hand labor for preparing the soil, planting, thinning, chopping, and picking cotton. There was ample labor available, but upon return of better economic times, industry would drain off human resources and the plantation system would become short-handed. During this time the Agricultural Adjustment Administration began a program of laying idle many acres of cotton land in an attempt to bolster cotton prices. In order to keep the idle acres from going back to forest, cover crops had to be planted or alternate crops grown to keep the land tillable. With all inputs of a cotton crop already having been made as resourceful as possible, the only avenue with which to continue to make a profit was to improve the efficiency of production. In order to compete successfully with industry for the much needed labor force, cotton plantations had to "mechanize, systemize, and streamline" their efforts. This system was to introduce new and untried crops to the idle acres. Within a few years, the old plantation sharecropping system was turned on its head as new management and supervision techniques were employed, different crops were planted, and the operation of plantations was mechanized so that the displacement of hundreds of thousands of families occurred. And it was during this time that the great northward migration of tenant families took the blues from deep within the Delta to Memphis, St. Louis, Chicago, and Detroit.

"61 Highway...longest road I know,
goes from Chicago to the Gulf of Mexico"

Piston-driven motive power had long been tinkered with as a replacement for four-legged brawn. Regarding the standard of agricultural propulsion, William Faulkner once stated, "a mule will work faithfully for you for years, just to have the opportunity to kick you once." However, mules were heading to Missouri and animal rendering plants

HOPSON FAMILY COLLECTION

as gas-operated tractors were developed for farm use. The hand operations of thinning, chopping, and picking cotton had to be replaced in order to continue the streamlining of farm operations. Mechanical planters, disc harrows, hippers, cultivators, and dirt drags were being developed, but the one area that was the most worrisome to perfect was the picking of the cotton.

The first U.S. patent to be issued on a mechanical cotton harvester was granted in 1850. According to Noel Workman in *Staplcotn: The First 75 Years,* by the 1930s, eight hundred patents had been issued on various mechanical cotton harvesting devices and hundreds of patents issued covering many types of mechanical pickers. J.D. Rust had first introduced a wet spindle machine in 1927 in Weatherford, Texas, and by 1932 that picker was in operation near Lake Providence, Louisiana. The following year Rust's machine picked five bales of cotton at the Delta Branch Experiment Station at Stoneville. Also being developed at Stoneville was a flame cultivator that used fire to burn down weeds and grasses in the cotton rows. Delta Aviation, predecessor to Delta Airlines, began using converted bi-planes to spray crops for bugs and weeds. Mechanization was on the way in and mules and sharecroppers were on the way out. By 1948, labor displacement ran as high as 55 to 65 percent as machines took over labor-intensive jobs. In 1940 there was one family for every twenty-seven acres of land, and by 1948 there existed only one family every one hundred acres. "Where a hundred families had provided the labor needed to weed and harvest a typical pre-war Delta cotton crop, a half dozen tractor drivers and mechanics now performed the same task." And Hopson Plantation led the way, replacing 140 mules with twenty-two tractors. Only five of the old mules remained sentimentally as pets, each being over twenty years old. Hopson Plantation was the first Delta plantation to become totally mechanized.

International Harvester Corporation had teamed up with the Hopson Plantation and Memphis-based Mid-South Oil Company to develop and experiment with a mechanical cotton picker suitable to use in the Mississippi Delta. A basic Farmall tractor could be used all year long as a row-crop tractor and converted to a cotton picker by having the picking mechanism and basket attached. The steering wheel was remounted, and the tractor then run in reverse to pick the crop. Total cost of the one-row machine was $3,750 with $1,000 for the tractor and $2,750 for the seasonally mounted picker. As stated by Dick Hopson, "This machine is not an invention in the true sense of the word but the result of a long, slow, tedious process of evolution." By 1948, Hopson Plantation had eight pickers that were each averaging six acres of cotton picked a day and sometimes at night.

The entire operation at Hopson was totally mechanized. All houses were removed from the separate twenty-seven-acre tracts to roads that cut through the property. Four headquarters were demolished and one huge headquarter complex was built with commissary, offices, cotton gin, warehouses, tool and tractor sheds, seed storage, and grain bins scattered about several acres that ran alongside the Illinois Central Railroad and Highway 49. It took a centralized servicing station three minutes to totally refuel, service with lubricants and oil, and check all fluid levels and tire pressures on each of the twenty-eight tractors running on Hopson Plantation. According to a cotton trade publication, *Acco Press* from Texas, Dick Hopson reported, "the Hopson Plantation has become almost like a tourist sightseeing land this fall with eight mechanical cotton pickers in the field, each of them picking in a day what it would take sixty hand pickers to do. Our plantation has been a testing ground for mechanical equipment for a number of years. We have always wanted to see progress in this direction. Last year we bought four McCormick-Deering cotton pickers and this year got another four. It's no longer an experiment with us."

Each year after ginning season, Hopson Planting Company certified seed was in great demand, and many tons were shipped each year throughout the cotton belt.

Coahoma County Agricultural Agent Harris Barnes stated, "Hopson has the best accounting system for farming operations I have ever seen and I am a thirty-year veteran in the Clarksdale area. Hopson Planting Company has kept an accurate cost record on mechanical picking operations that have been published and distributed by International Harvester."

Hopson was truly a model and trend-breaking plantation with varying results. Dick Hopson, always aware of the needs of his employees, stated, "One of the most gratifying results of the new plantation system has been the fact that although comparative production costs have declined, higher wages have been consistently paid than would have otherwise been feasible. And it is anticipated that additional benefits will accrue to those employees who remain, now that cotton production is becoming completely mechanized."

Hopson further stated, comparing the old system to the new: "Sharecropping was a product of the times, a result of cause and effect, and it was as it should have been. In all fairness, most of the outstandingly successful planting operations continue under the old plan. However, the many advantages and opportunities for more efficient operation promised for agriculture in the post-war era cannot be utilized as readily under the old system." Today, the changes to agriculture brought about by Hopson Plantation leading the way continue worldwide.

The Great Bear Hunters of the Mississippi Delta

Long before the Delta was covered with cotton, corn, and catfish, it was a primeval hardwood bottomland that abounded in deer, turkey, wildcats, panther, and bear. Girdled by the Yazoo and Mississippi Rivers, the exterior and interior streams flooded and flushed the fertile forest annually. Raccoons, opossums, cottonmouth water moccasins, and rattlesnakes intermingled with alligators and monstrous snapping turtles. Alligator gar and huge catfish swam in the lakes and streams, and migratory waterfowl blackened the sky during their fall and spring flights. Huge cypress trees stood sentinel at the edges of lakes and in bayous and sloughs with red oak, white oak, pecan, persimmon, and gum trees towering above all else. Canebrakes stretched along ridges bordering the streams, sometimes for miles, and could have been as much as a mile wide and so thick and dense that a man could only walk into them by hacking his way with a heavy bush knife. Visibility was limited to possibly fifteen feet, and the canebrake was the favorite lair of wild and dangerous animals. Into this jungle stepped some of the most notable sportsmen of all times—the Southern bear hunters.

Southern Plantation Owners

"The planters of the South, more than the citizens of any other section of the Union, indulge in the manly excitements of the chase; they are, without exception, excellent horsemen, and have a thorough knowledge of woodcraft," stated *Harpers New Monthly* in October of 1885. The celebrated wealthy Wade Hampton family of Columbia, South Carolina, came to Washington County, Mississippi, in the early 1800s and bought several plantations outside of Greenville, close to Lake Washington. Wild Woods, Walnut Ridge, Linden, and Bear Garden were among them. Some of their holdings were used extensively for hunting. A large section of Bear Garden is now a part of the Yazoo National Wildlife Refuge.

It has been noted by Paul Schullery in *The Bear Hunter's Century* that the aristocratic flair of the Southern gentlemen enabled them to hunt with "the British formality of the fox hunt and the aboriginal wildness of the bayou alligator hunt. Bear hunting for those ardent sportsmen was almost a religious activity." Wade Hampton III has been considered one of the greatest bear hunters of all time, and his prominence as a horseman is legendary. He was, as Schullery also notes, "admired throughout polite society not only as the killer of many bears, but as a fine gentleman."

Hunting bear in the thick canebrakes required dogs to strike and run the bear. Crashing and mauling their way through the cane, the dogs trailed the scent of the bear until at last the bear became tired or he was ready to stand and fight. Sometimes, lanes were cut through the thick cane, and bears were shot at as they crossed openings. Most of the time, once the bear was bayed, the hunters came scrambling and ripping in on horseback to find the bear viciously fighting off the marauding dogs. In an effort to limit the possibility of hitting one of the prized hounds if a gunshot were taken, many bears were killed with a heavy hunting knife, wielded by the fearless sportsman, jumping into the melee.

THEODORE ROOSEVELT COLLECTION, HARVARD COLLEGE LIBRARY

Returning home from the Civil War with "little more than the clothes he wore," Robert Eager Bobo found his family land holdings in Coahoma County inundated with tepid water. He got in a canoe and headed south to high ground and staked his claim on the spot where the small town of Bobo now stands. He ran a model plantation yet spent as much time as possible during the fall and winter hunting bear. In an 1887 interview in *Forest and Stream*, Bobo stated, "One year we rented a farm and spent the entire time out in the swamp. We didn't come out for three months at a time. We killed 304 bears, fifty-four deer, forty-seven wildcats and nine panthers." Mrs. Fincher Bobo, daughter-in-law of Robert Bobo, recalled, "the festive mood in their setting out for the wild country, with the string of four-mule wagons, the dozens of dogs racing here and there, and the hunters themselves, mounted on their fine-spirited horses. The men were gone for weeks and lived on bear steaks and stew." The bear meat, she said, was "quite coarse and tough, but good."

Captain Bobo was an overly anxious sportsman who was eagerly involved in most of the kills, even in front of his invited guests. He just became overwhelmed in the excitement. Bobo often used his knife to save his hounds. Carrying a Colt pistol instead of a rifle, he found that in order to be effective, a pistol had to be fired from close range, often spooking the dogs and causing them to run away. The dogs would sometimes back off when they saw him coming. "A bear not distracted by dogs is a hard bear to kill with a knife," Bobo claimed.

Holt Collier

"In the old days we came in wagons: the guns, the bedding, the dogs, the food, the whiskey; the young men then who could drive all night and all the next day in the cold rain and pitch a camp and sleep in wet blankets and rise at daylight the next morning and hunt. There had been bear back then." – William Faulkner

William Faulkner has given us possibly one of the most in-depth insights into the minds of hunters in his collection of hunting stories entitled *Big Woods* (1955). Sam Fathers was "the son of a negro slave and a Chickasaw king, and had trained the boy and taught him how to use a gun with care and respect, in order to enter the Big Woods when his time came. The Big Woods, the Big Bottom, the wilderness."

Minor Buchanan, lawyer and author of the definitive book *Holt Collier*, believes that Sam Fathers could have been based on a true-to-life, legendary man named Holt Collier. Holt was born a slave in 1846 into the family of General Thomas Hinds, a preeminent "first family of Mississippi." Holt was raised on Plum Ridge Plantation one mile south of Greenville on the banks of Rattlesnake Bayou. Plum Ridge consisted of a little more than a thousand acres and was loaded with wild game of all kind. Young Holt was given a pony to ride and an expensive Scott 12-gauge shotgun and instructed to provide meat for the plantation. He learned to shoot from both shoulders and often gave excess game to the neighbors as well. It was in the swamp known today as the Cypress Preserve in Greenville that young Holt Collier killed his first bear at the tender age of ten. Because of Holt's prowess and intense, innate abilities, his duties were limited to the hunt. He kept all the plantation guns cleaned and oiled, the dogs and horses fed and trained. "He was known to have kept the kitchen at Plum Ridge and all the neighborhood tables supplied with ducks, geese, and squirrels." The Hinds family moved to Kentucky in the summer to escape yellow fever and intense heat, often staying away from the Delta from May 10 to October 10. Young Holt was taken with them. He learned to jockey racehorses in Kentucky and that ability would forever enhance his life. In later years, his qualities as a horseman, a hunter, and a noble gentleman preceded him.

At the outbreak of the Civil War, Thomas and Howell Hinds left for Memphis to join the Confederate cause. Young Holt was left at Plum Ridge Plantation and told to take care of the ladies. Holt was fourteen years old and crying as the two men that meant more to him than anything in his life left him at home for his own safety. That evening Holt Collier disobeyed Howell Hinds for the only time in his life and stole away on a steamboat to join his masters in Memphis. He went on to become a full-fledged Confederate soldier and rode with the Texas Calvary seeing action in Mississippi, Alabama, and Tennessee, while serving as a scout, sharpshooter, and spy. Holt Collier was later granted a pension as the only black man to serve in the Confederacy from Mississippi.

Returning home from the war, Holt found that he could make a living supplying deer and bear meat to the growing frontier camps in the Delta. These camps housed laborers who were logging the land for timber and to produce more cotton fields. Thousands of laborers were building levees to keep out the ravaging Mississippi River, and finally they were building the railroads that connected the plantations and towns to the outside markets. An average-size field-dressed deer brought only twenty-three dollars where a full-grown bear could bring sixty dollars or more. However, according to Holt, "Money don't buy nuthin' in the canebrake, and a man's dog don't care whether he's rich or po'." It is reported that Holt Collier in his lifetime killed more than three thousand bears—most of them to feed hungry men, but some were killed for sport, with sporting gentlemen.

Delta Men and the Famous 1902 Hunt

Holt Collier had become legendary as possibly the greatest bear guide and hunter of all time. Upon the death of Thomas Hinds, Holt took up with Senator LeRoy Percy and brothers Harley and Clive Metcalfe. They hunted together, spent many nights in wilderness camps together, and shared the same tables. In 1902, President Theodore Roosevelt was invited to come to the Delta to hunt bear. Holt Collier was to be his guide. Encamped on the banks of the Little Sunflower River, President Roosevelt noted that Holt Collier was "a man of sixty and could neither read nor write, but he had all the dignity of an African Chief." The next day, Roosevelt missed his opportunity to shoot a bear that Holt had run across a clearing where he had been stationed. (Hunger and boredom had caused him to walk back to camp for a bite to eat!) Later, Holt bayed the bear and rushed in and tied the exhausted bear to a tree. President Roosevelt refused to shoot the tethered bear, and a political cartoon depicted the scene as "Drawing the Line in Mississippi." From that hunt came many jokes and a small toy bear that is known all over the world as the Teddy Bear.

Roosevelt was indignant and not happy with the hunt and vowed to return and "with Holt Collier as his only guide, chase bears and come up with one and kill it, running free before the dogs." In 1907, the President joined his friends across the Mississippi River in Louisiana for the second hunt. Another guide showed up early to help in the hunt. Ben Lilly was infamous in his tracking ability and marksmanship. However, he was described by Roosevelt as a "goofy old coot whose oddness went far beyond anything that could safely be called eccentricity." Lilly had walked forty miles to camp and had not eaten nor drank for a day. He slept that first night "perched in a crooked tree in the beating rain, much as if he had been a wild turkey." A few days later, with no luck so far in the hunt, the Metcalfe brothers showed up with Holt Collier and his dogs and took charge. According to Roosevelt, "the Metcalfes were young men, swampers, planters, Mississippians, gentlemen in the old English conception of the term...and bear hunters from the heart." Based on the advice of Ben Lilly, the camp was moved about fourteen miles away to Bear Lake. After ten days the President had not gotten a bear, and he asked Holt what to do. "Cunnel, ef you let me manage the hunt you'll sho' get one tomorrow." The President replied, "Whatever you say goes, Holt."

Holt Collier instructed Clive Metcalfe to "take the Cunnel and bum around wid him in the woods like you an' me always does, and don't put him on no stand. He ain't no baby. He can go anywhere you kin go; jes' keep him close to the dogs as you kin. Mr. Harley and me'll follow the hounds; when we strike a trail, you and the Cunnel come a-running."

The next day about six miles into the cane, they jumped a bear, and Roosevelt did just as Holt Collier had told him to do. Hearing the lead dog at bay in the thickest of cover, Clive Metcalfe and the President of the United States galloped into the dense quagmire and dismounted. Roosevelt got ready as the bear broke away and "turned, walking forward very stiff-legged, almost as if on tiptoe, now and then looking back at the dogs." Roosevelt took close aim and fired a fatal shot through both lungs. The bear fell and the dogs rushed in. Writing later of the hunt, the President recalled, "The bear went down, stark dead, slain in the canebrake in true hunter fashion." According to Buchanan, "The final count of the 1907 hunt was three bears, six deer, one wild turkey, twelve squirrels, one duck, one opossum, and one wildcat. All of the game animals were eaten by the hunters except the wildcat."

After the 1907 hunt, Holt Collier continued to hunt bear, but he slowed down a good bit. Very possibly the last bear that Holt Collier was involved in killing came at the hands of his dear friend Clive's son. Albert Gallatin Metcalfe killed his first bear in 1912 on the banks of the Bogue Phalia River north of Leland. He was ten years old, and Holt Collier was sixty-six. Most of the Mississippi Delta had been cleared for farming, and a way of life was forever changing. Gone were the Big Woods...and gone were the bear.

Lindsay Dennison, one of the journalists accompanying Roosevelt on the famous 1902 hunt, might best describe the relationship between the men and animals, rich and poor, aristocrat and slave, common and sublime: "There was the instructive picture of Holt Collier and some of the white men, too, on bended knee, dipping their horns into the water hole where the first bear had died, and drinking their fill of a puree of bear and dog and mud, all held in solution in water that had been standing for at least eight months."

Those were the bear hunters of the Mississippi Delta.

Holt's Feisty Friend
Catching an American icon on the Mississippi Delta's most famous hunt

Jocko was a little dog, of a breed commonly called a feist, a centuries-old lineage of small Southern hunting dogs. He probably weighed less than twenty-five pounds, yet he had the heart of a lion. And because of his tenaciousness, he alone was the cause of a phenomenon of endearment to millions of children all over the world.

In 1902, President Theodore Roosevelt had read about and wanted to go to the South and hunt the Louisiana Black Bear in the jungled swamps of the Mississippi Delta. A hunt was organized and preparations made to travel by train to the deep virgin wilderness of the south Delta, yet to be cleared and turned under by plow and the last stronghold of the elusive Louisiana Black Bear. Not wanting the hunt to turn into a press riddled picnic, the guest list was kept small, and Roosevelt was met at Smede's Landing, a cotton shipping platform south of Onward, Mississippi, on the Illinois Central Railroad. The hunt had been arranged by prominent plantation owners and important businessmen and placed in the hands of the ex-slave and Confederate cavalryman, fifty-six-year-old Holt Collier from Greenville, Mississippi. Holt had grown up hunting in the woods and swamps of the Delta and knew it like the back of his hand. After the Civil War, he had supplied the labor gangs of the burgeoning railroad and levee building camps with wild game. By this time he had killed almost three thousand bears, mostly with his knife. If anyone could guarantee the president a bear it was Holt Collier.

Willa Johnson's studio photograph of Holt Collier captures him standing "with the dignity of an African chief," and clutching his cherished 45-70 Winchester lever action rifle, a gift from President Theodore Roosevelt.

Holt spent several weeks locating the bear he wanted to hunt. On the banks of the Little Sunflower River, he and fellow guides hacked out a primitive campsite and cut trails through the almost impenetrable canebrakes in order for the president to get a clear shot at a bear running before the hounds. Several hundred people met the train at Smede's Landing, mostly children and grandchildren of slaves. In the words of Collier, the president emerged from the train and walked straight to him with an extended hand saying, "So 'dis is Holt, de guide. I h'yar you's a great bear hunter." Immediately, the hunting party got on their horses for the fifteen mile ride through cotton fields, briar and vine entangled forests, and finally along Coon Bayou to camp.

Sitting around the campfire that night, President Roosevelt made it clear he expected to see a bear the next day and orders were given to let the "Colonel," as he asked to be called, kill the first bear. The next morning, Holt placed the Colonel on a stand close to a water hole and next to a big fallen tree, a location where he knew the bear he had seen earlier would emerge once the chase was on. Holt gave explicit instructions to the Colonel to "stay there 'til I get back."

Holt and his fellow guides turned their pack of forty bear hounds loose, led by "Old Remus," his oldest and most experienced hound. According to Minor Buchanan's book, *Holt Collier, His Life, His Roosevelt Hunts, and The Origin of the Teddy Bear,* Old Remus had a "foxhound's body and a bloodhound's head." Hanging in a burlap bag on Holt's saddle horn was a small yellow Scotch terrier feist dog. He was "a valiant little scoundrel that would harry the bear and bite his flanks and run away to bite again as soon as the bear had turned his head."

Holt followed his dogs on horseback until they jumped a bear and the chase was on. The Colonel and his companion, Huger Lee Foote, grandfather of novelist and Civil War historian, Shelby Foote, heard the hounds in hot pursuit as the bear crossed the Little Sunflower several times. About mid-afternoon, the barks and wails of the hounds drifted far away and faded out of hearing. Foote told the Colonel, "Holt has either gone across Big Sunflower or the Yazoo River following his dogs." The Colonel asked, "Do you reckon Holt crossed the river?" Foote replied, "Holt will go anywhere his dogs go." At Foote's suggestion, they abandoned the stand and broke for camp and a late lunch.

Of course Holt stayed on the hunt, stating years later, "I could have killed that bear a thousand times, but we'd been warned not to shoot, to save ev'y chance for the Cunnel. I sweated myself to death in that canebrake. So did the bear."

Holt relayed the hunt, "By me keeping between the bear and the river, I knew he'd make for that water hole where I left the Cunnel. After a while the bear started that way and popped out of the gap where I said he'd go. But I didn't hear a shot and that pestered me…It sholy pervoked me 'cause I'd promised to bring him a bear to that log, and there he was, bayed up against the very log where I'd left the Cunnel sittin."

When the bear turned at bay, Holt was left with a serious predicament. The president had been promised the first bear, but he was nowhere near. Holt became angered that the Cunnel had disregarded his very specific instructions. The bear began to fight and maul the dogs as they circled the bear. Something had to be done to prevent a useless slaughtering of his favorite hounds. Holt had only one recourse—he untied the string that held the little feist dog in the burlap bag on his saddle. "Catch him, Jocko, catch him!" The little yellow dog leapt from the horse and jumped on the bear from behind.

Lindsey Denison, a Washington correspondent along on the hunt, described the scene. "There was a flashing confusion of black, hairy forefeet beating off the dogs—of white teeth snapping here and there at the squirming mass: squeals of wrath and pain from the dogs were lifted in a deafening chorus, then the bear rose straight up on his hind legs and stood waist deep in the water. In the grasp of his mighty forelegs he had a curly yellow cur that was Holt Collier's especial pet."

"Leaping from his saddle, rifle in hand, Holt howled, 'Leggo mah dog, bear!' The bear and the little dog fell backwards into the muddy pool. Holt could not shoot for the risk of killing two or more of the pack as well as the bear. He clubbed the rifle and waded into the melee. 'Leggo mah dog!' Holt shouted again and swung the stock of his gun through an arc that landed at the base of the bear's skull. The bear let go of the dog, but it was too late, the dog was dead."

Needing to further restrain the bear for fear of his killing any more dogs, Holt grabbed his lariat, and in the mud and the blood and ruckus and chaos, he lassoed the bear and tied him to a willow tree. After being beckoned by hunter's horns, Roosevelt came hot footed on horseback to find the hunting party and hounds exhausted and a two hundred fifty pound bear tied to a tree. As he dismounted and ran into the water, Holt humbly suggested to him, "Cunnel, don't shoot him while he's tied." Roosevelt, of course, had no intention of shooting a tethered animal stating, "Gentlemen, no magazine bears for me." Holt had the bear dispatched with a knife.

Dennison recalled the scene, "There was the instructive picture of Holt Collier and some of the white men, too, dipping their horns into the water hole where the first bear had died, and drinking their fill of a puree of bear and dog and mud, all held in solution in water that had been standing for at least eight months." Later that night at camp, President Theodore Roosevelt, founder of the Boone and Crockett Club, told Holt Collier, ex-slave, that he "was the best guide and hunter he had ever seen."

Soon, Clifford Berryman, Pulitzer Prize winning cartoonist for *The Washington Post*, ran a cartoon depicting Roosevelt in his hunting attire. The much teased and macho President was shown holding his rifle with his other hand up, refusing to shoot a small bear cub held on a rope. The title of the cartoon was, "Drawing the Line in Mississippi." The small bear cub began to symbolize Roosevelt in his ensuing political career in a comical way. Other political cartoonists picked up on the cute little creatures, and they were fondly called "Teddy bears."

Morris Michtom, a Russian Jewish immigrant living in Brooklyn, New York, saw the cartoons and designed a soft cuddly toy bear, and with the president's permission, called it "Teddy's bear." He immediately began mass producing the toy bears, displaying them in the window and selling them out of his candy store. Thus was the beginning of the Ideal Toy Company. When Michtom died in 1938 his company was a multi-million dollar industry producing and selling over one hundred thousand teddy bears a year.

As a young man, William Faulkner would venture into the south Delta, that diminishing primeval wilderness along the Little Sunflower, on hunting expeditions. He certainly heard the stories and tales of the 1902 hunt. In *Go Down, Moses*, Faulkner wrote of the "small fyce dog killed by a bear..." Some scholars believe the venerable character and Indian guide, Sam Fathers, immortalized in *The Bear*, is no less than Holt Collier.

President Roosevelt came to Bear Lake in Louisiana in 1907, directly across the

Mississippi River from his previous hunt, and got his bruin while riding his horse to the hounds with Holt Collier. The bear, according to the press, weighed 375 pounds. The actual weight was probably less, but Roosevelt was proud that it was "slain in the canebrake in true hunter fashion." In his chronicles, President Roosevelt stated that Holt Collier "was a man of sixty and could neither read nor write, but had the dignity of an African chief, and for half a century he had been a bear hunter."

Upon his return to Washington, the president had 45-70 Model 1886 Winchester lever action rifles delivered to brothers Clive and Harley Metcalfe who were instrumental in both hunts. According to Roosevelt, they were "young men, swampers, planters, Mississippians, gentlemen in the old English conception of the term-and bear hunters from the heart." He also sent one to their dearest friend and mentor, Holt Collier.

In December of 1908, President Roosevelt invited Holt and other hunters to the White House for a bear hunter's dinner, but Holt declined the invitation. "I didn't have no friends in Washington other than the Cunnel, an' I couldn't hunt up there. So I thought the best thing for me to do would be to stay right here among my own people."

Holt Collier's favorite little dog, Jocko, by his willingness to bid his master's command, caused the creation of a world icon. When asked what it was like to hunt and be associated with some of the most powerful and influential men in the world, Holt simply stated, "Money don't mean nothing in a canebrake, and a man's dog don't care whether he's rich or po.' "

Bootlegging—The Oil of Conversation
Mississippi's controversial path to legalizing liquor

Mississippi officially became a dry state on January 29, 1920, when Prohibition was voted in as federal law. (Although Mississippi had been dry since 1908 when a state-level prohibition was imposed.) It remained dry until July of 1966 when the state legislature voted to legalize the sale of bonded liquor in approved package stores. Mississippi was the last state in the Union to repeal Prohibition. At that time, each county could vote for the sale of liquor by the bottle or by the drink or not at all. Is there any wonder that the Mississippi Delta had the first legal package store license #0002 granted to the Jigger and Jug owned by brothers Joe and Machan Azar on Highway 82 in Greenville? The Broadwater Beach Hotel in Biloxi was granted license #0001 as the first legal establishment allowed to serve liquor by the drink.

Until then, liquor was readily available in bootlegger houses and shacks. Normally located out in the county, these businesses stayed open twenty-four hours a day, seven days a week. Soda crackers and sardines and a few sundry items were also available so the establishment had the guise of a legitimate country store. There were fifteen wholesale liquor dealers in Mississippi to service the 1,500 federally licensed bootleggers selling illegal liquor! One of the largest wholesale liquor warehouses in the Southeast distributing "illegal whiskey" was in Ruleville. It contained over ten thousand square feet of storage and had a package store attached to it. The Feds didn't bother the operation because the federal tax had already been paid on the liquor. The sale of illegal bonded whiskey was a state issue.

Even though Mississippi was a dry state, the legislature had enacted a "black market tax" on illegal liquor sales. William Winter was appointed the state tax collector for this tax and was paid ten percent of his receipts. It was a very lucrative job. *TIME Magazine* stated that the position of the Mississippi Black Market Tax Collector was the highest paid public servant in the United States. Later, as a legislator, and before he became governor, Winter was instrumental in abolishing this position having realized the flaws in the system. County sheriffs were also very aware of the sale of illegal whiskey, and many maintained amply stocked liquor cabinets in their homes. It was up to them to see that a black market tax receipt was posted on the walls of the bootlegger's store. The sheriff's position was a coveted job, and many went straight into early retirement after serving several terms.

In a *TIME Magazine* article in September of 1963 regarding liquor in the United States, it was reported that Mississippi received $4.20 per case and an additional 9 percent sales tax on all "illegal liquor" sold in the state. The black market tax added $3,302,385 to the state's treasury based on the sale of over a million gallons of liquor. However, there was no "official" gallon consumption figure because, according to state law, Mississippians did not drink.

After Oklahoma voted to legalize liquor, Mississippi remained the only state in the Union that had not repealed Prohibition. During a speech given to the joint session of the Mississippi Legislature in early February 1966, Governor Paul. B. Johnson urged the state to legalize liquor stating, "Mississippi's liquor laws are shameful and disgraceful." He said the time had come to end the hypocrisy by either "legalizing liquor or drying up the state like the Sahara Desert!" The weekend after his speech, Governor Johnson attended the King's Reception at the posh Jackson Country Club held immediately after the biggest social event of the year, the Jackson Junior League Charity Ball. Unbeknownst to anyone, Hinds County Chief Deputy Thomas Shelton, known locally as "The Untouchable," also showed up at the reception with a search warrant, four deputies, and a sledge hammer. After the key to the liquor closet would not be produced, the chief deputy gave the order to smash the door down. Hundreds of cases of fine scotch, bourbon, gin, and French wines were hauled off to the dismay of the many tuxedo and gown-clad socialites. Patrons included doctors, lawyers, bankers, politicians, and businessmen. According to an article in the February 5, 1966, *Jackson Daily News*, one lady in a full-length mink coat grabbed the governor's arm and pleaded with him, "Paul, can't you do something about this?" The governor replied, "I made my stand, I took my chance." The raid had netted a whole lot of illegal liquor, about $10,000 worth, but most of all, it was considered to be the final straw that pushed the legislature towards legalizing liquor. Four months after the Jackson Country Club bust, the legislature convened, a vote was held, and the state went wet.

However, during the 1952 session of the Mississippi Legislature, there were hot debates as to whether liquor should be legalized. Certain areas of the state were adamantly dry and vehement in their opposition. Other areas, including the Delta and the Gulf Coast, were roaringly vocal for legalizing liquor, or at least maintaining the status quo. The church community (minus some Episcopalians) wanted liquor to remain illegal; however, they wanted the bootleggers to stop selling it on Sundays. The wet side of the state didn't care because now they could get their toddies 24-7. The state was receiving the black market tax, and the bootleggers' and sheriffs' pockets were jingling merrily and everyone was happy. Two or three weeks before the vote was to be held, the churches came out in full force against legalizing the sale of liquor and gave out bumper stickers that read "For the sake of my family, vote DRY." The son of one of the most prosperous bootleggers in the state drove around town in a brand new Buick with three of those bumper stickers on the front and three on the rear of his new car.

According to Willie Morris in his book *North Towards Home,* "Every so often there would be a vote to determine whether liquor should be made legal. Then, for weeks before, the town (Yazoo City) would be filled with feverish campaign activity. People would quote the old saying, 'As long as the people of Mississippi can stagger to the polls, they'll vote dry.' A handful of people would come right out and say that liquor should be made legal, so the bootleggers and the sheriffs would not be able to make all the money, and because the state legislature's 'black market tax' on whiskey, a pittance of a tax that actually contradicted the state constitution, was a shameful deceit."

Noah S. "Soggy" Sweat Jr. was a one term legislator from Corinth when he was asked to address the combined House and Senate, along with their wives and guests, at a

FRED BLACKWELL

Hinds County Deputy Sheriff Bill Russell cleans out the Jackson Country Club storage room case by case the night of the infamous liquor raid.

banquet being held at the King Edward Hotel in Jackson. "Soggy" Sweat later served as a lawyer, district attorney, circuit judge, and college professor. He was twenty-eight years old on April 4th, 1952, when he delivered what has become a classic example of "political double-talk." In a 1989 interview with the *Daily Corinthian*, Sweat said his copyrighted speech was a "tour de force." As he began talking, the crowd sat in silence. "When I finished the first half of the speech, there was a tremendous burst of applause. The second half of the speech, after the close of which, the wets all applauded. The drys were as unhappy with the second part of the speech as the wets were with the first half!"

47

Following is the infamous "Whiskey Speech"by "Soggy" Sweat:
"My friends,

"I had not intended to discuss this controversial subject at this particular time. However, I want you to know that I do not shun controversy. On the contrary, I will take a stand on any issue at any time, regardless of how fraught with controversy it might be. You have asked me how I feel about whiskey. All right, here is how I feel about whiskey.

"If when you say whiskey you mean the devil's brew, the poison scourge, the bloody monster, that defiles innocence, dethrones reason, destroys the home, creates misery and poverty, yea, literally takes the bread from the mouths of little children; if you mean the evil drink that topples the Christian man and woman from the pinnacle of righteous, gracious living into the bottomless pit of degradation, and despair, and shame and helplessness, and hopelessness, then certainly I am against it.

"But; If when you say whiskey you mean the oil of conversation, the philosophic wine, the ale that is consumed when good fellows get together, that puts a song in their hearts and laughter on their lips, and the warm glow of contentment in their eyes; if you mean Christmas cheer; if you mean the stimulating drink that puts the spring in the old gentleman's step on a frosty, crispy morning; if you mean the drink which enables a man to magnify his joy, and his happiness, and to forget, if only for a little while, life's great tragedies, and heartaches, and sorrows; if you mean that drink, the sale of which pours into our treasuries untold millions of dollars, which are used to provide tender care for our little crippled children, our blind, our deaf, our dumb, our pitiful aged and infirm; to build highways and hospitals and schools, then certainly I am for it.

"This is my stand. I will not retreat from it. I will not compromise."

Cheers!

Cotton in the Delta

I remember well from my childhood days the many trips we took to Ruleville, watching the "Daddy Longlegs" of straight, lush, green cotton rows flitter by on either side of Highways 61 or 49. Each route was the same distance from Greenville. But normally, Mama would go up through Indianola and return through Cleveland so we could stop at Lehrton Cemetery on the way home to visit with and learn about our kinfolks. My grandmother, Mama Rule, was still alive back then and running the Rule Flower Shop, but we went to the cemetery anyway. And I still do today, every time I am close by.

I don't remember seeing miles and miles of corn or the verdant and deep-green, almost purple fields of soybeans we see today. Sure, there were patches of beans scattered here and there, but it was COTTON that was planted as far as your eyes could see. And it was dusty, hot, and always busy. Not many mules were around back then, except off of Bayou Road in Greenville at the rendering plant. I kept my horses close by at Mrs. Carlton's pastures, and as I would brush and clean hoofs and saddle Ole Joe or Sweet Janie, I could hear the incessant pop every five minutes or so as another mule that had been bred to spend his entire life, which he painstakingly and reverently did, plowing cotton and pulling wagons, went down because the tractor had taken over his job. And the tractor not only displaced the mule, it sent thousands and thousands of Delta families packing their bags and heading north for better work and at least a chance for a better life. There were factories that needed help in St. Louis and Detroit, and as Delta bluesman Howling Wolf found out, jobs to be had on the killing floors of meat packing plants in Chicago.

During the fall in the 1950s, I remember the pungent and sweet smell that permeated the air in all the small Delta towns, and especially at the headquarters of the large plantations scattered about our beloved flatland. The smell of cotton defoliant went along with the whine and hustle and bustle of harvest time in the Delta, when the cotton was harvested and wagons and trailers of white gold ambled down highways and country roads on the way to the gin. Highways were lined with fluffy white blankets of cotton on either side, and back then there were no triangular orange fluorescent signs or shimmering, blinking caution lights on the rear of every moving farm vehicle. You knew it was cotton-picking time in the Delta, and you drove slow and careful, and you were always aware. And when the gins shut down about midnight, another smell that never went away, and is sorely missed, was that of the gin trash as it slowly burned and glowed in the big cone shaped cages as the gentle fall breezes drifted the sweet smell of money all over the Delta. Yes, it was good times back then. Soon, new Cadillacs were being driven, and diamonds were noticed on slender fingers…of the landed gentry.

"October sunrise on Pantherburn, cotton lint confusion all around…
Summer's gone now it's picking time, gins are humming with the sound…
Works never done 'til the crop is in, and the cotton market just keeps going down…
Dawn to dusk, seed to bale, Saturday night in Hollandale, as we turn our weary backs on Pantherburn… – Jimmy Phillips, "Pantherburn"

The sharecropping days in the Delta are now long gone, as are the sharecropper and tenant shacks. According to William Alexander Percy in his autobiography *Lanterns on the Levee,* in 1936 the Percy plantation east of Arcola, known as Trail Lake, consisted of 3,343 acres of which 1,834 acres were planted in cotton, with fifty-one acres of pastures for the mules and fifty-two acres of gardens. The remainder of the place was planted in hay and corn to feed the almost two hundred mules, with enough woodland left to supply firewood and stove wood. On the place lived 149 families, each with their own house. These families lived and worked on a share basis, with the plantation supplying everything to make a crop including credit at the plantation commissary store. When the cotton was picked and sold, settlement day cleared the books and a new year was started.

Just about the only old swoop-roofed tenant houses and shotgun shacks left today are preserved at the Shack Up Inn outside of Clarksdale and the Tallahatchie Flats on Money Road a little ways from Greenwood. I recall one winter in the late seventies when the ladies group of a prominent Delta organization pushed to "clean up all the unsightly shacks and country eyesores." I saw many of the old cypress shacks and barns in flames as I traveled up old Number 1 Highway from my cabin on Lake Ferguson to visit my cousins in Hollywood. A tear went up in the smoke with every one of them as they burned. The shacks remaining today may cost you seventy-five bucks a night to stay in them, but it is money well spent for the glorious experience you will have reliving and sleeping in history.

It's ironic that it was on the Hopson Plantation, where the popular Shack Up Inn, Shackdale, and the Hopson Commissary are located, that the first real mechanization in the Delta took place. International Harvester teamed up with the Mid-South Oil Company (Pure Oil) to develop, prototype, and demonstrate the mechanical tractor that was to replace the mule. By 1948, each tractor displaced about sixteen families from the farm. A typical sharecropping family could look after and farm about fifteen to twenty-seven acres of land so when mechanization took over, twelve mules were sent either to Missouri or the rendering plant for every tractor that was bought. An International Super M cost $1,000 and would run in forward gear as a row crop tractor all year long, but for another $2,750 you could buy a basket and picker to be placed on top, and the tractor would also run in reverse and could be used as a cotton picker.

Today, row crop tractors cost around $300,000, and these huge behemoths pull implements that disc, till, and cultivate forty to fifty-foot wide swaths. All systems are run by computers, and the machine is guided and programmed into a GPS system that electronically steers the tractor with signals from a satellite. Herbicides, pesticides, fertilizers, and chemicals are precision calibrated and applied precisely with huge

Primitive mule powered fumigation wagon used in hopes of controlling the boll weevil.

mechanical applicators that resemble spiders as they crawl across the fields. A new combine to cut the rice, corn, and soybeans costs over $300,000 with each of the different headers costing almost $100,000 each. A new six-row cotton picker will set a farmer back almost $900,000. Each of these harvesting machines will be used only about six to eight weeks out of the year.

There was a time when most plantations of a thousand acres or more had their own cotton gins. Fortunate were the farms that straddled a railroad that could ship their cotton to the compress where the bales were pressed by steam power into much smaller bales for shipment to the mills in Virginia and up the East Coast. Today, gins are scattered few and far between, but they gin a lot of cotton.

In 1950, a five hundred acre farm was a good sized and profitable operation. Today, it takes almost three thousand acres for the farming economics to work out considering the price of equipment, seed, fertilizer, and chemicals. That's a long way from the old black gentleman farmer I saw plowing twenty acres of his own cotton with a mule along Highway 61 at Lyon in 1972. I stopped and talked with him as he made his turn and left his mule hitched up in the field to walk over to his shotgun house for a drink of cool water from a pitcher pump in his yard underneath a catalpa tree. I commented on how good his cotton looked, even though his rows were noticeably serpentine, comparing them to the field across the road being plowed with tractors in almost half mile long rows. He tipped his straw hat back on his head as he wiped his brow and said, "Just look at them straight rows over there, thowed up by dem tractors, and look at mine what me and that ole mule is working. Boss, you know, you can make more cotton on a crooked row." My, how times have changed.

Paving the Way

Over the millennia of time, the Mississippi River, with the help of the northern Ohio and smaller rivers rushing out of the Loess Hills to our east, carved and created what we call our Delta.

As floods came, the riparian banks would overflow, catching the heavier sandy particles as the overabundance of water sought lower ground. It was on these high banks that the Indians hacked their trails through canebrakes along the rivers, streams, and bayous. As the great river, and lessor ones, built up steam coming around a bend, sometimes the swirling waters created a cut-off, leaving in its wake an oxbow lake. And the process was repeated thousands of times, gnawing at the land, building ridges and sloughs, and slicing into the hills all the way from the Chickasaw Bluffs at Memphis to Walnut Ridge at Vicksburg. The procedure was continued year after year until the Delta as we know it today was created.

Early travel in the Delta was by water. Access to the interior of the Delta was by river, then stream, then bayous and sloughs. It was a long and slow trip upstream from Vicksburg on the Yazoo, Tallahatchie, and Sunflower Rivers, Deer Creek and Steele Bayou. But if you made the trip with an empty barge or packet boat, you could return to the markets of Vicksburg and New Orleans loaded down with virgin timber or bursting bales of cotton from Rolling Fork, Hollandale, Leland, Greenwood, Belzoni, Ruleville, Marks, Cleveland, Clarksdale, and all the smaller towns scattered throughout our beloved flatland. The railroads were the first to nudge into the Delta, following the timber companies as they gobbled up the prime hardwood trees. Mainline railroads crept south along the high ridges while short dummy lines snaked their way off into the lower swamplands. Dirt wagon roads were plowed up along the railroad rights-of- way as more land was cleared and more cotton was planted.

Life in the Delta was clipping along, and as William Faulkner forlornly stated *"this land which man has deswamped and denuded and derivered in two generations"* was aching for development. In 1916, the Washington County Board of Supervisors voted to pave 144.6 miles of roads throughout the county. A bond issue was approved by the voters for $950,000, and the first contracts for a nine-foot-wide concrete road were let to C G Krenshaw Company from Birmingham, Alabama. From Greenville south to Glen Allen and north to Winterville, then out east to Leland on the C&G then north and south on the IC and later to Tribbett and Tralake along the Black Dog Line, the concrete roads hugged the steel railroads and commerce flourished. Graveled roads searched out and tied into the concrete roads, and soon tar was being placed on the gravel to keep down the dust before asphalt plants were set up in sand pits and the arterial roads began being paved.

Washington County led the way, but the rush was on to get products to market, and the paving process was being copied in every county in the Delta. As the roads developed, so did our highway system, and the small Delta towns' cash registers rang. Highways 61, 82, 49E, and 49W ran alongside the railroads as Henry Ford ushered in

Employees of Burdine Construction set forms and prepare to pour concrete on North Broadway in Greenville in preparation of the opening of Greenville Air Force Base in January 1943.

the Age of the Automobile. Dollar cotton came and went, and soon the Delta was swallowed up by the Great Depression. *"Forty cent cotton and ninety cent meat, how in the world can a po' man eat?"* was being sung in back alleys and juke houses as the Delta folk tried to cope with hard times. One way to help bring an economy out of a depression is by work relief programs and infrastructure development that puts people to work. Highway and bridge construction employed a multitude of strong men, and their wages fed many hungry mouths. Oftentimes there would be a hundred men sitting along a railroad track watching the paving crew. If one man tired out and lay his shovel down, there would be ten men scrambling and rushing to pick it up. There was not a shortage of labor in those days.

One pioneer in Delta highway construction was my daddy, Hal Burdine from Greenville, South Carolina. While watching a paving crew as a child in front of his house on McDuffie Street, he hired on as a water boy pulling a wagon with an oak barrel filled with water and a gourd dipper. Later after leaving Washington and Lee University, he went to work for Southern Paving Company out of Chattanooga, Tennessee, and headed south with his own crew. A contract to help build the seawall in Biloxi brought him to Mississippi and then to the Mississippi Delta. Highways 49, 82, and 61 were being paved with concrete, and in 1934 he was given the opportunity to "buy out his spread and pay for it as he could" from the owners of Southern Paving. Settling in Shaw, before moving to Greenville, he was instrumental in the road and bridge construction programs in the Delta during the Depression. In order to help the entire country out of the devastating era, President F. D. Roosevelt enacted his New

Deal administration, and federal and state contracts were being let and men were going to work. During the 1930s, this program was an economic boon to the Delta and the state of Mississippi. By 1937, New Deal projects had pumped over forty million dollars into the state with a good bit of that going into the Delta. The WPA Program was soon created to help develop state infrastructure and recreational facilities. Burdine Construction Company was awarded many contracts during this time. One was to build Highway 12 through the lowlands of Black Bayou as Leroy Percy State Park was being developed by the WPA. Burdine Construction was awarded the contract to build Highway 454 from Highway 1 to the new Benjamin G. Humphreys Bridge connecting Greenville with Lake Village, Arkansas, along with all concrete paving and culvert work on the approach roads to the super structure on either side of the great bridge. WWII brought much construction to the Delta as Greenville Air Force Base was built and gas pipelines were laid from the oil and gas fields of Louisiana and East Texas, facilitating thousands of pilings to be driven and many yards of concrete poured at the numerous pumping stations along the routes. Burdine Construction, Burdine & Ross, Burdine & Ross Concrete Products, Greenville Ready Mixed Concrete Company, and Greenville Materials helped pave the way for progress. The Delta was on the move again, and the price of cotton was coming up. Elected president of the Mississippi Road Builders Association by his peers in 1950, Hal Burdine helped bring leadership, development, and innovation in the heavy construction industry to the Delta and our state.

In 1941, a young Jesse Ferguson acquired a new Ford dump truck. He remembered the days of his youth in Carroll County plowing, planting, picking, and hauling cotton. He knew well the cool streambeds of the creeks that flowed out of the hills, and he also knew they were full of sand, gravel, and red clay. With that one truck as a beginning and a 15-B Bucyrus dragline, Jesse Ferguson built a company that would later own hundreds of yellow Mack trucks and dump trailers; asphalt and ready mix concrete plants, sand, gravel, and clay gravel pits; and Ferguson Brothers Construction Company. With his motto of "a company is no better than the top men that lead it and the people within it," J. J. Ferguson's legacy continues today with an employee-owned company manufacturing pre-stressed bridge beams and a construction company.

In 1935, a group of forward thinking farmers and businessmen got together and formed an organization to solidify efforts and progress of the eighteen counties in or a part of the Delta. Delta Council was founded, and one of its main purposes was to further implement and develop a viable transportation system within our region. Highway construction and development was, and still is, one of the main efforts of this nationally recognized body that has done much to afford progress to our great region. In 1914 there were 5,700 cars and trucks in Mississippi, but by 1920 there were almost sixty thousand. In 1922 the state legislature authorized a tax of one cent per gallon of gas, allocating 60 percent for county and 40 percent for state road construction. In 1932 that tax was raised to six cents. The heyday of road construction in Mississippi was from 1934-1956. The federal government had contributed $107 million by 1951, and the highway system throughout the state was moving forward.

Many of the highways constructed in the early days of the Delta are still being used today. Progress of the current state and federal funded four lane highway programs is ongoing, and the International Highway 69 is scheduled to slice through the middle of the Delta connecting Canada with Mexico. Chip Morgan of Delta Council states, "The early leaders of Delta Council identified our state highways among its highest priorities. Without river navigation, flood control, and a good highway system, safety and commerce would have no access to the Delta. Just as it was in the early days, we find ourselves in a situation where Mississippi and the Delta have a modern and sound transportation system; however, without a strong commitment and adequate funding for new construction and maintenance, Mississippi and the Delta will suffer economically."

Indomitable
Delta
Characters

The Bride of Annandale
The legend of the tragic love story of Helen Johnstone and Henry Vick

Early one cold December morning in 1858, Colonel H.W. Vick, prominent Delta plantation owner and banker from Vicksburg and of the founding family of that town, dispatched his son Henry Grey Vick to Madison, Mississippi, to pick up some important family estate papers needed to complete the sale of Haywood, a large plantation in Madison County. Dressed in his riding habit and shiny black leather boots, young Henry Vick lit out for Madison after being handed a gold handled buggy whip by Old Jake, the family retainer and Henry's personal attendant. Slowing down only to catch the ferries at the Sunflower and Yazoo Rivers, Henry was clipping right along anxious to return to his home at Nitta Yuma, as he was to catch the steamboat *Vicksburg* and head down to New Orleans for several days and nights of partying before returning on Christmas morning.

Later that day, after picking up the papers in Madison and with his horses rested, fed, and watered, Henry headed home into the setting sun. Traveling down a long west facing rolling hill, Henry was dreaming about the frivolity and fun times to be had in New Orleans when he hit a rut and his right front wheel collapsed. The buggy fell over on its side, and Henry was able to stop the frightened horses before much damage could be done to the chassis. Realizing all that was needed was a blacksmith to fix the broken wheel, he was trying to decide whether to go back to Madison or Canton to have the wheel repaired when he remembered a beautiful mansion that had been under construction close to a quaint Gothic church that stood overlooking the entire countryside. Henry Vick headed back up the hill in search of the plantation, hoping it had a blacksmith shop that could fix his broken wheel. The outcome of that decision was the beginning of a romance that endures today as the legend of the "Bride of Annandale."

After riding bareback and carrying the broken wheel to the top of the hill, Henry dismounted and laid the wheel aside. As he walked up the wide brick walkway, Henry noticed the stately mansion was adorned with huge holly wreaths and in full dress for the holiday season. Tidying up as much as he could, the most eligible bachelor in the Mississippi Delta knocked on the massive white entrance door. According to Dorothy Vick Phelps in her book *Nitta Yuma*, "After a few moments, to Henry's amazement, the door was opened by a beautiful young lady, the loveliest he had ever seen in all of his travels, even in New Orleans!" Realizing he was a gentleman in need of assistance and asking for his hat, Helen Johnstone, the Belle of Mississippi and descendant of the Scottish Earls of Annandale, went to fetch her mother. Henry greatly admired Helen as she walked away in her lacy red-hooped skirt with her long auburn curls flowing gracefully over her shoulders.

When Helen returned with her mother, Mrs. Johnstone realized that Henry was the son of her recently deceased best friend, Sarah Vick. They visited quite frequently on Sarah's many trips to her father's plantation, Haywood. The blacksmith was summoned

COURTESY OF GAY YERGER

The Chapel of the Cross in Madison was consecrated in 1852.

and Henry was asked to stay for dinner while the repairs were made. After dining, Henry Vick was no longer in a hurry to race back home and on to New Orleans. Sitting on the "chaperone couch" in the parlor, with Mrs. Johnstone close by in the library reading her Bible, the young admirers talked and laughed until the chimes on the mantel clock rang midnight! Mother came in and reminded the enamored young gentleman that his buggy was indeed fixed and he should be getting on his way. Rushing home in the cold evening air, Henry's mind was racing with thoughts of the courtly invitations he had just received to the forthcoming gay balls, picnics, house parties, and hayrides.

During the course of their courtship, Henry Vick and Helen Johnstone fell madly in love. Both very prominent families were delighted when their wedding date was announced. Henry had presented her with a beautiful five-carat diamond ring. They were to be married at the family church on the hill across from Annandale. The Chapel of the Cross had been consecrated as an Episcopal church in 1852, and its original parishoners were the members and servants of the Johnstone and Britton families of Annandale and Engleside Plantations. The church was built in 1848 "with slave labor, hired artisans, grim determination, and three thousand dollars." The "river bottom" bricks were hand made and cast on site using area clay. The walls of the gothic church are two feet thick with the massive wooden beams and timbers cut and milled from huge oak trees growing in the surrounding hills. Colonel Vick was so delighted and pleased with the commitment, and especially with the choice of the bride, that he deeded one of his family homes on Cherry Street in Vicksburg to his son as their honeymoon house.

By the middle of May 1861, the honeysuckles, wild roses, sweet olives, and magnolias were in full bloom, and the hills around Annandale were not only filled with the sweet smell of spring but with the joyous excitement of the upcoming nuptials. Family members, friends, and servants were busy with the happy preparations. Invitations had been mailed, and the wedding dress had arrived from Paris. The church had been duly decorated, and the silver candlesticks held white candles, as everyone awaited the arrival of Henry from New Orleans, where he had gone to take care of last minute preparations and bring back the caterers, cooks, waiters, musicians, food, and French champagne.

As was customary, a jovial bachelor's party was held at Henry's lodge at Vickland prior to his departure for New Orleans. As the packet boat blew the whistle for the landing on Deer Creek, Old Jake brought the usual horse around for Henry's childhood best friend James Stith from Vicksburg. In an effort to keep from missing the boat, James hurriedly grabbed the reins from the old family servant and ordered him into the house to fetch his bags. Not realizing that Old Jake had not had time to tighten up the girth on the saddle, James attempted to mount the horse only to have the saddle slip, with him in it, underneath the rearing and frightened horse. Humiliated and embarrassed, James demanded that the old man be thrashed. Henry refused, knowing full well that Jake would never intentionally not tighten the girth on any horse about to be ridden. In a fit of rage and anger, James Stith stormed away from the house exclaiming that he would never speak to his lifelong friend again.

Once in New Orleans, Henry stayed busy collecting all the items on his list of last minute preparations. He stopped by a local billiard hall for a bit of enjoyment with his buddies before he was to catch the boat back up the Mississippi to Vicksburg. While chalking up his cue, a familiar voice was heard, and James Stith walked in. He was invited to have a drink with all the old pals, to which he refused indignantly! Pointing to Henry Vick he replied, "I will not drink with him, because he is no gentleman!" According to Phelps, "Mr. Stith, with both gloves, slapped them back and forth across Henry's face in a most disrespectful manner." Henry drew his gun, but re-holstered it as he remembered an oath to Helen that he would never use his gun against another man to settle a dispute (as he had obviously done on several previous occasions). "Mr. Stith made another pass with his left fist. Dodging this time, but to save his honor, Henry challenged Mr. Stith to a duel."

Along with their surgeons and seconds, the men took a steamboat to Mobile, as dueling was forbidden in Louisiana. Kentucky long rifles were chosen as weapons with a distance of thirty paces and a count of three. Henry was well known for his prowess with a firearm and could hit a running rabbit or deer handily with a rifle. In order to save his honor and also to honor his promise to his bride to be, on the count of "one" Henry raised his rifle and fired into the air. Not realizing what had happened, James Stith turned, aimed, and fired, the bullet hitting Henry's rifle barrel and deflecting, entering his forehead and killing him instantly.

Later that evening a telegraph was dispatched informing of what had happened, and it was agreed that the boat carrying Henry's coffin, which unknowingly included all the trappings and caterers, would be met at Vicksburg and then travel by train to Annandale where many of the wedding guests had already arrived. The burial would not be at Henry's ancestral burial grounds but at the chapel in Helen's family plot. At precisely the appointed time for the wedding ceremony, a solemn torchlite procession arrived at the little Chapel of the Cross as the church bell was tolling from the tall steeple. Bishop William Green said prayers for the dead in front of the beautiful altar, lit with candles and adorned with Henry's favorite flowers, red roses.

Dressed in her pure white Parisian wedding gown, Helen Johnstone walked slowly down the aisle and tearfully leaned over into the open coffin and kissed her Henry on his lips stating, "You shall always have my heart, for I promise never to give it to another." With that she produced a pair of scissors and cut her beautiful long auburn curls and placed them over his heart.

Helen went into severe mourning, and her mother decided a trip to Europe would do her good. She was squired by nobility with matrimonial requests made by several eligible gentlemen, all to be refused. Soon after she became known as the "Bride of Annandale."

Soon the Civil War broke out, and Helen was busy supporting the cause. She furnished an entire regiment with uniforms and even had her gorgeous wedding dress cut up for bandages.

Helen was later introduced to a handsome young rector who had preached at the Chapel of the Cross, and he, too, fell in love with her and asked her to marry him. Helen explained, "My heart still belongs to Henry Vick, the gentleman out there in the grave. I could never forget him, Never! Even when you would call my name, I shall be remembering his dear love!"

Helen eventually married Reverend George Carroll Harris, and they produced five children, two of whom lived to be adults. They moved to Rolling Fork where a sister Chapel of the Cross, had been erected. There they built a huge and beautiful mansion a few miles north of town atop a large Indian mound. And it was at Mont Helena amongst the cotton fields where Helen lived to be almost eighty years old with her husband preceeding her to the grave. In 1917, on her deathbed, Helen seemed to be the lively girl of her youth, exclaiming, "He is coming back. He has come back for me!"

Helen is not buried by the side of her beloved Henry but in Rolling Fork next to her husband Reverend Harris. However, outside of Madison, amongst the oaks and pine trees "when the warm spring nights come, and the roses, honeysuckle and magnolias are in bloom, it is said that the sweetest heavenly music can be heard, and Helen returns to the chapel at Annandale and to her sweetheart, Henry Vick."

In his definitive work, *Shadows of a Chapel*, Glenn S. Smith writes: "What was in Helen's heart will never be known, as only one thing is certain, Henry Grey Vick lies alone in a strangely wide grave...in the shadow of a chapel."

The Enigma of Willa Johnson

Born of landed gentry, Willa Adams Johnson was an enigma to her family and friends, acquaintances, and possibly herself. Reared a Southern belle on the north shore of Lake Washington around 1900, she grew up with a silver spoon in her mouth and a deck of cards in her hand.

Her father, Colonel Matt Johnson, inherited Chatham Plantation from his father, Captain Henry Johnson, a prominent pioneer of Washington County. Born in Kentucky in 1794, Captain Henry came by keelboat to Worthington Point on the Mississippi River. While camped there, he bought, from a disreputable fellow named Bunch, the "tomahawk improvement" rights to three thousand acres of prime cotton ground, paying fifty dollars and a keg of Kentucky whiskey. Later he acquired title to the land from the state of Mississippi. Admiring greatly the freedom-loving qualities of the Earl of Chatham, England, Johnson named his plantation after Lord Chatham. Facing the lake was the plantation home, a large two-story house surrounded by brick servants' quarters.

Willa's mother entertained lavishly. A breakfast for twenty or more was not uncommon at Chatham. According to Noel Workman in a 1964 *Delta Review* article, "Colonel Johnson enjoyed Lake Washington society. He maintained his social obligations, often at the expense of his responsibilities, as was customary of gentlemen farmers. It was a good life while it lasted."

Young Willa Johnson grew up enjoying the lifestyle of the Old South. She couldn't be beat in swimming and canoeing races, and as a horseman she had few equals. With a rifle or pistol, she was a crack shot. According to an essay by Willa's cousin, John Erwin, "The family had mistakenly chosen Mississippi as Eden...she and her brothers led the sporting life of country gentlefolk."

Her childhood nickname "Willie" stuck as she spent a year or two in a New Orleans finishing school. Later she went to New York and studied photography under the noted Impressionistic portraitist Arnold Genthe. In later years, Genthe would recall Willie as "a violent spirit."

Returning home, she found the curse of many Delta families and financial difficulties had set in. Crops and entire plantations were lost at the drop of a card. Gambling addiction very possibly could have been the reason for her animosity at times. Willie had moved home to Chatham as an enlightened young woman in the ways of the world. New Orleans and New York City had left their mark, and her eccentricity began to bubble. The flamboyance of the "good life" and the inability to finance it became a problem.

Willie began to dress in a manner unheard of a Southern belle. She was quite the character in her "panama hat and narrow four-in-hand tie, a severe black suit and a man's white shirt, black stockings, and flat black shoes." Erwin wrote, "Her stride was set—quick and heavy for such a small person. The anomaly? She was completely feminine. There was something else in her face that was paradoxical, something hard

COURTESY OF CHARLOTTE HAYS

A rare portrait of Willa Johnson, right, taken in Greenville in the early 1900s.

and pugnacious that made one think of some quality beyond beauty or ugliness."

Willie kept her hair dark brown, almost black—a cropped coiffure Willie said resembled "a black iron kettle set to boil on a too-old face." She rolled her own Bull Durham cigarettes and "had a vocabulary unlike any lady of the day...She was often referred to as scandalous!" She had "two personalities, wildly divergent and cloaked by a somewhat hard exterior into which it seemed little light entered." Erwin's mother had always been fond of Willie, "finding stimulation in her raucous humor and uncommon intelligence."

Before the plantation was either lost or sold, Willie opened a shop in the general store with a young woman named Pearl Moritz, a divorcee from Natchez. Erwin noted, "Only once did Willie ever meet a person with a disposition that complemented her own in its rancor and general cussedness." They lived together and became the talk of the community dealing in Oriental commodities and novelties.

Workman stated that by then the "Johnson family was reduced to less than modest means and the role of family provider fell to Willie. She accepted misfortune without complaint."

Willie and Pearl opened a business in downtown Greenville that was a bookstore and gift shop. Frequented by enlightened luminaries, the shop had a bohemian air about it. According to Willie's cousin, author Charlotte Hays, "Her shop became both gossip central and a sort of literary hangout."

William Faulkner's first literary agent, Ben Wasson, often held court there with Anne Grasty and William Alexander Percy, noted poet and author of *Lanterns on the Levee*. "There was a lending library of forbidden literature of the day," Erwin wrote, "and the conversation was often too provocative and outspoken for the general wayfarer."

Will Percy remembered Willie and Pearl stating, "I have always known Willie and found her amazingly talented, a rare character, but utterly unbalanced, a pot that is always boiling. And Pearl is a sort of oasis in this town, that at times is a barren waste as far as conversation, mores and general outlook is concerned. Both of them, coming to grips, probably have the most deadly, intractable, vile dispositions ever put in the female body."

Befriending and intriguing Will Percy's mother, Camille, with their Orientalia, the pair inspired an entire room at the imposing mansion on Percy Street. Unfortunately, the relationship between the two erudite women came to an end. "The bookstore, or any business...was too small for two such molten spirits," said Erwin.

Hays adds, "Amid fearful battles, Willie and Pearl parted but not before Willie chased Pearl with the butcher knife!"

Pearl kept the shop and Willie opened her own photography studio—one door away!

Strapped financially, Willie and her parents moved from flat to flat as she supported them with her meager photographic earnings. She became heavily indebted as her gambling desires moved from poker tables to slot machines in local, raunchy Delta joints. While living in the old Greenville Military Academy that had been carved into small apartments, which Willie called "rat holes," her friend Ben Wasson set up a photo shoot of the up-and-coming writer from Oxford, William Faulkner. Faulkner wanted a portrait to be made for publicity in his forthcoming publication of *The Marble Faun*. He was elated about the possible success of his new book. Upon settling down in her cramped studio, the young man commented, "They're reading poetry again. I believe my book will be an escape for poetry lovers from the scribblings that some authors are presumptuous enough to call poetry."

A poet herself and author of a small book of poetry titled, *Poems that Mean Something*, Willie replied, "Doggerel! I call it free worse!" Faulkner smiled as he pulled out his briar pipe and Willie hand rolled another Bull Durham. Sharing the box of kitchen matches that lay on the table, they lit their respective smokes as they admired each other's wit. In his book, *Count No Count*, Ben Wasson recalled them "looking each other over carefully and liking what they saw." She showed Faulkner some of her work, and he was especially interested in a study of the local blacks, stating, "Good straight stuff, nothing fancy here. It's honest." Wasson wrote, "Before he left, she told Bill she'd like to get in a poker game with him sometime, promising she'd beat the tarnation out of him and teach him how the game should be played."

Willie had reverted to selling family silver and portraits. The land was gone, and it was all she could do to feed herself and her parents. "We're remnants of one hell of a family," she commiserated to Erwin one day. He later reminisced, "Willie felt free to criticize the South and family, but woe to anyone outside the circle who trespassed in such a manner. If she took offense, real or imagined, at any individual, that person might well have walked up the steps to the guillotine!"

Willie was often a guest at Percy's house as she was considered to be a "kindred spirit." She had a certain air about her and a dignity in her art that came out in the photographs she took. Some shots she liked, and some she considered balderdash. She photographed Holt Collier, the legendary guide on President Theodore Roosevelt's famous bear hunt. And she photographed William Alexander Percy and William Faulkner and harlots and little children. She adored children, and they in turn "seemed to adore her, somehow seeing through the opaque shell to the nebulous beauty that lurked inside."

Once Willie took some photos of Erwin. The results were outstanding, but she disapproved saying, "You are too young to show any character and what character it does show, shouldn't be seen at all."

Years and hardship would later take its toll. She moved to New Mexico and lived with her niece, a prominent former concert violinist. She moved into a convent nursing home run by Catholic nuns. Erwin wrote, "The sisters must have all needed a refresher course in their calling when Willie passed on."

No one knows how old she was when she died in 1950. Willie considered it "none of anybody's damn business." Hearing of Willie's death, Faulkner quipped, "I hope she taught the nuns to play poker!"

Willie was shipped back to be buried in the Greenville Cemetery. Family and friends were on hand that sweltering day when a cousin drove by in an automobile and waved, "Yoo hoo, Willie missed the train in Albuquerque! Come back tomorrow!"

Photographic genius or eccentric bohemian? We have only to look at what's left of her flamboyant life to answer that question.

How Matsy Made History

A premier female fashion photographer of the 1930s, Wynn "Matsy" Richards Taylor paved the way for women in both fashion and the arts.

For years, the much-ballyhooed season ending awards of the Greenville/Leland little theater were the Matsy Awards. In the late '50s, the Twin Cities Theater Guild built a facility and named it the Wynn Richards Taylor Playhouse. It was painted "Matsy pink" in honor of Matsy Wynn's favorite color.

Wynn Richards Taylor was born in Friar's Point to Judge and Mrs. J.H. Wynn in 1889. She moved to Greenville as a young child when her father became a circuit court judge and later mayor of Greenville. Nicknamed "Matsy," she grew up as a privileged child and attended finishing school, marrying when she was eighteen years old to levee contractor Dorsey E. Richards. She had one child, Harper Richards, born in 1908.

As a young mother in Greenville during the early part of the last century, Matsy was quite adept at living the good life. She entertained creatively, staging home talent shows and decorating lavishly for parties. She became interested in the arts and was well known for her charity benefits, especially on behalf of King's Daughters Hospital.

In the spring of 1918, Matsy received a call from a friend wanting her to come over and look at an article in the Christian Science Monitor about opportunities in the new and rapidly expanding field of photography. An impulsive woman, and excited about a possible new career, she hurried over to her friend's house. After reading the article, Matsy went home, packed her bags, and headed north. She searched for an instructor for weeks until she located Clarence H. White, a New Yorker who was teaching a summer course in Connecticut. The engaging life of a premier fashion photographer was born that very day.

The Clarence H. White School of Photography was known throughout the art world as one of the premier photographic schools and today is well respected as one of the earlier cutting edge pioneers in photographic techniques. Turn of the century artists were struggling to elevate photography to the realm of fine art while embracing an avant-garde attitude. Acknowledged as a master of fine art photography, Clarence White was best known for his teaching abilities. A leader of pictorialist photography, he stressed the importance of composition and design, encouraging his students to make their own pictorial decisions. Several of his students have become photographic history's most well-known artists.

Matsy learned rapidly and returned home on May 5, 1919, to open "Ye Ole Barne Studio." The makeshift studio was behind her parents' home in Blanton Park, which adjoined the business district on Washington Avenue in Greenville. Brodie Crump recalled in his "Mostly Old Stuff" column in the local newspaper, "She fixed up the carriage section and hayloft of the barn to where there wasn't an interior on Royal Street in New Orleans that her studio would have to back away from." According to an article in the *Democrat Times* by her friend Miss Lillian McLaughlin, "Her darkroom was an old tool closet covered with brown paper, painted black." Matsy often collaborated with her

Matsy and Bert Taylor aboard the "Matsy" in New York, 1943.

friend and fellow New York educated local photographer Willa Johnson. They shared ideas of different photographic techniques, Willa having been schooled in the Impressionistic style. They also entertained together putting on plays and theater productions. Matsy persevered through her early career stating, "I was forced to work out many fundamental problems of photography the hardest and best way...by myself!"

In 1921 Matsy's work became nationally known when she won the second place prize in a *New York Evening Post* camera contest. "Old Aunt Maria," a portrait of an elderly cook smoking a corncob pipe, garnered her the whopping sum of ten dollars. A year earlier, her work had gained international fame as three of her photographs traveled to Copenhagen, London, and Liverpool in a traveling exhibit of the Pictorial Photographers of America. One of those images was of a small child with a short bob-tailed hairstyle. "Caledonia" was Caledonia Jackson (Payne), the daughter of her dear friend that showed her the newspaper article that began her career.

Moving to Newport, Rhode Island, in 1922, Matsy and a friend opened a studio and were soon receiving assignments from *Vogue* magazine. She returned home to the Delta briefly that fall but moved to New York when a job was offered and accepted as a staff photographer for *Vogue*. Matsy was unfamiliar with studio lighting and the aspects of studio techniques, and after about a year she came back home. It was then that a lifelong study of lighting began. "My experiments with lighting led me straight to fashion photography, for I found out that correct lighting was the secret in bringing out textures and other qualities of material."

As a professional photographer, Matsy's lighting skills became her single strongest characteristic. Through experimentation and hard work, she soon began to understand the different angles and exposures that portrayed the effect she wanted in a shot. Matsy packed her bags again and moved to Chicago to open a studio with friend Bettie Frear. The Richards-Frear Photography Studio concentrated on the advertising world, shooting catalogs and ads for Marshall Field & Company, Maurice L. Rothschild, Piggly Wiggly, and Johnson's Wax. According to Greenvillian Louise Mayhall, "Matsy used her given name 'Wynn Richards' for her business name so she would seem to be a man. It was sort of a taboo against women competing with men...It was a long time before some people realized that she wasn't a man."

Matsy and Miss Frear moved to New York City in 1927, continuing their business expansion during the Roaring Twenties. According to an April 1982 article in the *Delta Democrat Times* written by her granddaughter Holly Richards, Matsy remained in New York until the mid-'30s when her partner, Miss Frear, moved to Florida. Matsy then took a penthouse in Tudor City near the river. There she met and married a former British Naval Officer, Herbert Taylor. He became her manager and assisted her in much of her photographic work. Matsy's New York days were considered her finest and most prolific. Fashion photographs were included in magazines such as *Vogue* and *McCall's* with cover photos adorning *Bride Magazine* and the *Saturday Evening Post.* New York based advertising clients included Old Spice, Warner's Foundation, Elizabeth Arden, Nicole of Paris, Pequot Percale Sheets along with Dorothy Grey and Orloff Cosmetics.

In 1934, Matsy exhibited a collection of photographs of women executives in the fashion industry. The "arbiters of fashion for the country" included editors of *Vogue* and *Harper's Bazaar,* renowned fashion coordinators and Lilly Dache, milliner. So well known had she become that in 1943 the National Cotton Council in Memphis commissioned her to do a series of photographs to run as full page ads in twenty-six fashion magazines as part of a national fashion advertising campaign. The governors' wives and their children of seventeen cotton-producing states posed for her 8x10 camera. Eight thousand watt lights lit up governors' mansions from coast to coast as fashionable cotton dresses and suits were proudly modeled. Photographic shoots were set up in cotton gins and mills throughout the country. Fashion designers exhibited their creations, and the story of cotton from the field to the mill was told. Matsy went on to become quite popular on the lecture circuit, speaking about photography and encouraging other women to pick up a camera and pursue the field of photography. Because of her notoriety in the fashion industry, she was invited to be the first woman judge for the Miss America Pageant in 1948.

Matsy's second husband died in 1945. According to her nephew, the late Doug Wynn, "Bert's death and funeral was the only time I ever saw Matsy break down." Mr. Taylor's coffin was draped with a Union Jack and buried in the Wynn family plot in Greenville. The following year a water pipe burst above her New York studio and destroyed much of it.

In a paper on file at the Library of Congress written by Doug's stepdaughter, LeAnne Gault, "The combination of Bert's death and the flooding of her New York studio left her both at a loss and lost. Again she returned home, like she did whenever she faced a life change, only this time, she would not leave."

Matsy bought a lot on South Main and commissioned her son, in Chicago at the time, to design a studio for her. Harper Richards was a renowned architect in Greenville, having lived there as a child and recently returning to design a number of homes in Gamwyn Park and Leland. The studio, currently the long-time residence of Rabbit Jenkins, was a contemporary building with a towering roofline and floor-to-ceiling windows that took advantage of available light and allowed room for very large light stands. The studio was expertly designed and served its purpose well. From her studio/home she took formal photographs of "prominent and not so prominent" citizens of the Delta. According to her granddaughter Holly, "She was the official portrait photographer of the Delta Debutante Club. Young women in their long ruffled tulle dresses came to the studio to stand before her camera, either inside or outside in the adjacent gardens." Doug Wynn remembered, "She was always kind to her subjects calling them 'Darling' and 'Sweetie Pie.' She was also willing to hide their flaws or 'remove some of their chins' with a soft lead pencil." Matsy was known to have stated, "I am making them look the way they want to look, rather than the way the negative shows them. The lens doesn't lie and they don't like that."

Her love of gardening had led her in 1922 to form the Greenville Garden Club, the first garden club in the state. That club is still in existence today. And in 1956, at Matsy's urging, the Greenville Garden Club was instrumental in the preservation of the Winterville Indian Mounds north of town, now a Mississippi State Park.

Matsy's love of the arts and theater caused her to become heavily involved with Ben Wasson, Louise Eskrigge Crump, and others to form the Twin Cities Theater Guild. According to Holly, "This love for theater, for drama, had always been with her, and it blossomed profusely after her return from New York. 'Matsy' awards for best performance or direction during a season were as coveted by members of the clique as were Oscars."

Matsy was a staunch Christian Scientist and regularly attended the church her son had designed close to her home and studio. "Perhaps," Holly Richards suggests, "it was from her religious refusal to accept fear that she was able to conquer obstacles and to accomplish so much in her life." Matsy was always involved in her passions, either the arts, the theater, her photography, or gardening. And in the end, Matsy died as she had lived, pursuing her passions. Following a board meeting of the little theater, she was sweeping her studio, preparing for a photo shoot the next day and suffered a fatal heart attack. At seventy-five years old, Matsy, the Mother of the Arts in Greenville had her final curtain call at 5:30 in the afternoon on March 20, 1960. LeAnne Gault reflects, "Wynn Richards was more than just her work and her sacrifices. She was a stylish and beautiful lady who helped pave the way for generations of women in both fashion and the arts."

The Life of a Delta General
Three Wars, Three Stars, and the '27 Flood

In the spring of 1927, it rained. By the time April came around, the Delta was totally saturated, and the Mississippi River was at full capacity and bulging against the protection levees. Ten thousand or more laborers frantically attempted to sandbag low places on the levee and weak areas in the berms and sand boils along its base. On April 16, the Greenville National Guard Unit was placed on state active duty, and Major Alexander Gallatin Paxton was given charge of all operations. The weakest point of the levee was found to be about twelve miles north of Greenville. According to John Barry in *Rising Tide*, "At Mounds Landing the levee was particularly and unavoidably vulnerable. Just above the landing, the river ran in a straight line for several miles, gathering force and momentum. Then it curved around a 90-degree bend. The water was in a tumult; it boiled. It collided with the bank and generated terrific, literally terrifying, currents. Their swirl threw up waves that made no sense, which came from opposite directions and crashed against each other. The surface of the river rose and fell from one spot to the next, exploding into eddies and whirlpools."

On the night of April 20, it rained six inches. The next morning, Major Paxton answered the phone at headquarters, and his duty officer at Mounds Landing said, "We can't hold it much longer." Then followed three words that Galla Paxton said he would remember as long as he lived: "There she goes!" The levee had collapsed and billions upon billions of gallons of rushing, seething, foaming, yellow river water began pouring through the almost mile-wide crevasse.

Moving his headquarters into the second story of the old Opera House, Major Paxton found local poet and lawyer Will Percy hard at work in his new position as commander of the local Red Cross. Senator Leroy Percy, Will's father, had taken over as general advisor for the entire operation. The first order was to safeguard the city water supply and maintain law and order to prevent any looting. Volunteers were abundant and Major Paxton delegated authority where he felt it would do the most good. Voluntary martial law was imposed and an 8 p.m. until dawn curfew was placed on anyone without a pass. Motorized boats were dispatched each day to go out to save refugees clinging to rooftops. Cattle and mules were herded to the remaining dry levee areas, and hay was brought in by steamboat. Huge levee camps were built along the levee that housed and fed eight thousand refugees.

In June, the tepid, stagnant, disease ridden water slowly began to recede. Coordinated operations to clean, disinfect, and inspect all public places before re-opening also began. Clean up efforts were so successful that the American Legion was invited to have their annual state convention in Greenville later that summer and the invitation was accepted. Through close personal attention and the display of professional leadership, Major Galla Paxton had brought Greenville through high water hell. At thirty-one years old, he was awarded the Mississippi Magnolia Medal by the state for his service during and after the Great Flood of '27.

COURTESY OF THE PAXTON FAMILY COLLECTION

General Paxton maps out a plan with Lt. General Palmer Swift and General Joe Stilwell.

Growing up in Greenville

Galla Paxton had grown up in Greenville wanting to be a soldier. A true "son of the South," he went to Washington and Lee University in Lexington, Virginia. During his junior and senior years, he was president of the Alpha Chapter of Kappa Alpha Order, the fraternity founded by Robert E. Lee in 1865. VMI cadets often came over to the KA house and drilled W&L students giving young Galla his first taste of military life. Short of stature, bowlegged, and weighing only 155 pounds, Galla started most football games as fullback and earned his letter his senior year in 1916.

Talk of war was raging as graduation rolled around in the spring of '17. Galla applied and was accepted as a first lieutenant in the National Army. After training he reported for duty at the 8th Field Artillery Unit at Camp Mecon near Vannes, France. According to his biography *Three Wars and a Flood*, "I was hardly dry behind the ears and commanding a battery of artillery in France." His superiors recommended his promotion to captain because of his "proficiency in gunnery and demonstrated ability to fire the batteries without reference to a notebook and outstanding leadership capabilities."

His next move was to Brest, France, and then home. WWI was over.

Galla returned home in August of 1919 and went to work with Hubert Crosby classing cotton. He soon started his own business as the A.G. Paxton Cotton Company.

71

Receiving a commission in the Mississippi National Guard in 1926, Captain Paxton accepted the command of a 155mm howitzer battery being organized in Greenville. His armory was an unused section of the Delta Compress. Acquiring five used Model A Ford trucks from the post office and two old howitzers, the unit received federal recognition as a Field Artillery Battery in the Mississippi National Guard. Galla Paxton was granted the gold leaf of a major in the Mississippi National Guard and made commander of the 1st Battalion, 178th Field Artillery. Within a year, his leadership and organizational abilities would be taxed in the worst natural disaster to ever befall the Mississippi Delta.

After the Flood

Soon after the Great Flood, life returned to normal in Greenville, and the National Guard unit continued to build in strength and equipment. A new armory on Walnut Street was built and units drilled one night each week and two weeks during the summer. Smaller 37mm guns were mounted on the barrels of the 155mm howitzers, and the guns were laid and fired as if the 155s were being used. The artillery pieces were pulled on top of the levee, and the guns fired across the Mississippi River to sandbars on the other side. Major Paxton was promoted to colonel and given command of the re-designated 114th Field Artillery Regiment in September 1933.

During this time Galla Paxton began to expand his cotton brokerage business and planned a trip to Europe to develop contacts for an international marketplace to export Delta cotton. With his wife Ruth, the Paxtons flew from Liverpool to Paris and by train traveled to Belgium, Holland, Italy, and Switzerland. In Germany, he saw young brownshirted boys in Hitler's Youth Corps being indoctrinated into the Nazi party. The trip marked the beginning of an export business that was soon to make the A.G. Paxton Company known throughout the cotton markets of Europe.

In 1936 Colonel Paxton was placed on the War Department General Staff Eligibility List. By this time, Camp Shelby in South Mississippi had become a training camp for the National Guard and was soon to be a full-time Army post during WWII. The 114th was inducted into the Army in November 1940, as part of the 31st Infantry Dixie Division. Colonel Galla Paxton was promoted to brigadier general in 1942. When WWII broke out, his first assignment was to defend the major Hawaiian Islands from invasion after the attack on Pearl Harbor. A favorite pastime during off-duty hours was pheasant hunting. Pheasants were considered pests and did considerable damage to the pineapple and sugarcane fields. General Paxton kept his staff and friends amply supplied with this delicious bird.

Later, having participated in the very successful invasion of Kwajalein, General Paxton went on a speaking tour informing officers of the proper way to invade a Pacific island. He was soon ordered to New Guinea and the Philippines. While fighting on Baguio, the going was slow and always uphill. The artillery was able to lay down a "preparation fire" up the hillsides with the infantry scrambling right behind. During these island campaigns, General Paxton flew in his small L-4 observation planes so often and extensively behind enemy lines that he received the Air Medal for his numerous flights. The Japanese dreaded seeing these small planes because they knew of the bombardment that would soon follow.

During one battle, a large number of enemy artillery pieces were captured along with many rounds of ammunition. Organizing "J Battery" with a small group of American and Filipino soldiers, four howitzers were able to take the fight to the Japanese with their own guns. Having earlier criticized Japanese equipment, one officer commented, "It ain't the guns, brother, it's the technique!" Soon the bombs over Hiroshima and Nagasaki ended the Pacific War.

General Paxton returned home and began to re-organize his cotton business. In July of 1948 he was promoted to major general of the Mississippi National Guard. One of his greatest prides was the Dixie Division Band. Dressed in Confederate uniforms, the Dixie Division Band was approved by the Department of the Army. The band performed at football games, parades, conventions, and as the official band for Derby Day at Churchill Downs. Every performance began with the song "Dixie."

The Dixie Division was called to active duty during the Korean Conflict and was told to prepare to go overseas. However, the division never shipped out to Korea. Major General Paxton retired from the military in 1958 and was given the Mississippi Magnolia Cross at his final review of troops as commanding general of the 31st Infantry Division. The headquarters building at Camp Shelby was dedicated Paxton Hall.

In the fall of 1958, a festive "Galla Paxton Day" parade was given by Greenville's Mayor George Archer. The Dixie Division Band led the parade. Among the many floats and bands and military units were several jeeps carrying a bunch of neighborhood kids known as "Galla's Gang." The gang spent many Saturday afternoons in his upstairs study in Gamwyn Park marveling at war memorabilia and listening to his stories. Hubert Crosby's youngest son, Barry, was riding in one of those jeeps. He later lost his life in Vietnam defending his country.

The afternoon of the parade, the third star was pinned on General Galla Paxton's shoulders making him the first lieutenant general in the history of the Mississippi National Guard. Hodding Carter, owner and editor of the *Delta Democrat Times*, presented him with a bullwhip. For some reason, and one can only imagine, he had gotten the nickname "Bull Whip Shorty" during WWII.

In his retirement speech after forty-one years of military duty, General Galla Paxton stated to the assembled officers and men of the 31st Division, "Three times have I seen the Dixie Division organized from the ground up. Twice it has been honored by a call from the President of the United States to active duty, taking its place of honor in the defense of our nation in times of great emergency. In each tour it has served with great credit and distinction. To each of you officers and men of the 31st Infantry Dixie Division, I present my most honorable salute."

Rosedale Moon and the Untouchable Perry Martin

Al Capone considered Perry Martin's moonshine the best there was. He sent specially designated boxcars with armed guards down from Chicago to load cases upon cases of what was known as PM. To those who remember it, PM was arguably the best moonshine in the country.

In any speakeasy in Chicago, New York, Pittsburgh, or New Orleans, all you had to do was ask for "PM" and you were given the finest moonshine whiskey there ever was, straight from Rosedale, Mississippi. There are heirloom bottles today that are passed down from generation to generation, with a sip taken on special occasions. Judge Bard Selden from Hollywood, Mississippi, recalls his father telling him, "Each month, you could set your watch by the arrival of a long black Twin Six Packard limousine with District of Columbia plates headed south on old Highway 61. Later that afternoon, it would make its return trip to Washington, D.C., through Hollywood, loaded, with its rear fenders low to the ground. Franklin D. Roosevelt was the president back then."

During the days of Prohibition, moonshine was made in back country stills all over the South. Federal revenuers were kept busy locating and busting up illegal whiskey stills and carting off those that got caught to jail. Even though Perry Martin from Rosedale was fined a few times, it is doubtful he ever went to jail for making moonshine. It was illegal to make whiskey within the city limits of Rosedale, those limits extending across the levee and to the river. The offense carried a $100 fine. Perry Martin paid his fine in advance each year on January 1. Mr. Charlie Capps, who was sheriff of Bolivar County during the last years of Perry Martin's life, recalls, "I would receive a gallon of PM each year around Christmas, and I never even met Mr. Martin."

Bolivar County had never offered a bounty on finding and destroying moonshine stills. "The only trouble with local law is them drinking up my whiskey," a retired moonshiner told William Sullivan in *Perry Martin, Mississippi Moonshine*. During Prohibition, the local lawman was viewed as a defender from the federal revenuer who was "a foreigner messing in what was not his business!" One Rosedale law officer offers, "We were all in moonshine back then, either making it, selling it, or drinking it." Charlie Crawford, at one time the town marshall of Rosedale said, "Perry Martin had a reputation for being dangerous, but he was the most honest man I ever knew. He tended to his own business, left everybody else's alone. Perry Martin's business was on the river side of the levee, and except to get a haircut or to vote, he stayed away from Rosedale, on his side of the levee." A former chief of police of Rosedale adds, "Perry Martin wasn't bothered by the law because he was as good a man as he was a moonshiner."

Martin was the son of a wealthy rice farmer and had been educated for the ministry. As a young man he was involved in state and local Arkansas politics. In 1920 he left the rice farm with his wife and two children and settled on Big Island, a 121,000-acre wilderness area across from Rosedale at the confluence of the White, Arkansas, and Mississippi Rivers. He went into the timber and logging business. Big Island was reported to be the "largest whiskey producing area in the United States." Earl Drury, a retired moonshiner from Big Island that served twelve years as Rosedale's constable, said that when he sat in front of his still on Big Island he could see an additional twenty-one stills in operation. When asked if life was dangerous on Big Island, Drury recalled, "There was plenty of law and order on Big Island. Simply, if there was an argument, somebody got killed." According to Drury, the main law enforcement figure on Big Island was Perry Martin himself. The sheriff of Desha County, Arkansas, had sworn him in as a deputy, and he wore the badge with pride.

Not many people bothered Perry Martin because he had the reputation of being a violent man. This was possibly untrue unless he was provoked. One hot summer night he was guarding a raft of his own logs tied up on the river

Perry Martin on his houseboat, as photographed for The *Delta Review* September/October 1965 issue in "Rosedale on the River." Printed by permission.

awaiting a boat to pick them up. Five men came up with guns and tried to steal the logs. A gun battle ensued, and Perry Martin killed all five of the robbers. He turned himself in to the sheriff's office and was acquitted for "simply protecting his own property." It is also believed that he killed his own stepson during an altercation. According to Henry McCaslin, Perry Martin and his stepson were in a rowboat in the river, and the stepson started rocking the boat, either to try to throw him out of the boat or to just scare him. "Perry Martin pulled his pistol and shot him because he could not swim."

Melvin Martin, Perry Martin's grandson, states, "My grandaddy was a very educated man. He was an ordained minister, a self-made man, and he was as good as gold. But if you crossed him, he would kill you."

After killing a man for stealing his hog and only serving one year of a ten-year sentence, Perry Martin gave up logging and went into the moonshine business. He moved to the east side of the river in 1929 and lived on the banks of the Mississippi in a fairly ornate old wooden houseboat set up on blocks in a grove of cypress trees. In 1950, Perry Martin bought his wife Lou a house at the foot of the levee in a place called "the pasture." He spent the first night in the new house with his wife and became ill and was not able to sleep. He never stayed another night on the dry side of the levee. Yet each day he could be seen walking across the levee to have lunch with his wife. He slept on his houseboat every night to be close to his stills. Perry Martin's houseboat had electricity but no air conditioning and possibly no running water. But when his grandkids walked to the picture show in Rosedale on Saturday afternoon, they were flush with cash. Bill Parker recalls, "My daddy would give each of us twenty-five cents, which was enough for admission, popcorn and a Coke. Whenever Melvin and James Perry showed up, each of those boys had two or three dollars in their pockets."

Will Gourlay remembers that as a boy growing up in Rosedale, camping and hunting on the river, he would see him often. "Mr. Perry was a tall and slender man. He walked slowly, and he talked slowly, making sure you heard and understood everything he was telling you. He drove an old green Jeep pickup truck, and you never knew where you might see him along the river. He had stills all over those woods."

According to Martin's daughter-in-law, Mrs. Myron Martin, "one of the most frightening things about him was that you never heard him in the woods until he was face to face with you."

Bill Parker says that according to Alfred Welsan, "Each time you went out to the houseboat to buy a gallon of moonshine, Perry Martin would have you come in the kitchen where he would pour you half of an iced tea glass of PM. You were expected to drink it right then and there to ensure its quality. With the heat of summer, and no air moving at all in that sweltering houseboat, after you drank your sample and paid for your gallon, it was all you could do to make it back up to the top of the levee!" One imbiber recalled PM as "so smooth, but so strong, it would make a little rabbit walk right up and spit in a bulldog's face."

The whiskey did not have the crystal- clear appearance of most moonshine, otherwise known as white lightning, because it was aged in oak barrels giving it a deep amber color and wonderful tannin flavor, much like good bonded Kentucky bourbon. There were wooden kegs of PM buried all over the woods, their secret whereabouts known only to Perry Martin. Melvin Martin recalls, "That whiskey Grandaddy made was as good, if not better, than Crown Royal. It would go down real smooth and then there would be a real good fire." According to William Sullivan, "People who weren't even whiskey drinkers drank PM when they could."

Many moonshine stills operated out of the dense and almost impenetrable Arkansas River bottoms across the Mississippi. Even today, Big Island is a virtual wilderness area with several possible sightings of the illusive Ivory Billed Woodpecker being reported. Unless you were a river rat or a moonshiner, you didn't venture into that area for pleasure. And if you were a government man, looking to bust up moonshine stills, sometimes you didn't come back out. In 1928 Federal revenuers raided Big Island using a gunboat and hauled in about two hundred area moonshiners. Captain George Reid of the Brent Towing Company remembered in 1951 helping out the Federal Barge Line when a tow ran aground on Concordia Bend right across the river from Big Island. Federal Barge was wholly owned by the U.S. Government, and a full barge of sugar with government seals on the covers was tied up on the Big Island side of the river in order for the towboats to free the other barges aground on the sandbar. When the government boat returned to the sugar barge to put it back in the tow, the barge was almost completely unloaded by the moonshiners on Big Island! Locked hatches and U.S. Government seals meant nothing to those men.

Perry Martin operated out of his own territory on the Mississippi side of the big river. According to Mrs. Myron Martin, "Those were Perry Martin's woods. Nobody came out there that didn't have business there." He paid whatever Mississippi black market tax he was supposed to and nobody bothered him much. It is a fact that during Prohibition, every four years surrounding the gubernatorial inaugural week, a Mississippi Highway Safety Patrol double escort could be seen coming down the levee, surrounding a truck, loaded to the gills with moonshine and being driven by Myron Martin, turning south on Highway 1 heading to Jackson.

There were several reasons for the quality of Perry Martin's whiskey. Using the basic Kentucky recipe, one part corn to one part sugar, he adjusted and blended rye malt in with the corn. He got his water right out of the Mississippi River. His stills were pristine and immaculate with the bright copper works glistening in the sunlight filtering through the tall oak trees. He always made small batches and cooked it very slowly. Yet according to some, the most important thing was the use of white oak barrels that "rocked gently under willow trees by the ebb and flow of the Mississippi River along its banks."

At ninety years old, Perry Martin made his last batch of whiskey. He had just built a brand new still and run off his first batch when he was raided and his still destroyed. In a moment of frustration he got out of the business that had made him famous all over the country. Grandson Melvin Martin was with him that day: "I helped him make his last batch of whiskey. It was a beautiful still, and when they chopped it up, well, it just broke his heart. He told the revenuers he would never build another still and never make anymore whiskey. They believed him and just gave him a fine. He was too old to go to jail." He suffered a stroke the following year and died on September 9, 1968.

Perry Martin has been remembered as a good man, often giving his money away freely to those in need. He raised a little girl who had been abandoned on a shanty boat and sent her to college. He reared another young man outside of his family that continues to live in Rosedale. He entertained visitors, customers, and politicians alike, often telling humorous stories. One such story was about a revenuer that destroyed his still with an ax and poured the broken bottles of moonshine over his slick bald head as he claimed it helped his hair grow. Perry Martin knew better. "He just wanted the chance to drink the whiskey that dripped off his pointed nose and onto his long outstretched tongue!"

Martin did not fit the local vernacular of a "river rat," according to William Alexander Percy in *Lanterns on the Levee*, "illiterate, suspicious, mean, clannish, blonde, and usually ugly." Perry Martin was well educated, honest, proud, generous, self-confident, self made, and independent. He may have spurned genteel society, yet he demanded its respect. He has been recorded in history as the most famous moonshiner in Mississippi, and very possibly, of all times.

Hot Moore—Super Cowman of the South

Hot Moore was HOT indeed. To cattlemen all over America, and possibly the world, he was known as the Super Cowman of the South. From a meager beginning in the eroded red clay hills of Tate County, Maurice P. "Hot" Moore built his Circle M Ranch into what was undeniably the world headquarters for the Polled Hereford industry. Cattlemen from all over America and many foreign countries would attend his auctions held in an enclosed pavilion large enough to hold a thousand or more patrons. Stetson hats and dusty cowboy boots adorned cigar-chomping cattlemen with money to spend on the finest Polled Hereford bulls and heifers in the world.

Born in 1905, Moore graduated from Senatobia High School and went to the University of Alabama to play baseball. While there he acquired the nickname "Hot" for his pitching abilities, especially his fastball. Behind his arm, his team won every game but one during his three-year college career as a pitcher. He graduated in 1926 and returned home. The young robust and energetic Moore decided that with the price of cotton and related headaches and indebtedness of farming, he would do better playing semi-pro baseball. He left the large plantation owned by his family and was hired as a pitcher in the Delta Bush League.

After a few years of traveling around playing baseball, the young Hot Moore took $3,800 in savings and bought a rolling, nutrient-depleted 380-acre farm outside of Senatobia. His daddy, along with others, said that the land was not good for "field mice or tickle grass," much less a cattle operation. Nevertheless, he went to work revitalizing the tired and worn out ground with plant foods, fertilizers, good grasses, and stock ponds. According to a 2006 article in *The Heritage of Tate County*, Hot Moore bought nine cows, including two heifers and two Rollo bulls from well-known Western breeders and started a cow calf operation. Soon he bought his first herd sire, Pawnee Rollo 44 from Hugh White of Keller, Texas. This would be the beginnings of the world famous CMR Rollo Domino and CMR Advance Domino families, the great and deep foundation of the CMR Herd. Moore's philosophy was "the South is for cattle as well as cotton."

Always looking to the future and what could make the best breeding stock for his operation, Hot Moore spied what he considered to be a truly great herd mother for his Polled Herefords at an auction in 1940. As he jumped in on the bidding, his aunt began to shake her head. When his name was called out as the top bidder at $3,500 for the cow, his aunt threw up her hands and fainted. The highbred heifer, V. V. Bonnie Burton III was to be instrumental in making the Circle M Ranch known as one of the top Polled Hereford herds in the nation. A local newspaper, *The Democrat*, stated in November of 2000: "Moore felt that Bonnie would be capable of producing herd bulls, and she did not disappoint him." She came from the same lineage as CMR Rollo Domino, grandson of Victor Domino, who according to legend was the greatest bull in Polled Hereford history. Between the two, they produced four offspring including CMR Rollo Domino 12, the Fort Worth Champion dubbed "Sire of Sires," and the

Circle M Ranch, "The Headquarters for Hindquarters."

National Champion CMR Rollo Domino 28. According to Hot Moore, "Better cows and steaks don't just happen; you've got to design 'em and build 'em."

For years he built his herd, improving it at every breeding. In doing so, he was able to breed the middles, that part that does not bring much at the meat market, right out of them. In developing his herd, he improved the marbling, the veins of fat that make steaks tender, and he increased the size of the lean ribeye area. In 1959, measuring by ultrasound, one of his Hereford bulls had the largest lean ribeye (30.06 square inches) ever measured in a bull of any breed. Hot Moore would boast, "Circle M is the headquarters for hindquarters."

By 1965, the CMR herd had produced and sold the world's record priced Polled Hereford bull named CMR Rollotrend 5th. He sold for $320,000. Interviewed in *The Polled Hereford Hub* in June of 1975, Moore stated, "I had a desire to be a true breeder and a master breeder if at all possible…so I decided to dedicate my efforts to a planned breeding program with practical and fundamental goals in order to make real progress and profitable success."

According to his daughter Louise, as reported in the July 1996 issue of *Hereford World*, "Daddy always was a little different. He never did anything in a half-hearted fashion. He was a visionary."

Those practical and fundamental goals led Hot Moore to become possibly the greatest of Polled Hereford breeders in the world at that time. In the mid-'60s after competing in National Polled Hereford Shows for twenty-three years, his blue ribbons included nineteen National Grand and Reserve Grand Champions, ten Best of Six Head, nine First Prize Get-of-Sire, nine Premium Exhibitor, and two Premier Breeder (that class only being held for six years). By the time of his death in 1991, Hot Moore was the first Polled Hereford breeder to have his prefix "CMR" patented by the government. Three times he served as president of the American Polled Hereford Association and three times on its board. He was named Champion Farmer of America, and in 1951 he was selected as Man of the Year in Mississippi Agriculture.

In order to market his cattle, Hot Moore began having picnic and production sales in 1942. By 1991, he had held seventy-five sales attracting buyers to the intensely popular events. Huge barbecues were held, and Polled Hereford buyers from all over America and the world showed up, daring not to miss a CMR sale. Always by his side was Hot's wife, Annie Louise, who was reportedly as knowledgeable about cows as any cattleman. Hot's leadership preceded him everywhere he went. His large stature and presence in a sales ring, along with unprecedented salesmanship ability, established him as a merchandiser un-paralleled in the livestock industry.

Today, the CMR herd continues to be a dominate factor in the Polled and Horned Hereford cattle world. Hot's son-in-law Walter McKellar, along with his wife Louise, look after the farm and the commercial beef cattle operation while grandson Walt McKellar is in charge of the registered cattle business. According to an article in the 2006 publication *Welcome to Tate County,* Walt believes that farm life is good for his three sons. "Raising cattle has given my boys a good work ethic. Growing up around the farm teaches them to appreciate a good day's work."

Walt's philosophy is a lot like his grandfather's. "Cattle in Mississippi can go anywhere in the United States and work for anybody," Walt says. "In the last two years, I've sold cattle into thirty states. It's hard for cattle to come from the north into our humid climate, but cattle grown in the southeast can stay here or go north and thrive. Raising cattle from here gives me a really good area to sell to."

Graduating from Mississippi State with a degree in business has given Walt a wide marketing and professional expertise that has been instrumental in the continuing success of the Circle M Ranch. "Walt basically put CMR back on the map and has brought it out as one of the front-runners of the Hereford breed today," says Jil, Walt's wife.

At age twelve, Walt bought his first heifer on his own, picking her out and then showing her on to become the grand champion at the popular Jackson-based Dixie National Rodeo. He has dedicated a great deal of his time to the youth in the industry. In a July 1996 *Hereford World* article, Walt said, "When a junior buys a calf from us, I'll be there to help out as much as I can."

Each year, CMR hosts a two-day youth clinic, offering instruction in selection, fitting, and feeding. Recently, forty kids from fifteen Mississippi counties attended. Walt also participated in the Mississippi Rural Rehabilitation Program. The program allowed farm youth to receive a registered bull to take home to improve their family's cow herd. The youngsters also got a chance to exhibit their purchases, and CMR was very proud of the championships the juniors garnered. After a brief show career, these young cattlemen began to develop a base for their own herds. Walt said, "We realized how worthwhile this program was when heifers by these bulls started producing quality calves."

In November of 2014 CMR, in conjunction with partner Grandview Farms, held the largest Hereford bull sale in the Southeast. Buyers were expected to be in attendance from all over America and as far away as the Central Asian country of Kazakhstan. "We're moving in a positive direction right now," according to Walt. "We're seeing more calves with the kind of muscling the industry needs, and the cows can make it on grass. Herefords work just about any place, and the docile temperament is sure a plus in our market."

Hot Moore had a vision many years ago, and that vision is being perpetuated now at the Circle M Ranch outside of Senatobia. With Circle M cattle being produced and sold all over the world, Hot's favorite saying continues to ring true even today, "The sun never sets on CMR."

Larry Pryor—Delta Bon Vivant

Webster's defines bon vivant as "a person having cultivated, refined, and sociable tastes, especially in regard to food and drink." The literal French translation is "good living." Lawrence Bellfield Pryor, Squire of Silver Lake Plantation in south Washington County, was the embodiment of such a life. Internationally known, Squire Pryor entertained with the best food and drink wherever he was. Whether ensconced in his sprawling country home on the banks of Silver Lake, at his townhouse in Greenville on Washington Avenue amid a sea of azaleas, or seated at a gin rummy table, drink in hand, on the Queen Elizabeth heading to France, he entertained. And on the boat it was always high stakes rummy, at a dollar a point.

Said Mr. Pryor, "Like Omar Khayyam, I'll take the cash and let the credit go!"

Reared in Memphis during the halcyon days at the turn of the last century, young Larry decided to pursue fun in everything he did. He felt it his mission to "keep up the hurrah." His parents were well-known Memphis realtors. They sent Larry to Cornell University thinking that a demanding Ivy League school would keep his mind occupied and his interests focused. He graduated in 1923 with honors in animal husbandry and a yen for the good life, having burned a little midnight oil in worldly endeavors along the way!

PRYOR FAMILY COLLECTION

Larry Pryor returned home and soon acquired a plantation in the heart of the Mississippi Delta a few miles east of Longwood and close to the Mississippi River. Nestled between Whiskey Chute and Swan Lake, Silver Lake Plantation was a showplace. Cotton and soybean fields were interspersed among lush pastures where fine beef cattle grazed.

The original plantation home had been built around 1820. Larry began adding onto that structure rambling libraries, sun porches and sitting rooms, game rooms, dining areas, and places to rest and drink. The pecky cypress walls were adorned with fine art and a complete collection of duck stamps and autographed prints. The bookcases became a depository for original copies of John James Audubon bird books, Nash Buckingham's hunting chronicles, Englishman Crawford H. Greenwalt's *British Gamebirds and Wildfowl,* and many more sought after editions of sporting, wildlife, and fine art books. An outstanding collection of Chinese bronze pieces was bought from the respected Wanamaker Estate and shared space with local and other esteemed artists' work. Outside, among the stately oaks and flowering gardens, he built a large pavilion and dance floor, big enough to hold two orchestras. Beyond that was beautiful Silver Lake, with its still water and towering bald cypress trees.

The parties at Silver Lake Plantation were quite the hurrah with orchestras and acclaimed musicians coming from Memphis. According to Robert Carpenter in the 1964 summer issue of the *Delta Review,* "Larry's parties were well known, some really fine musicians kind of stood in line hoping to be picked. It was a musicians holiday, a jam session with pay!" Daytime parties were *de rigueur* and usually "started at 2 p.m. and lasted until milking time or first dark, as he defined twilight." Thirty or more servants tended the indoor and outdoor bars, and a typical overflowing southern buffet was served. Larry invited his guests by phoning them himself. To decline an invitation was "unthinkable."

The parties were what Larry Pryor called his "seasonal rituals." The spring ritual was his favorite. He described it as "some sort of fertility rite." A fall party was also planned each year with occasional gatherings interspersed at his whim. His propensity for party giving began during the Depression years in an effort to celebrate July 4th. Bad times had settled in over the Delta, and he thought that a little fun would not cost much and everyone could use some lightening up. After several cocktails one evening, he decided to host a mule race at Silver Lake. Mules were everywhere in the Delta back then, and Larry selected eight of his best mules and hand picked his own jockeys. Farmhands raced bareback on a quarter-mile track he constructed on his plantation. Betting was heavy among his neighbors, and the hurrah continued with the annual Pryor Derby, a major attraction.

Serving as a lieutenant with the Army Air Corps during WWII, he had the perfect job as a "special service officer" with a mission to "keep everybody happy." After the war, Larry Pryor served four years as a state legislator. During this time, and while poking fun at the Illinois Central railroad, a publicity stunt was set up to challenge the perpetually late "Old Reluctant" in a race with mules from Cleveland to Greenville. Supposedly changing mules and riders at stations along the way, the one-sided race was neck and neck. "Old Reluctant" backed into Greenville from Leland, belching and smoking as Squire Pryor raced in ahead of the train atop his prize mule, Nature Boy.

According to a Sunday, May 23, 1948, front-page headline story by Hodding Carter in the *Delta Democrat Times,* "Nature Boy broke the tape amid thunderous applause. Mr. Pryor waved his black ten-gallon planter's hat and switched the long tails of his frock coat in triumph as he rode through the crowd. There pretty hoop skirted Margaret Turner gave the winner a stirrup cup—a trainman's oil can filled with an undivulged liquid." According to Jimmy Robertshaw, a gin martini filled the can.

As a "gentleman farmer," his attentions soon turned to the sporting lifestyle of trap shooting and duck hunting. He built a regulation trap field, forming the Silver Lake Gun Club, and hosted three state champion shooting tournaments. Larry enlarged Silver Lake and impounded a sizeable wooded area on his place where he could attract and hold thousands of ducks each year for hunting. Ornate duck blinds were constructed in the flooded timber and came replete with servants to attend to the visiting duck hunters' every need. His burgeoning gun collection inspired envy, and he freely gave guns away to young shooters interested in getting started at the trap field.

Larry Pryor believed "the greatest pleasure in life is helping people, but that's something I don't talk about." He helped many talented young people in the Delta and elsewhere. He gave freely to worthwhile causes and to St. James Episcopal Church. To be a friend of Larry's also meant that you very possibly were the recipient of gifts from him. To his family and many lady friends he bestowed gold Austrian Emperor medallions minted before WWI but never issued. These coins hung from the neck on thin golden chains and were quite the coveted jewelry of Delta ladies. According to his niece Ainslie Pryor Todd of Memphis, "Uncle Larry bought them by the gross from Peacock's in New York."

On his many trips to Paris he would return with parasols and fine silk scarves to pass out to the ladies at his parties, considering himself a true "dirt road sport." And with a handful of his closest gentlemen friends, he formed somewhat of a secret society. Pryor gave 14 carat gold "Ruttin' Buttons" to a few sporting sorts with whom he hunted, shot trap, and enjoyed the good life. The pin is a golden ring on which is inscribed the names of several shooting areas in Germany. Inside the ring is a figure of an animal with the head and body of a wild boar and the horns of a stag leaping over an ibis, the often regarded mythical bird of fertility! Bearers of this pin are supposed to have standing invitations at shooting boxes in the respective locations. These pins are seen on the chests of gentlemen at full-formal Delta Debutante Balls, funerals, weddings, and other special social events.

These pins are seen on the chests of gentlemen at full-formal Delta Debutante Balls, funerals, weddings, and other special social events.

Upon the death of Larry Pryor, and at the bequest of Jimmy Robertshaw, close personal friend, lawyer, and executor of his estate, Claude "Sandhawg" Powell and myself were given the rights to the "Fraternal Order of the Horny Hart" and charged with carrying on its traditional customs. This has been accomplished by gifting to other sports the pin in sterling silver. We are an honorable band of merry makers and cohorts, and the pin is often the topic of conversation with inquisitive ladies at country club bars.

As executor of Pryor's estate, Jimmy Robertshaw kept the townhouse active and fully staffed with household help each day during the week. As before, and for many years, Robertshaw and Dr. Lewis Farr met daily to have lunch with their dear friend. Martinis were passed around, and a hot cup of pot liquor from a steaming bowl of turnip greens was offered prior to the main course. For a year and a half, the lawyer and doctor met daily with an empty chair at the head of the table. When the estate was finally closed and the townhouse sold, the cherished tradition ended.

Larry Pryor lived the good life and lives on today in the hearts and minds of many people who knew him. When Ferd Moyse III graduated from high school in the early '60s, before venturing off to college, he was beckoned to the townhouse. A gold embossed leather bound copy of the Rubaiyat of Omar Khayyam was given to him. And in the summer of 1966, I was sent to the townhouse in some sort of rite of passage before I went off to Marion Military School. There was a silver bowl full of buckeyes gathered from the yard, and Mr. Larry plucked one out. Rubbing the large seed in his hands and then placing it in mine he said, "Go forth now, my young friend, and may the fortune of good grades and the grace of gorgeous girls follow you."

And so the life of the Delta's great bon vivant passed on in 1976. He is buried in Forrest Hill Cemetery in Memphis next to his wife Hattie who had gone before him in 1959. Larry Pryor, Squire of Silver Lake, kept the hurrah going, often expressing his own personal philosophy in his favorite Latin phrase, *"dum vivamus biberimus et edimus,"* (while we live, we eat and drink).

The Birth of An Industry

How Greenville, Mississippi, became known as the Towboat Capital of the World

Shortly after the end of the Civil War, the burgeoning railroad companies began buying up all the steamboat companies and shutting them down in an effort to eliminate competition in the transportation of bulk goods in America. The movement of large quantities of materials on the Mississippi and her tributary rivers came virtually to a standstill, as the railroad industry grew even larger and more powerful, politically and structurally. The huge and oftentimes very ornate steamboats ceased to travel the Mississippi, Arkansas, Tennessee, Ohio, Allegheny, and Missouri rivers.

As WWI came to an end, it was realized that the immense need to move bulk goods in large quantities during national emergencies could not be met by the railroad industry currently in existence. However, no private concerns were willing to take the risk and try to restart the river transportation business. The Mississippi River was a virtual wilderness area with shifting sandbars and flood and drought cycles changing the course and depth every year. The Inland Waterways Corporation was established by the Transportation Act of 1920 to build and own boats and barges in order to move cargo on the Mississippi River and its tributaries. Major General T.Q. Ashburn, head of the IWC, stated, "By 1890, common water carriage, as it formerly existed on the Mississippi River, had disappeared. It's revival began in 1920 and by 1926 more freight was transported upon the Mississippi River than ever before in history." From the Inland Waterways Corporation came the Federal Barge Line.

Following the Great Flood of 1927, and because the Mississippi and its tributaries drain 41 percent of the land mass of the continental United States, covering 31 states, Congress passed the most comprehensive flood control legislation ever. The Flood Control Act of 1928 authorized the Mississippi River and Tributaries Project, a major flood control and navigation act. The four major elements of the act were building and maintaining a levee system, building floodways for excess run-off, establishing channel improvements and stabilization, and finally developing tributary basin improvements. This act effectively turned the responsibility of the Mississippi River over to the Corps of Engineers. It was on several Corps boats on the Lower Mississippi around Vicksburg that three young men were working during the Depression.

Having worked with his brothers and cousins on their grandfather's packet boat on the lower Yazoo and Sunflower rivers, eighteen year old Jesse Brent went to work for the Corps for two dollars a day. He soon worked his way up to pilot on a workboat. Percy Lemay was also a boat pilot, and Gilder McCool was a dredge captain. When they decided to start a towing company, Gilder McCool's father, a cotton planter around Lake Washington, agreed to finance the young and energetic river men with a capital infusion of $3,000. In 1941, Greenville Towing Company was formed with the little wooden hulled boat named the *Gilder Fay* and a one-year contract to haul gasoline for the Goyer Company of Greenville. From that point on, the history of Mississippi River transportation was forever changed.

River Kings: Owners, managers, and the founder of the Brent Towing Dynasty.

For the paltry sum of $800, a small boat was acquired and rebuilt. Greenville Towing began working for the Goyer Company hauling gas and diesel from Galveston, Texas, to Greenville, Mississippi. There were no sleeping quarters on the boat, and the crew slept in tents erected on the oil barge that belonged to Goyer. During construction of the boat, a credit application had to be filled out in order to finance the engines and reduction gears. The zealous salesman, realizing a problem with the collateral value for such a loan, added a zero to the value of the $800 hull making it $8,000, and the loan was approved. Years later, Captain Jesse Brent realized what had happened and declared, "If it had not been for that salesman anxious to make a sale, I don't know if I ever would have gotten into the towing business." In 1948, the steel hulled towboats *Totty McCool* and *Ruth Brent* were added to the fleet.

Boats and barges were built on the protected side of the levee and before completion were drug over the top and slipped into Lake Ferguson. It was during this time of expansion and trial and error that several of the original entrepreneurs branched out on their own to form competing companies. The Greenville towing concerns became well known for helping others join in the business by offering engineering and launching logistics to newcomers.

Anxious to go out on his own and provide a place for his two sons, Jesse Brent formed Brent Towing in 1956 with one of the original boats called the *Betty Brent* and two gasoline barges. He had acquired a contract from Cities Service to deliver fuel from Lake Charles, Louisiana, to Vicksburg, Memphis, and Nashville. Two box barges were added to make a four-unit tow. Jesse Brent's sons Lea and Howard grew up on the river and were both pilots. Lea went to Mississippi State to become a mechanical engineer, and the firm began building its own boats and barges as the operation grew. Howard stayed on the river as a boat captain before coming ashore and into the office. In 1965, a major contract was signed with Mobil Oil to build an anhydrous ammonia barge and three all aluminum tank barges. The second *Ruth Brent* was built in 1966. The Mobil Oil deal was a long-term contract haul and the one contract that catapulted the Brent name into towboating history. At that time the firm owned seven barges and eight boats. Over the next fifteen years, several other Brent entities were formed to complement the towing company. Brent Marine Supply was incorporated to supply the rapidly expanding Brent fleet and to take advantage of better prices for parts and equipment. Brent Shipbuilding and Repair had several dry-docks on Lake Ferguson, refurbishing, rebuilding, and repairing the Brent fleet and others. Superior Boat Works was acquired and brought into the Brent family of companies. By 1980, Brent Towing Company owned sixty tank barges and twenty-four towboats, becoming one of the largest privately owned towing companies on the Mississippi River. Jesse Brent died in 1982 at the age of seventy. Howard and Lea Brent continued operating all companies until 1989 when they sold Brent Towing Company to Dixie Carriers.

Meanwhile, up and down Lake Ferguson, boats and barges were being built and new operations started to service the rapidly expanding inland waterways business. The east bank of Lake Ferguson, where the offices and shipyards of the growing towing industry were located, was known up and down the river as the Million Dollar Mile. At one time there were thirty-five towboat and barge companies operating out of Greenville. And in Washington, D.C., Greenville, Mississippi, was known as the Towboat Capital of the World.

One newcomer to the towing business got his start as a corporate airplane pilot for several businessmen and towboat companies. Russell Flowers incorporated Flowers Transportation in 1970 with one boat, and by 1980, his fleet had grown to be the largest privately owned towing company in the country with fourteen boats and four hundred barges. Russell Flowers was forty-two years old and moving 8 percent of the bulk cargo transported on the Mississippi River.

In 2000, the *Waterways Journal* selected Captain Jesse Brent as the Riverman of the Century. Captain Jesse spent his entire working career on the Mississippi River, dedicated to its emergence as a vital force in the growth and security of our great nation. It all began with one small wooden hulled boat and a vision. The Greenville towing industry grew into a huge industrial complex that commanded over a hundred towboats and a thousand barges along with numerous shipyards and supply houses. On September 27, 1976, *TIME Magazine* ran an article titled "Brash New Breed of Entrepreneurs" profiling four businessmen in America. Captain Jesse Brent, who started out as a two-dollar-a-day deckhand and ended up with twenty-four towboats and sixty chemical tank barges, among other businesses, was featured. He had helped grow a major industry, nurturing it with his constant and ever-attentive involvement in political issues and river industry organizations. When asked by a prying young reporter from *TIME Magazine* about his personal financial holdings, Captain Jesse replied, "Son, I have enough to buy all the whiskey and steaks I want for the rest of my life."

Joe's Calling

Joe Call came to the Mississippi Delta to teach pilots evasive acrobatics during World War II. He remained, raised a family, and taught a multitude of pilots the proper way to fly—even upside down.

Often seen tucked away in farm sheds and on crop dusting strips is a small yellow airplane used occasionally to fly around the farm looking for wet spots in the fields or, for some sportsmen, to fly around and look for ducks.

These fore and aft seated planes are most likely the venerable Piper J-3 Cub produced between 1937 and 1947. Intended originally for flight training, the J-3's simplicity, affordability (a little over $1,000 in 1937), and its reputation made it perhaps the most popular and best known aircraft of all time. The J-3 Cub became the primary trainer aircraft for the Civilian Pilot Training Program, and by the end of WWII, 80 percent of all U.S. military pilots had received their flight training in Piper Cubs. During the war, painted olive drab and renamed the L-4, and because of its slow cruising speed and low-level maneuverability, the little J-3 Cub was instrumental as an observation and reconnaissance aircraft.

In the mid-1940s, a young Joe Call came to Greenville from Arkansas to teach aerobatics to the pilots at Greenville Air Force Base (GAFB). Joe was legendary in his acrobatic maneuvers and his ability to teach students the proper techniques to escape enemy aircraft by looping, rolling, diving, and doing just about anything that can be done in an airplane to evade the enemy and save your life. And he did it all in a J-3 Cub.

One of his students, ag pilot Larry Burns, recalls that Joe Call was national aerobatics champion three years in a row. "Joe was smart and an outstanding instructor. His able instructing kept me in one piece in many a tight corner in an ag plane."

Larry was one of Joe Call's last line boys at the Cypress Airport on Cypress Lane in Greenville. From 1966 until 1968, Larry washed and fueled planes, cut grass, and did minor repair work in exchange for lessons. Too young for a driver's license, he would run errands on an old Ford tractor. "We had to round up pillows to put under my rump and behind my back so I could reach the controls," Larry says. "On my first lesson he taught me how to fly under power lines reasoning that I would one day be a crop duster. He figured you couldn't start too soon whipping somebody into shape."

Clyde McGee of Greenville also learned to fly from Joe Call, he too working at the airport for lessons. Clyde remembers Joe "Eagle Rock" Hour approaching Cypress Airport in his Waco biplane doing a loop or two before landing for fuel and, when asked, would give a repeat performance upon taking off.

Clyde also remembers the story of an Arkansas crop duster that had a rack built in the cockpit of his Stearman so he could enjoy a cold beer while flying. When he began having some close calls, Joe Call and a few others asked him to stop drinking and flying. Two weeks later he was killed in an airplane crash. Joe Call regretted the talk because he said he was a much better pilot while drinking than when sober.

One of Joe Call's sayings was, *There are old pilots and there are bold pilots, but there are no old-bold pilots.* Clyde recalls another favorite. *Crop dusters usually die one of three ways: stall on a downwind turn, hit a wire or tree, or starve to death. And most of them starve to death.*

Lelander Jimmy Reed was taught to fly by Joe Call. "After familiarizing me with the controls, we shot touch-and-go's at Cypress Airport. To show me I was actually doing the flying he would hold onto the cross-members above his head and prop one foot on the open door hinge."

One day they saw some folks fishing in a large drainage canal. "Watch this," said Joe Call. He cut the throttle so that the plane was quiet and drifted down into the canal, gliding around the bend. When he got so close to the fishermen that they saw nothing but yellow, he firewalled the engine. "I can still see those horrified people throwing their poles in the water and scrambling up the bank," Jimmy says.

"Another time we had flown upriver to Montgomery Island. On the way back we saw a water skier on Lake Ferguson. Once again, he cut the throttle and glided down so low that the wheels couldn't have been a foot above the water. When he was right beside the skier—the wingtip was over the guy's head—he throttled up. Terrified, the skier let go of the rope and tried to run across the top of the water! When Joe Call strapped into a Cub, man and machine were indistinguishable."

The first time Gil Worth ever saw Joe Call fly was in 1955 at the GAFB during an Armed Forces Day air show. The military part of the show was rather bland, but Joe Call astonished the crowd in a modified for inverted flight J-3 Piper Cub. For about fifteen minutes, he wowed the crowd with loops, barrel rolls, and upside down fly-bys. It would be eight years though, before he actually got to know Joe Call.

Jesse Brent asked Gil Worth to take his own Cub up several times a month to keep it in shape, but first he should get checked out by Joe Call. Gil was told to meet Joe at Jesse Brent's strip behind his house on Highway 1. "I was told to get in the front seat while he climbed into the back and said we should go to his airstrip off Old Leland Road for fuel. When he took over the controls to land, I thought it was curtains for me as there was no strip to speak of, just a patch of grass at the end of a pecan grove with the trees spaced out just wide enough for the wingspan of the J-3 to fit between and under the limbs! We stopped just short of a fence and taxied up to his gas tank where we fueled. We had to pull the airplane back to the fence in order to have enough room for take-off. And we did take off, almost hitting a car on Railroad Avenue.

"Once I got the hang of the Cub, Joe had me make several landings at the Municipal Airport on Raceway Road. My first landing was less than adequate. He took the controls to show me what to do, yelling, 'Are you afraid of this airplane?' Once adjusted, he had me land on a county road close to his house so he could walk home, and I delivered the plane back to Jesse Brent's strip."

Joe Call's pecan grove airport was infamous among Delta ag pilots. "Big Skeet" Edwards accepted a steak dinner bet that he could not land his Stearman bi-plane underneath those pecan trees. "Little Skeet" Edwards recalls one evening sitting in a local watering hole next to Joe Call and bringing up the bet. "Well, yes, son, I did make

A young Joe Call as flight instructor at the Greenville Air Force Base teaching evasive flight maneuvers to pilots.

that bet with Big Skeet, and he did in fact land that big airplane underneath those trees. But he's gone now, and you ain't him, so I don't have to pay you a steak dinner."

One legendary air show stunt was the Grandma Act. A free airplane ride would be given away to a ticket holder in the crowd. A little old lady would come hobbling out of the hanger on a cane with the winning ticket, approaching the J-3 Cub that was idling on the tarmac. The announcer held the crowd's attention, as the little lady in stubby heels and a sun bonnet walked to the plane and fell into the back seat while peering over into the cockpit. At that time the plane would begin to wildly taxi up and down the runway until it took off spinning, rolling, flying upside down and scaring the crowd while they scattered as the plane headed straight towards them, all the while with Joe Call flying the plane as the little old grandma that fell into the back seat.

Of all the pilots that Joe Call taught to fly, one stands out. On a sunny afternoon after eighteen holes of golf, Dot Etheridge, along with her husband and another couple went by Joe Call's airport to go for a ride. Remembering the airport as a short grass strip, upon take-off with Dot, Joe Call performed an aerobatic maneuver "loop," a one turn spin and a "full stall," all from an altitude of five hundred feet. "I remember telling him that I wanted to learn to fly and that I enjoyed the introductory flight immensely," Dot says. "Had he been trying to scare me away from flying because I was a woman and he thought I wouldn't stick with it? Did he doubt my intentions?"

Dot showed up at dawn the next morning and after basic ground instruction climbed into the J-3 Cub. "My first lesson consisted of almost the same maneuvers as the introductory flight. If Joe Call thought you were really interested in learning how to fly, he would spend the time to teach you no matter who you were."

During her lessons, Dot was thrilled with the aerobatics, learning later that wasn't the normal curriculum. However, she especially enjoyed the loops, spins, and split-8's and anything else Joe Call would throw in. One afternoon, he taxied to the side of the runway, got out, and very nonchalantly said, "Take it around, don't get higher than five hundred feet, do your loop, circle the field, and come in for your landing." She did just that. Later on she learned how very proud Joe Call was of his young female student that did a loop on her first solo flight!

"Joe Call's ground instruction was as excellent as in the air at the controls of the airplane. He was an exceptional, talented, and unafraid airman." she says. "He never dwelled on his many accomplishments, some almost unbelievable, such as landing his Cub on the top of a station wagon as it raced down a runway. Joe enjoyed life and didn't see the purpose of negative thinking—the reason so many people were drawn to him, not only because of his pilot prowess but for the happy-go-lucky person he was."

Dot Etheridge went on to become a professional pilot winning many air shows and pylon races and soon became known as the Queen of the Powder Puff Derby, a transcontinental air race. "All of my flying was a result of Joe's instruction. It's the reason I am alive today."

Local author Gayden Metcalfe soloed when she was thirteen years old. Joe Call, her father, had taught her well. She was almost born in a J-3 Cub. Not having time to drive to Greenwood when her mother went into labor, they loaded up in the Cub, landing on River Road and taxied into the parking lot at the hospital. "Dr. Lucas, there is an airplane in the parking lot!" a nurse exclaimed. Doc Lucas replied, "I told y'all not to be drinking while on duty!"

Gayden was born as the Yazoo River spilled out of its banks, overflowing the road before mother and child could leave the hospital. Joe Call flew his J-3 Cub back to Greenwood, landing on the Yazoo levee to bring his wife and newborn home. According to Gayden, "Daddy flew inverted half the time. He would truly rather have been flying upside down than right-side up!"

Viva, La King Silky!

The King of Beale Street is B.B. King. The king of rock 'n' roll rests at Graceland. But there is another King in Memphis, "SILKY, King of the Irish!"

Thomas "Silky" Sullivan was born a May baby in 1942 and grew up in Memphis, Tennessee. He and his brother were reared in a stately pseudo castle that overlooks old Highway 61 on a hill south of Memphis. His mother "Miss Mary" Sullivan, ninety-five years old, still lives there and is visited by her son King Silky each and every day. Silky admits, "Like Hemingway went around fighting bulls, I go around collecting Kingships!"

"I was a roads scholar, R-O-A-D-S, I stayed on the road a lot. Every time I failed out of one school, I went to another." After high school, Silky attended the University of Tennessee and flunked out his freshman year. His parents sent him to Sunflower Junior College in Moorhead, Mississippi (now Mississippi Delta Community College and referred to by his majesty as "Harvard on the Highway"). After his tour of duty in the Delta, Silky went on to the University of Paris-Sorbonne. (Once settled into the lifestyle at Moorhead, he claims he learned that socializing with his teachers, along with a little heavy book work, was grease enough for an A in most classes. After attaining the honor roll at MDCC, his parents sent him on to Paris to further his education, realizing he was such an astute and honorable student.) Upon

returning from Europe, where he learned some of the "finer things in life," Silky went on to the University of Georgia, Louisiana State University, and even the real Harvard University. He was accepted there with some trepidation, based on a letter dated June 17, 1963, from Harvard University, Cambridge, Massachusetts. "With only some reservations, the Committee on Admissions has voted to accept you for the 1963 session. We trust you will at minimum have learned to handle formal applications with some degree of seriousness!" His majesty finally earned an honorary degree in Culinary Arts from the University of Oxford, England, in 1991. "You only go to school once, so why not have some fun?" King Silky has just recently been inducted into the Christian Brothers High School Hall of Fame in Memphis, his alma mater. "Sometimes it's life's experiences that teach you a lot more than books do." Presently, Silky is spearheading a foundation effort—as so many past presidents of our great

93

nation have done—to open a Silky Sullivan Memorial Archival Library in Moorhead, on the campus of MDCC, to hold his boxcar load of memoirs, barbecue trophies, and worldwide fun time memorabilia.

In 1970, after matriculating around the globe, Silky settled into Memphis life and worked for his family's concrete curing and paint business. Overton Square was the hot spot in Memphis at that time, with T.G.I. Friday's as the anchor bar and grill. Silky became upset one day when he couldn't open a tab because he had left his coat with his wallet in it at home. "I spent about $10,000 a year entertaining my clients there, and I couldn't open a $50 tab! I decided to open my own damn bar!" Which is exactly what he did, right across the street in the old Pappy's Lobster Shack. "As I nailed up partitions, tore down walls, and drug furniture around, everybody at Friday's would point out the windows at me and laugh. After about a year, they weren't laughing anymore."

Silky began his lifelong determined charge of promoting Memphis, the blues, and down home Southern barbecue. He is well known all over the world, having been around it about twenty-five times, but Memphis is his home base. During the height of the Cold War, he spread good cheer and lip-smacking barbecue to Ireland, Estonia, Costa Rica, Russia, Cuba, Bangkok, Sweden, Jamaica, and many more far out places. He is Memphis's premier ambassador of good times, good food, and good drink, and he is relentless. According to a close friend, "Silky is a cross between P.T. Barnum, Rhett Butler, and Muhammad Ali."

Once his "Silky Sullivan's" bar was running in Overton Square, and quite successful in competing with Friday's, he realized that the movement to re-open and re-energize Beale Street was in the making. Not one to ever be left behind, he was able to negotiate and acquire a lease on a premier building on Beale Street. The Gallina building was over one hundred years old and at one time was an all day and night saloon with fourteen bartenders. Upstairs were hotel rooms and gambling parlors that catered to the "theatrical and sporting world."

The wonderful old corner building was refurbished, and "Silky O'Sullivan's" was opened, the "O" meaning "son of the original Silky's" on Madison. The Irish Pub is used as his theme, and the great goat "Killian" is the pub's mascot. He is stabled on the patio. Silky's goats are world famous. Maynard (the goat) was on Jay Leno to predict the Tyson/Lewis world heavyweight fight. Maynard also flew to Chicago in an unsuccessful effort to break the curse on the Cubs. A documented Blarney Stone from the Blarney Castle, Ireland, is entrenched on the patio by the moat around the goat castle, and patrons are allowed to kiss it for "good luck and eloquence."

When he was King of Jamaica, subordinates called him "Silk Mon," and they named a Caribbean island "King Silky Island" in his honor. In 2004, at the 400th reunion of the O'Sullivan Clan, he was dubbed "King of Ireland" in Castletownbeare, the ancestral home of the "5 fighting Sullivan brothers." They were all killed on one ship during WWII, and the US Naval Destroyer USS *The Sullivans* was brought in at Silky's request to the County Cork for the celebration. He was made "Commander Silky" for a day aboard the gallant fighting ship! He has since been given the title "Chieftain of the

O'Sullivans in America." Silky was founder of the Irish Eyes of Memphis, which has been responsible for all St. Patrick Day festivities for over thirty years.

I first met Silky in the early '70s when he and my dear friend and rambling cohort, Claude "Sandhawg" Powell, now deceased, were traveling together setting up barbecue festivals all over the world. Both were blessed with Irish ancestry and elegant oratorical skills. They were well received and admired for their grandiose appearance—Silky, with his cigar-chomping largese and deep bellowing voice, and Sandhawg, with his long and thick, bright red flowing handlebar moustache, tipped with a little grey on the perfectly curled ends. As self-appointed members of "Her Majesty, the Queen of England's, Barbecue Team" they were, tongue in cheek, "Her Majesty's subjects spreading cheer and good will." And I can personally attest that much good cheer was spread. Today, the globe is speckled with many barbecue festivals, in places where hickory and oak smoke, infused with sweet and savory spices, never before lingered low to the ground. Without Silky's ever-demanding desire to spread the good will of barbecue, these fun-filled times would not be in existence.

Silky's wife, traveling companion and business partner, Joellyn, recalls, "With the Berlin Wall still standing, Silky decided that barbecue was the answer and recommended that the Soviets come to Ireland for a barbecue festival. He suggested that disarmed nuclear warheads would make great barbecue pits and proceeded to invite the Soviets to join him and dubbed the effort Pits for Peace. His idea was declared 'pig-astroikia,' and the following year three Soviet teams did come to Ireland, and there was even a pit resembling a missile! The Estonians came and participated in the Memphis in May World Championship Barbecue Festival and invited the American teams to come back to Estonia for their own barbecue festival. A fun-seeking group of devoted revelers traveled to Moscow and then on to Estonia where twenty American teams competed with twenty Soviet teams. While in Estonia, there was an announced end of the Communist Party there and Lenin's statue was removed! And in Moscow, Silky cooked pork chops on Red Square and passed them around to the comrades. He even attempted to hand deliver a personal invitation to Mikhail Gorbachev to attend the barbecue in Estonia but was turned back on the front steps of the Kremlin at the point of a rifle and bayonet!" After Sandhawg passed away, Silky continued to carry his spirit with him, and the cheerful message was spread from nation to nation.

In 2000, Silky decided to open a Silky O'Sullivan's bar in the French Quarter of New Orleans. He chose a good location on Decatur right across from the old Jax Brewery. Soon established and with a loyal following, Silky decided at the last minute to run for Lt. Governor of the Pelican State. He thought the race needed a little spicing up. Silky had been made an honorary member of the Huey P. Long family at their reunion in Winfield, Louisiana, in 2001. His personal choice for chief of staff was a blues singer from Memphis named Little Howling Wolf. In recalling his attempt at Louisiana politics, Silky replied, "It's the flea on the rear of the dinosaur that made him fall off the cliff." Two weeks before the election, Silky had garnered 8 to 12 percent of the polled votes and he decided to withdraw and join forces with Mitch Landrieu who had 38 percent.

At the end of the state election, Landrieu won by 2 percent of the actual votes. Today, Silky is one of the Lt. Governor's standing colonels.

Silky O'Sullivan's Vieux Carre was successful, but wanting to concentrate on Beale Street, Silky sold the business two months before Katrina hit and wrought devastation to businesses and livelihoods. However, during that time, he was honored by being picked as King of the Krewe of Iris in 2001, Grand Marshal of the Krewe of Shangri-La in 2003, and most recently he was the King of Shangri-La. The name Shangri-La means "eternal youth, peace, and tranquility." Silky readily adheres to that notion.

While being honored this past Mardi Gras as King of Shangri-La, he and his entourage were wined and dined at Commander's Palace, Galatoire's, Arnaud's, and Antoine's, certainly fitting venues for a King! At the major Saturday night Mardi Gras parade, King Silky recalls turning onto Canal Street atop his float, "You feel like Julius Caesar coming into Rome. You feel a chill, and for a moment, you can be anything you want to be. Wanting to pinch yourself, you just look at whomever you are with and say, 'If only the boys back home could see me now!' "

Last year Silky was the King of a krewe in San Francisco and this year has been asked to be King at Mont Tremblant in Quebec, Canada. And what is Silky's next ambition? After bringing the Minnesota Vikings back home to the motherland for an exhibition game in Goteborg, Sweden, against the Chicago Bears, the first NFL game to ever be played in Europe, Silky wants to do the Ultimate Game. He even contacted the New Orleans Saints about the idea. "Look, I got the Pope Bowl in Rome, I'm going to have your quarterback riding around a coliseum in a chariot throwing footballs up to the crowd!" And guess who the Saints opponents are going to be? "Why the Detroit LIONS! of course."

VIVA LA KING SILKY!

Buckwheat Wade—The Blond Bomber
*Belzoni's indomitable boxing champ, legendary poker player,
and fun-loving nightclub host*

In 1931, Jenny and Preston Wade left the hills of Coxburg, Mississippi, and moved to the Delta. They bought one hundred acres of timbered bottomland in Humphreys County. With them came seven kids and the dream of a better life. The Depression hit hard in Mississippi, and especially the Delta, for a man with a family trying to make a new start.

To develop cultivatable land you first had to remove the timber, ringing and then cutting the trees, creating a deadening as you farmed between the stumps. Preston Wade cleared the land with his older boys at his side and his two girls in the cabin doing household chores. Everyone old enough did their part. The younger boys did all they could, but mostly they played and kept out of the way. Leisure time was spent playing ball, playing chase, and going to church. The Wades were dirt poor, but you couldn't tell it because they were always smiling and playing. They wore hand-me-down clothes and spent the summers barefoot, but the first bale of cotton brought new shoes and coats for the winter. Luxuries were a trip to town to the picture show or to watch a baseball game. The Wades had to walk to Belzoni, but once there, there was always lots of action on a Saturday afternoon and night.

Most of the year, the older boys were working in the fields, preparing, planting, plowing, chopping, or picking cotton. They worked hard so the younger ones could go to school. And as the younger ones began to grow up, they found that playing sports kept them out of the cotton fields. A baseball practice was very important and a relief from plowing mules or chopping cotton. The girls found that basketball kept them busy, and both the Wade girls became champions at the sport.

Older brother Darry Wade excelled in all sports with baseball and football being his favorites. He went on to become an all-star at Sunflower Junior College in Moorhead before transferring to Delta State. In 1941, he was to be the first of the Wade boys to become a Mississippi State Golden Gloves Boxing Champ. He went on to coach sports at Ruleville and then Oxford High School. So very highly was he thought of that he was later inducted into the Mississippi Coaches Hall of Fame.

Boxing was big in Belzoni, and the Wade brothers grew up as scrapers. They had to be to survive. At twelve years old, the youngest, Larry Arlington Wade, was a stand out. During a very early bout, the boxing announcer Red Solomon could not remember the boy's name. He knew he was a Wade, but which one? All of the Wade boys were fighters! Noticing his blondish red hair that resembled a field of wheat, he said, "And in this corner we have BUCKWHEAT WADE!" It ended up in a knockout, one of many by Buckwheat Wade, and his nickname stayed with him the rest of his life.

Buckwheat Wade went on to win three Mississippi State Golden Gloves Championships and was called by many to be the best amateur boxer Mississippi has ever produced. During this time he acquired another moniker, "The Blond

Bomber," because he knocked almost everybody out. Mrs. Winkie Allen remembers him in high school. "He was the cutest little thing! Everybody just went crazy when he got in the ring."

Family members recall 163 fights and only fifteen losses, with many knockouts to his credit. He finished his amateur career with a phenomenal ten straight knockouts, the last three he fought with a broken hand.

Buckwheat was also an outstanding offensive tackle in football, losing weight in the summer to be classified as a welterweight boxer. A football shoulder injury cut short his boxing career.

Buckwheat's brother "Squirrel" was a superb baseball and football player. He too was a Golden Gloves Champ in 1956. The Wades knew the meaning of the cotton patch, you either played hard and excelled, or you went home to work behind a mule. All the Wades were champs.

Buckwheat soon drifted to New Orleans but ended up in Chicago as the sparring partner for the two times Welterweight World Boxing Champion Tony Zale. Zale was best known as the "Man of Steel" who wore his opponents down before knocking them out. Rocky Graziano was his most famous and formidable opponent.

Eventually his shoulder injury retired Buckwheat from boxing. In 1954, he moved to Texas and the oilfields. After breaking his back in an oilfield accident, fate presented itself to Buckwheat in the form of an old time gambler that needed a chauffeur and bodyguard. He took Buckwheat under his wing and taught him how to play a poker game invented by a West Texas road gambler. The game was a variance of seven card stud and soon became known as Texas Hold'em. The old gambler taught Buckwheat and many other professional poker players the essence of Texas Hold'em.

Buckwheat moved back to the Mississippi Delta in 1963 with a wife and three children. He became a polished and seasoned gambler. It is considered by many that Buckwheat Wade was the first to introduce Texas Hold'em east of the Mississippi River. In 1970, the first World Series of Poker was held at Benny Vinion's Horseshoe Casino in Las Vegas with Johnny Moss the winner. At a prior inaugural meeting, it is thought that sixty players put up $10,000 apiece for a total take of $600,000. Buckwheat Wade was picked to be a finalist; however, Crandell Addington won.

Buckwheat came back from Las Vegas to open up a nightclub and restaurant business in Belzoni. Sometimes he served as many as three hundred guests on a weekend night. In those days of Prohibition, almost all the towns in the Delta had nightclubs that featured big name bands and lots of liquor, even though it was illegal at the time. And if you forgot to bring your own bottle, good bonded whiskey was never too far away to buy. It was not rare at all for some of those nightclubs to have a back room where the shuffle of a deck of cards or the clinking roll of a pair of dice could be heard. That's just the way it was in the Delta during those days.

Local attorney Cham Trotter remembers the Twin Gates Supper Club after prohibition was repealed. "It was a wonderful place to go! We called it 'Buckwheat's,' and he cooked the best steak in this part of the Delta. During the Christmas and Fourth of July holidays, they had big bands come in, and you better get your reservation early because the guest list filled up very quickly."

Bill Allen also remembers those wonderful dances at Buckwheat's. "We all just had so much fun! Buckwheat himself would get carried away and get onstage and take the mic. His favorite song was 'Behind Closed Doors.' I can assure you that Buckwheat was a fighter, not a singer. He tortured that song!"

This year will mark the fiftieth anniversary of Buckwheat's family restaurant businesses. Many patrons can still remember the excellent steaks, spaghetti, hamburgers, and Greek food that Alex Frenn and Earline Gallion prepared in the kitchen with expert finesse. Buckwheat's son Jerry and his wife Alison with grandson Anthony continue that delicious tradition at Alison's Restaurant in downtown Belzoni today.

LARRY "BUCKWHEAT" WADE

As an amateur Mississippi State Golden Gloves Champ, Larry "Buckwheat" Wade fought 163 fights with only fifteen losses. His career ended with ten straight knockouts, the last three given with a broken hand.

WADE FAMILY COLLECTIONS

Buckwheat Wade is still talked about around Belzoni and other parts of the Delta. While in elementary school, Dr. Mack Gorton remembers the high school senior as being a hero. He kept the name Buckwheat all his life, but his wife, Sofie, would only call him Honey. He was a handsome man that was always smiling and had a heart as good as gold, and he would help anybody. Oftentimes, he and his gambling buddies would pool their resources to reach out and help a family in need or someone down on their luck. His card playing abilities were and still are renowned and admired among patrons of the games of chance.

Buckwheat Wade always carried a solid punch no matter what he was doing. And as folks would often say when they saw the Blond Bomber on the streets of Belzoni, "There goes Mr. Buckwheat; he walks hard."

The Lady Behind the Levee Who Wouldn't Leave
For 61 years, Melba Parker lived with the threat of floodwaters at her feet and was known for her indomitable spirit whether teaching in a one-room schoolhouse or defending her property rights.

Melba Parker moved to the south Delta on the north end of Eagle Lake on January 1, 1950. The home she moved into was built in 1816 by Andrew Jackson's friend Alexander Gwin when he bought the surrounding land for twenty-five cents an acre. The house is located on the unprotected side of the mainline Mississippi River levee and subject to flooding each year. Melba had been courted by F.G. Parker for eight years before she agreed to marry him and move to the remote farm with the levee running through the middle of it. Originally, the house rested right on the east bank of the Mississippi River but was moved by mule team and logs to a mound atop a high ridge before natural causes changed the course of the river, cutting off Terrapin Neck and creating Eagle Lake.

Raised in Bay Springs, north of Laurel in south Mississippi, Melba grew up learning how to live off the land. Her father was a "bear of a man" and well known for his doggedness, according to Melba's son Lou Parker. "My grandmother was a small, ninety-five pound Indian woman. She could sit in Grandpa's hand and he could pick her up." Melba grew up shooting squirrels and other wild animals to eat along with their farm stock and vegetables from the family garden. The milk from the dairy cows was kept cold stored in a well or placed in a creek. Melba learned to depend on herself and was finely attuned to good and hard work habits, and she practiced those ideals her entire life.

Graduating from Mississippi State College for Women with a major in home economics, she wanted to get into the business world but had promised her father she would try teaching. Melba was given a job without sitting for an interview or even giving a resume at the Oak Ridge High School in Vicksburg. One day, a student threatened to throw her out the window when she disciplined him. He backed down when she replied, "Come on! We'll both go together." She moved to Memphis at one point and began selling appliances in five states for the Wallace Johnson Distribution Company.

F.G. Parker raised cattle and hogs and also farmed corn, on the protected side of the levee. Their romance blossomed, and once they were married, Melba helped on the farm. However, when their son Lou was six years old, she took a job teaching again so she could drive Lou to school each day instead of having him go to school on the bus that crossed the Yazoo River on a cable guided ferry at Kings Point. In an article in the The *Vicksburg Post,* she stated, "I just couldn't put him on the bus crossing that river. Sometimes that cable would break and the ferry would end up downstream." The only other route was to take the levee road that was oftentimes very muddy and one would have to cross over a low water bridge that flooded frequently. After much pleading, in 1963, the Highway Commission and Warren County built Highway 465 between Brunswick and Redwood giving paved access to Highway 61 to the Eagle Lake community.

JOHN MONTFORT JONES/COURTESY OF DELTA MAGAZINE

Once retired from the Vicksburg school district, Melba was asked by the Madison Parish school district to replace a retiring teacher in the one-classroom school on Australia Island, one of the very last in America. This island was formed when the river changed course and even though in Louisiana, is located on the Mississippi side of the river. The children of the three tenants that lived on the 3,000-acre plantation on the island were the only students in the tin roofed, two-room clapboard building with adjoining "boys and girls" outhouses. Eight grades were taught to the twelve to eighteen students that attended each year. Parker accepted the job and was soon the bus driver (in her own pick-up truck), principal, dietician, counselor, maintenance supervisor, coach and teacher. She told a reporter for *The Vicksburg Post,* "A school doesn't have to be lined with gold to make children learn. And we've got our laboratory out there—in the cotton fields where we study the insects and the frogs, photosynthesis, and plant life-watching the cotton plants grow from seeds. I've always just wanted to teach in a school where all you did was be a teacher—not a record keeper or a clerk or referee. This is the place for me." She taught the way she liked to with no interference and no bureaucracy. Her rules were her own. She was a strict disciplinarian. Her students all learned and stayed focused as there were no frills, just school, and the students always scored highest in scholastic area testing. The school was closed when Parker retired in 1979, and the children were sent to Warren Central.

F.G. died in 1963 when Lou was twelve years old and in the sixth grade; therefore he grew up helping his mother on the farm. She sold the four hundred hogs they had and kept the three hundred head of cattle to graze on the levee and lush pastures comprising almost 850 acres along the Mississippi River. When Lou graduated from college, after attending Delta State and Mississippi State, he called his mother and told her that he was coming home but needed a new tractor, hay baler, and rake. And, if she would get it, he could have it delivered that day, and she agreed. Lou recalls, "She did just as I asked, but she only signed the note for the new equipment. She made me pay for it."

Melba Parker was a hands-on cattle woman. She drove tractors, baled hay, and mended fences. She maintained miles of levee right-of-way with her tractor and grass clipper. Oftentimes she would not wait on the levee board maintenance crew to come clean up debris after high water but do it herself, neatly stacking the logs and limbs at the base of the levee. She fed cattle every day, summer and winter, and during calving time would go out in the middle of the night in the sleet and cold rain to pull a calf. Every now and then she would butcher a two thousand pound bull by pulling him up in a tree and skinning him, then quartering him with a chain saw.

"Mother could ride the hair off a horse," Lou says. "It was nothing for her to swim across the river chute on her horse to herd a trapped bunch of cows and swim them back across to the levee." Once while they were across the chute working, Melba, in her seventies at the time, had to go to Eagle Lake for a meeting. Later in the day, Lou noticed that the boat was still on his side of the chute. Melba just swam across the chute to keep Lou from being stranded.

She loved her cows and her land, and *nobody* crossed her. She was adamant about her property rights and woe be unto the poacher or trespasser that tried to take advantage of her. "Mother could shoot the spades out of an ace of spades with a .38 caliber revolver," Lou notes. "In her eighties, she would not look through the scope on her rifle but sight down the side of the barrel while shooting armadillos that dug holes in the levee and pastures." Once she dug a hole around a tree in her truck chasing some duck hunters around it who were poaching in her front yard. When she got out of the truck with her rifle, she fired it into the air. "I'm not shooting at you; if I was, you'd be dead!" On another occasion, three lawyers with guns were poaching on her property. She walked right up to them and pulled a .38 Special out of her pocket and said, "How you?" She then took them to the justice of the peace who threw the book at them.

"Mother kept some kind of heat on her at all times. She had a 460 Weatherby Magnum by the front door with no intention to shoot anyone, but to make enough noise to run somebody off!" During the flood of 2008, her grandchildren asked her if she needed anything from Vicksburg as she was surrounded by water. She replied, "Please bring me two boxes of 30-06 bullets and two boxes of twelve-gauge double ought buckshot. With all this water, people might start looting around here, and I don't believe in the law. I am the law on this side of the Pecos."

Melba Parker had a pioneering spirit and was loved and respected by her beloved Methodist church and the Eagle Lake community. Newman Bolls, longtime chief engineer of the Mississippi Levee Board, often butted heads with Melba. They were both "bull-headed," but respected each other and were good friends. When the current chief engineer, Peter Nimrod (whom she called "Hot Rod" because of his habit of driving fast on the levee), met with her to tell her that the river was going to get inside her house during the epic 2011 flood, she told him, "No problem, I will just move up into the attic and live there until the water goes down. I have done it before."

Melba was an adamant supporter of flood control. Chip Morgan, executive vice president of Delta Council, remembers her with admiration. "Mrs. Parker was the original Steel Magnolia," Chip says. "I have never met a person with a stronger constitution than Melba Parker. I will always remember her for her fairness and her compassion for the land, the animals, the crops, the birds, and the legacy of firm convictions which she protected with every ounce of her being."

Assistant engineer of the Mississippi Levee Board Bobby Thompson met Melba in 2004. "She was a smart, no-nonsense, tough-as-all-get-out kind of woman, but very much a lady."

Retired chief engineer Jim Wannamaker relates, "She was a true and loyal supporter of flood control for the south Delta, despite the fact that her home was on the unprotected side of the levee. She was no stranger to floods. She was a gracious hostess and opened her home for meetings with supporters, regulators, and opponents of constructing the Backwater Pumping Plant."

On April 4, 1989, Melba joined the Mississippi Levee Board and Delta Council in Washington, D.C., to testify before the House Committee on Appropriations. Mississippi Congressman Jamie Whitten was chairman and very attentive to the testimony. However, there were some there that were dozing off, chatting with staff members, or reading a book. At one point in her testimony, she slammed her fist on the podium and exclaimed, "I don't want to be up here before you, but I am, and, dammit, you are going to listen to me!" Not one member missed another word she spoke.

For sixty-one years, Melba Parker lived with the threat of floodwaters at her feet. She baled hay and cut her own grass on a Cub Cadet until she was eighty-eight years old. She never moved out of her house until the water rose almost three feet into the ballroom where she used to host dances on Sunday afternoons, and the power company cut off the electricity. Her philosophy on life included the way she lived: "I try to leave everybody else alone and tend to my own business and hope they do too." Her son Lou took all the guns out of her house when the floodwaters crept in. He was on the porch of his own house, built on stilts and being run off a generator, when he noticed his ninety-year-old mother wading across the floodwaters in her housecoat with something shiny in her pocket. It was a .38 caliber stack barreled derringer. She moved in with Lou until her health required her to be hospitalized in Cleveland to be looked after by family friend Dr. Brock. Anxious to get back to her home on the river, yet realizing that she never would again, she died on July 16, 2011, shortly after the greatest flood of our recorded history crept back out of her house. Her death came much like the death of the great and immortalized Sam Fathers of William Faulkner's *Big Woods*:

"He's all right," the doctor said. "He just quit."

"Quit?" McCaslin said.

"Yes. Old people do that sometimes…"

Muddy Water Ruskey

To paddle with John Ruskey is like slipping into another realm—a realm of love and respect for the River and a continuous awareness of the churning, life-threatening power you are riding upon. It is that respect that allows you to realize and become a part of the influence and grace and magnitude of the Mighty Mississippi River.

It's the River, the Big River, the Father of Waters, and its boiling, churning, swirling, sucking, rolling, and nourishing currents that are enlightening to John "Driftwood" Ruskey, whenever he is on it, in a hand-built wooden canoe. He winks at towboats whose captains sometimes shake their heads at him and offer disparaging remarks to other boats on their VHF marine radios about the safety of canoes on the River. There is an adventure around every bend in that big body of water.

John almost drowned in that river one cold night south of Memphis back in the '70s, when his Huck Finn-type raft came apart and he and his buddy clutched onto slippery flotation drums until they were washed ashore on a desolate island. A tin of waterproof matches salvaged from the debris saved them from hypothermia and possibly death on that sandbar. However, that near-death experience gave John a love for the River that has evolved into a passion and commitment to invite young folks and old adventurers alike to venture out and explore the River, enabling them to pull from those swirling eddies and whirlpools life itself. Life and inner strength is at our doorstep and waiting to be taken from the Delta's life-giver, the Mississippi River.

That Ole Man River, that Ole Man River,
He don't say nothing, but must know something,
That Ole Man River, he just keeps rolling along.

The third largest river in the world and one that drains 41 percent of the continental United States and parts of Canada is an awesome force. The River is somewhat uncontrollable during high water yet placid on calm and windless days, and Ruskey respects and stands in awe of its power and mystique. The Mississippi has been channelized, diked, buoyed, riveted, and leveed, yet, it is also allowed to go where its backyard used to be during peak floods, into its backwaters, before the Corps of Engineers began trying to control it. Mark Twain once said years ago:

One who knows the Mississippi will promptly aver—not aloud, but to himself—that ten thousand River Commissions, with the mines of the world at their back, cannot tame that lawless stream, cannot curb it or confine it, cannot say to it, Go here, or Go there, and make it obey; cannot save a shore which it has sentenced; cannot bar its path with an obstruction which it will not tear down, dance over, and laugh at.

Ruskey wants that very same river to just keep rolling along.

He don't plant taters, he don't plant cotton,
And them that plants 'em are soon forgotten,
That Ole Man River, he just keeps rolling along, rolling along.

Born and raised on the front range of the Colorado Rockies, the founder of the sixteen-year-old Quapaw Canoe Company has taken it upon himself to bring an awareness of the Mississippi River to thousands of people. "I've always been attracted to water," states John. "Water has always been calling my name." John feels he can change people's perception of the River by bringing them to it, by allowing them to experience the true wilderness and wildness about it safely, without a motor, the way Native Americans and the early explorers saw it.

He lives on the banks of the Sunflower River in Clarksdale, a very short distance from the Mississippi and its many life changing and enhancing experiences. "No one knows and respects the River like a paddler. When you paddle, you get a feel for the River you don't get in a power boat, and certainly not from the decks of the Mississippi Queen (one the largest paddlewheel excursion boats on the river). Canoeing is the most essential way of getting out on the water, the quietest, the most efficient, the most elegant, and the closest you can get to the spirit of the water, the River, and the lifeblood of our nation."

"Your arms are the motor in a canoe. Your eyes are the radars. This is as it should be. Americans need re-connection to the wilderness. It's in us; it's our heritage. The Mississippi is a wilderness in the heart of the South. Our ultimate goal is health and happiness. You gain health through paddling and caring for America's rivers and happiness through the experience of the wilderness. The human psyche blossoms on

MATTHEW DESPIAU, COURTESY OF JOHN RUSKEY

©Mathieu DESPIAU

River man extraordinaire John Ruskey is considered to be the most knowledgeable canoe guide on the lower Mississippi River covering a thousand miles of wilderness. Paddling with him is seasoned adventurer, expert guide, and Mighty Quapaw apprentice leader James "Woody" Sykes.

the River, your spirit soars, and your imagination is opened and you become closer to God. When you paddle, you are as weightless as a leaf blowing in the wind, and you are as heavy as the great River's boils and eddies."

John has been paddling the Mississippi since 1982. He is known as the most knowledgeable guide on the lower Mississippi covering almost a thousand miles. "The River has long been neglected, sidelined, put down, and disrespected. It was lonely and misunderstood. There was no one on the lower Mississippi who could escort people on her waters and bring them back safely. Many visitors to the South wanted to see the River, to experience it, to touch its currents, and learn its ways. Many residents grew up alongside the levee and never had ventured over it to the wilderness on the other side. There was no one to guide them, to show them the way."

The way is often paddled in hand-built canoes, some of them carved from huge cottonwood or cypress logs dropped off, or found, that look interesting. "Once water tested to find the bulk of the wood mass, the log is moved to the carving shed where days, weeks, sometimes months are spent studying the log, sketching it, visualizing the various possibilities. The primary job of the carver is to find the spirit of the log and create a new life for it in the form of a canoe."

Other Quapaw canoes are hand laid and are meticulously built beautiful works of art, sawed, sanded, glued, and molded into one-of-a-kind vessels, built exclusively for one-of-a-kind trips of a lifetime.

A trip with John Ruskey is one you won't soon forget. I have paddled kayaks and canoes in rivers and streams, lakes and ponds, and saltwater estuaries. I've even paddled for my dear life in a motorized sixteen-foot Boston Whaler, when a towboat hawser got tangled in my prop as I rounded the French Quarter with an ocean-going freighter bearing downriver on me. Yet to paddle with John is like slipping into another realm, a realm of love and respect for the River and a continuous awareness of the churning, life-threatening power you are riding upon. It is that respect that allows you to realize and become a part of the influence and grace and magnitude of Mess-ebbe, the Indian name for the Mississippi River.

Canoeing on the Mississippi, you silently slip along as part and parcel of the current, a sidestroke every now and then will keep you aligned with the River. The only noise is the bubbling and sloshing of waves lapping against the canoe, and maybe your own heartbeat. The low and steady drone of a chugging, digging, and smoking towboat heading upriver may break the silence, and, if you choose, you can thrust your paddle into the stream and cut off into a quiet and tranquil chute surrounded by towering cottonwoods and drooping willows. Herons and egrets perch regally in the treetops and gaze down as you slip underneath them. In the winter, mallard ducks leap into the air in front of your canoe, and wood ducks scream overhead, whistling and ducking and dodging as they seek safe haven. And in the heat of summer, the smell of cucumbers will make you aware of a cottonmouth water moccasin draped over a low hanging willow limb. Huge claw studded tracks with a smooth path drug between them will show you the escape route of an alligator that had been sunning beside the water when you rounded the bend.

Nighttime on the River with John and his guides is a guitar strumming, blues-infused culinary delight, cooked on a driftwood fire. History of the River is deliberated and philosophical ideas discussed. Sleep comes easy, only to think you have just drifted off into the sweet arms of Morpheus when you hear John scurrying about rattling coffee pots and cups, hooting like a hoot owl, and beckoning you to arise and watch the first rays of the breaking dawn. My mother would often say that the best coffee she ever had was prepared on cold early mornings, while goose hunting from water boiled hard and taken straight from the Mississippi River.

A canoe trip on the Mississippi is hard work yet relaxing at the same time. The silence of the River enters your soul as you reflect and become one with nature, aware of the cycles of the earth. You release the tedium of the daily hustle allowing your senses and natural instincts to come alive as you maneuver around rock dikes and shallow submerged sandbars, anticipating swirls and eddies, all the time keeping an eye out for the towboats…and the weather. Respect of the River is always of utmost concern as you learn discipline and the techniques it takes to survive upon its shoulders, and in return you reap the greatness and magnitude of it all.

Clarksdale, with its blues-grounded ecotourism engine running full throttle, is home base to the Quapaw Canoe Company with satellite operations in Helena and Natchez, offering canoeing adventures on the Mississippi and various other rivers and streams. And it is from this home base that the "Rivergator" project emerged. The forthcoming mile-by-mile description of the Mississippi River from St. Louis to the Gulf of Mexico is designed for paddlers as a travel guide to help ensure safety and success on canoe and kayak trips.

A very important part of Quapaw Canoe Company is the apprentice program for Clarksdale youth called the Mighty Quapaws. Teaching self-reliance and responsibility through canoe and paddle making, swimming and river guiding, the program has positively impacted many disadvantaged or underprivileged youth.

John Ruskey is a man of the river, as was Mark Twain and many others. He has a love of the river that equals their love, yet his is here right now, in the present, and his knowledge and experience is substantial and tangible to those who choose to partake of it. Respect and reverence, of possibly the most formidable natural force in our great nation, drives John and his guides every day. John has, as local singer/songwriter Jimmy Phillips once said, "…got muddy water, got muddy water in my blood."

The Duck Doctor

With a resounding snap of boot heels, and a stand-at-attention sharp salute, the morning duck hunt started at Fighting Bayou Hunting Club for twenty-seven years with the authoritative report of "Private First Class Edward Earl Tollison reporting for duty, SIR!" Millions of ducks have paid homage to the Delta's own Duck Doctor each year as he awaited their arrival after planting copious amounts of corn, milo, and rice for the overwintering waterfowl's use and enjoyment. It has been stated by the U. S. Fish and Wildlife Service that during a winter's stay, 80 percent of the ducks in the Delta spend at least a week on Fighting Bayou. And in December of 2003, a federal biologist from Grenada estimated close to 750,000 ducks were in the woods and fields. Fighting Bayou sits right smack-dab in the middle of Booger Den, five miles from the late Bubba Tollison's front door.

Bubba grew up in Doddsville and Ruleville. He spent his childhood playing on the Scruggs Place, where his daddy, Big Ed, kept the books on the plantation. His friends were the local kids living in the tenant shacks listening to the blues on radio station WDIA and playing outdoors. He was influenced in many ways by this country upbringing, which led to his absolute love of the blues and his endearing devotion to the old-time television series "Amos and Andy." His sister Cindy once said, "We didn't have a television back in those days, but we didn't need one, we had Bubba."

Bubba moved to Ruleville with his family and grew up sandwiched between the Ruleville Baptist Church and the Church of Christ. According to close friend Hugh Arant, "Bubba knew just enough about the stories of the Bible to be dangerous." One Sunday morning while sitting around the breakfast table at Fighting Bayou, Hugh got up quickly to go to teach a Sunday school lesson on the Prodigal Son. Skipper Jernigan, one of Bubba's closest friends, looked at Bubba and asked him if he knew that parable, and Bubba replied, "Wasn't that on 'Amos and Andy?'"

At Ruleville High School Bubba excelled at track and football because he was so fast. In the one hundred yard dash, Hugh said it was as if he was shot out of a cannon and no one could catch him when he grabbed the baton in the last leg of a 440, 880, or mile relay as Bubba hugged that inside lane and left everyone in his dust. Drew High School had the only track in north Sunflower County, and Bubba and Archie Manning grew up practicing and competing with each other. At a Sunflower County track meet in 1965, everyone eagerly awaited the one hundred yard dash as Archie ran for Drew and Denton Rogers ran for Indianola. According to Hugh, "When the starter fired his pistol to start the race, it wasn't even a race. Bubba blew Archie and Denton off the track as well as the rest of the field. It wasn't even close."

Archie recalls the year he and Bubba were invited to play in the all-star football game in Jackson and were being interviewed by Carl Walters, sports writer for *The Clarion-Ledger*. It was the biggest recognition either had ever had at that time. When asked if a lot of people were going to come to the game from the Delta, Bubba excitedly replied, "Mr. Walters, there ain't gonna be nobody left in Ruleville or Drew but the night watchman!"

Bubba was granted a football scholarship to Ole Miss along with some of his lifelong dearest friends and hunting companions, Archie Manning, Skipper Jernigan, Billy VanDevender, and George Lotterhos. Legendary freshman football coach, J.W. "Wobble" Davidson called the freshman class in to discuss mid-term grades, and some were less than sterling. Bubba was on that list. Coach Wobble got to Bubba and said, "What the hell is going on? Are you majoring in engineering?" Bubba very calmly replied, "No, Coach, I don't know nothing 'bout driving no train." According to Skipper, as stern as Coach Wobble was, even he couldn't take that and started laughing.

In the ESPN documentary, "House of Manning," Bubba recalled, "If you could make it through Coach Wobble's drills, you can run buck nekkid and barefoot through Hell and come out without a suntan." And Bubba did; however, a second hamstring tear and a detached retina cut Bubba's football career short in his sophomore year at Ole Miss.

While at Ole Miss, Skipper recalls, "Bubba was very intelligent, but he did not let that get in the way of his studying. Ole Miss had a Rhodes Scholar one year, and Bubba quickly let it be known that he too was a 'Roads' scholar, a 'Hit the Roads' scholar. He said he had made the dean's list every semester. When he got his grades, there was always a note at the bottom that said, 'Please go and see the Dean.'"

 Bubba was legendary in his 1967 Chevrolet Super Sport named Cecil. Cecil had no air conditioning because he thought it would decrease horsepower. Bubba said he had the 440 AC, four windows down and forty miles an hour. Roommate George Lotterhos remembers one summer Bubba going on "double dates." He would drive to Ruleville in the morning for a date and then return that afternoon for an evening date. Jane Carol Foshee was a Chi-O and the reigning Miss Mississippi when Bubba called the sorority house, "Hey, J. C., this is Bubba T! Would you like to go out and par-TEE with ME?

Playing sports was not the only thing Bubba did while in high school. Bubba hunted ducks. Wherever he could find ducks, he hunted them. Hugh Arant remembers the first time he ever went duck hunting with Bubba, beginning with a call one night. "Hey, Blackhand (Bubba had a nickname for everyone, and Hugh's came from his hands always being black with grease from repairing tractors), you wanna go duck hunting with me in the morning?" "Sure, Bubba! Where we gonna go?" "Well, there is a bunch of mallards over there on Sunshine right across from your house. Let's go get 'em!" It was also the first time Hugh was ever invited to go hunting on his own farm!

When the water rises in the winter on the Mississippi River, the ducks hit it in myriads. One season Lawson Holladay, Dud Burke, and Bubba were hunting out of Rosedale when the wind blew in big out of the south, hammering hard against a rising and very turbulent downward flow. Leaving the sandbar, the waves came crashing in. Lawson hollered at Bubba to turn around and go back to the sandbar. Bubba stuttered and said, "What, what did you say?" The next wave swamped the boat, losing all guns but one and everything else. Because they had on good life preservers and had good flotation in the boat, they survived but were stranded, wet, and very cold. A workboat came by and hauled them to the landing where a one-armed man they knew who lived close by met them. He came up to the wet hunters and said, "Bubba, you are just like a billy goat, you sure have a damned hard head." The next day they were back out on the river hunting.

East of Ruleville are the Tallahatchie River Bottoms. Each fall the Tallahatchie River comes out of its banks, and ducks flock to the flooded timber areas and fields. Bubba knew where these ducks would concentrate, and he hunted them hard. One year the scouting had been done and tons of ducks were located near Brazil and the hunt was set. Bubba invited Dud Burke and Lawson Holliday for the duck attack. Lawson, a lawyer, had a case before Federal Judge William Keady in Greenville the day before the hunt and had been promised it would be a one-day trial. However, it lasted into the day of the infamous duck hunt when Bubba Tollison was arrested by federal game warden Jimmy Pilgreen. Hugh Arant took Lawson's place on that hunt, and Lawson recalls, "The second day of participating in that trial kept me from standing in federal court before a federal judge with a game violation like Bubba and the rest got."

Hugh recalls, "Bubba blamed me for not hiding that second limit of ducks good enough, and I, of course, blamed him for not hiding the first limit very good. But it was the third limit that got us." Hugh and Dud (Son to Bubba) were picking up decoys while Bubba went to get the boat. Hearing him talking in the woods they both said, "Well, he's finally flipped out. He's talking to himself." Unbeknownst to them, two federal game wardens had paddled up and were watching their hunt.

Retired federal agent Jimmy Pilgreen speaks of Bubba with some degree of respect and admiration even though he tracked him on many occasions. "Bubba was an excellent duck hunter, maybe one of the best I've ever known. I had several encounters with him, and we were on a first name basis. I think the day Bubba stopped shooting over the limit I had been observing him in the Tallahatchie Bottoms. He walked into the woods to get his boat, and there I stood against a tree. He had a new shallow-water motor on his boat and said, 'Hey, Jimmy! You ever seen a rig like this? Let's go for a ride. Ain't no need to walk, I'll ride you around.'"

The two got into his boat and were just riding around in the woods when Agent Pilgreen noticed a bright orange duck foot poking up from underneath a log. He looked at Bubba and said, "Getting pretty close to pay dirt aren't we, Bubba?" And Bubba replied, "Jimmy, I believe you have finally got me." After that moment, Bubba Tollison never again shot over the limit on ducks for fear of what the federal judge later told him would happen to him if he did. According to Skipper, "Bubba became a reformed duckaholic. U.S. Game Warden Jimmy Pilgreen was his reformation, and he took the cure."

In 1987, the present day Fighting Bayou Hunting Club was formed and consists of three thousand acres of oak timber and ag fields. The one thousand acres of flooded woods have been a duck magnet since time immemorial and is renowned in Delta duck legend. No longer being chased by wardens, Bubba found a home and became known as the Duck Doctor because of his knowledge and experience with ducks. To Bubba, there were only three seasons, farming season, duck season, and the rest of the year. He often stated that any duck information more than twenty-four hours old is absolutely worthless.

Prior to the season, Bubba would sit on what is known as "Bubba's Prayer Bench" in the rest lake and watch the ducks as they migrated into the area. For twenty-seven years he called Skipper late in the afternoon and said, "The ducks are showing up, and I have just seen Mo and Elmo and all their cousins and friends, and they are all wearing little green baseball caps and their orange tennis shoes and carrying little duck grips under their wings so they can stay awhile." He described the migration some days as the ducks were falling out of the sky so fast that their "eyelids were peeled."

During the season, each afternoon at sunset, all members and guests go out around Sunshine with cocktails to watch the unbelievable display of thousands and thousands of ducks milling about and spooling into the woods. Bubba named this the "Benediction" as only God can orchestrate it. George "Goose Tatum" Lotterhos recalls one Benediction when Bubba, with cold drink in one hand and binoculars in the other, announced to the crowd that there were a half million ducks on the property. George immediately asked Bubba, "How do you know we have 500,000 ducks?" and Bubba's reply was, as he pulled on his chin, "Well, Goose, I just counted their feets and divided by two."

Often what was called "Bubba Math" was revealed. One day seven hunters were getting close to their four duck limit, and Skipper asked Bubba to count up. Bubba did and announced they had twenty-six and could kill twelve more as 7x4=38. Skipper told him that was not correct that 7x4=28 and they could only kill two more ducks. Bubba's response was "Are you sure?" Skipper wondered why Bubba had trouble with the game wardens in years gone by.

One evening no one was in camp, so Skipper decided to cook for himself and Bubba. Then members and guests started showing up. By raiding the freezer, a full-blown feast was soon prepared, and Bubba stated, "I want y'all to know that Mr. Clean (Skipper's nickname) is just like Moses, he's taken two fishes and five loaves and fed the whole damn boat!"

Goose Tatum is the Quartermaster at the club and decides the menu. Once the members became health conscious, their diets and the menu changed to salads, fish and less red meat. Bubba hungrily exclaimed one night that he was tired of eating "Johnson grass, Styrofoam, and cardboard!" Steaks went back on the menu.

The hunts will continue at Fighting Bayou, but Bubba won't be there to make his early morning salute, nor to holler "YEP" when it's time to shoot the ducks as they fall through the timber. Bubba is no longer with us. And as the last duck of the legal limit hits the waters of Fighting Bayou with a definite "phlop," to state the celebrated and often awaited command as the hunters begin to pick up decoys and head for camp, "Smell them biscuits, boys!"

Lil' Buck's First River Hunt

One cold winter night I received a call from one of my dearest friends from Cleveland, Colonel Thomas N. "Creeper" Sledge, Ret. USAF. "The ducks are covering up the cockleburr flat on Choctaw Bar in the middle of the Mississippi River," he said. "Meet me at Mounds Landing at 5:30 in the morning, and if that little brown puppy dog you have can pick up a duck, bring him with you. I'll bring my boat, and you bring something to eat." What could I say but, "Yes, sir!"

Lil' Buck was my Boykin Spaniel that previously had only picked up wood ducks on my Yankee friend Charlie Potter's place on Black Bayou. I awoke mighty early the next morning, kissed my Sallie, and told her I was going out on the river, not to worry as I would be with Creeper. I rousted Lil' Buck, and grabbing my boots, duck call, coat, and gun, we headed to Double Quick for a thermos of coffee and six sausage biscuits. It was going to be a long morning.

Hank Burdine with duck hunting buddies Skipper Jernigan and the late Colonel "Creeper" Sledge.

I arrived at Mounds Landing at five a.m. sharp, not wanting to feel the wrath of the Colonel for being late and proceeded to stretch back with the heater on low in my truck and took a nap. I was awakened by a gruff voice saying, "Wake up, the sun's coming up, and the ducks are flying!"

We hurriedly loaded our gear, jumped in the boat, and headed across the river as the sun broke day. In no time, we found our spot on the flat, and Creeper threw out five or six decoys as Lil' Buck and I found a big tree that had fallen in the water and set up our ambush point. Sure enough, as legal shooting time rolled quickly around, Lil' Buck was as anxious as ever, whining and shivering and excited to pick up his first Mississippi River mallard.

Here they came and because of my expert calling, (yeah, right!) the ducks cupped their wings. "Boom, boom!" and a fat drake hit the water. Not waiting on my command to "back," Lil' Buck hit that freezing river water like a tempered pro and swam straight for the duck. Once he grabbed it, he headed straight for the bank on the other side of the slash. Not wanting him to start off wrong on his first ever big water retrieve, I rushed out and grabbed him and drug him back, reprimanding him and setting him on the log. I made him drop the duck and commanded him to stay on the log. Lil' Buck started whining again.

Soon, Creeper asked for a bite to eat. "The biscuits are in the bag," I said.

He replied, "Ain't nothing in the bag but shredded paper." Uh, oh. Where, oh, where, did six sausage and biscuits go?

About that time a flock of twenty-five mallards started circling overhead, and as we hunkered down and began to call, Lil' Buck began to prance up and down that log, whining and running from one end to the other, doing a little pirouette on each end of the log. "Control that dog and shut him up!" my pal commanded. "These ducks are wanting to work!"

Then, two ducks committed, and BOOM, one fell to the water. Without waiting for my command, Lil' Buck lept off the log, swam rapidly to the duck, and, once again, lit out for the far bank. Upon reaching the sand, he scrambled up and down until he found a suitable spot and, with duck in mouth, took care of his bid'ness!

Creeper and I sat in awe as this young little retriever swam back across the water, dropped the duck next to me, and crawled back up on the log and looked at us as if saying, "Okay, boys, you want to go duck hunting, NOW, let's hunt!"

Matt's Journey
"When you set out for ITHAKA ask that your way be long,
full of adventure, full of instruction..."

It ain't much of a river; it ain't even a stream where the small flow of water trickles over the rocks at Lake Itasca, the headwaters of the third largest river system in the world. And almost 2,400 miles south it empties into the Gulf of Mexico after cutting through the heartland of the North American continent. Once she gains her headway, the Mississippi River is a romping, tromping, meandering, and gallivanting lady that once knew no bounds. But that was before man stepped in and dammed and locked her up and told her to go this way, go that way, and sometimes, she does...

My son, Matt Burdine, grew up on the banks of the Mississippi River on Lake Ferguson outside of Greenville. During several high water events, he, along with the rest of the children on the lake, would go back and forth to school on my raft because the roads were closed due to flooding. On summer weekends Matt would play along the sandbars and camp out with his friends around a big bonfire of collected driftwood, while listening to stories of the river, as towboats shined their searchlights on us and blew their mournful horns. I believe it was during these times the Big Muddy crept into his soul.

When we moved to the Wet Valley of the Sangre de Christo mountain range in southern Colorado, Matt spent many a day fly fishing and floating on the Arkansas River. Its headwaters are above Buena Vista which is close to where we lived. His love of water grew. And when his mama was diagnosed with breast cancer, we moved to the Florida panhandle to be close to her family and I could be closer to the Delta. Matt became a surfer on the sugar sand beaches of Destin, and I taught him how to fish in the deep blue sea. Again, he was surrounded by water.

Matt was almost eighteen years old when he lost his mama, but he never lost the love of water that she instilled in him at an early age as she herself had grown up on the beaches of Miami. After getting his MBA from Ole Miss, Matt somewhat pushed away the pull of Wall Street and headed back out to Colorado. He became a snow ski instructor for youngsters and a white-water rafting guide on the headwaters of the Arkansas River in the summer. During his visits back home to the Delta, he would meet and get to know paddlers that were coming down the Mississippi. He became inspired by "seeing their oceanic eyes and hearing their voices that sounded like water. I knew that regardless of age or occupation, anything is possible. By challenging one's self to learn something new, or to do something different, whole new arenas of perspectives open up and one's life can be changed."

The river pulled Matt like never before. He wanted to experience the sights and sounds and the feelings he had heard about. Matt realized he had to paddle the entire length of the great river, with or without a cause, for it tugged at his heartstrings. "Every person who goes on a long-distance trip, whether solo or as a team, is most likely after some kind of personal or spiritual transformation. One is not the same as he or she was

BURDINE FAMILY COLLECTION

before. One's perspective alloys their experience. Life becomes more vibrant and vast, gratitude fills the heart, and awe floods the mind." Matt could schedule his voyage with no time restraints. Bacon and beans are not that expensive, and five gallons of drinking water will go a long way. However, after losing his mother and grandmother to breast cancer, he decided to paddle for The Breast Cancer Research Foundation. "It gave me a little more fuel in each paddle stroke; it gave me inspiration during those times when my head was in my hands." He called his journey "A Million Strokes for a Cure." The trip "was by all means my personal Odyssey, in search of ITHAKA, of being immersed in the journey, and all of its trials and tribulations."

And so, his journey began.

Exuberant that he was to be sponsored by the Wenonah Canoe Company of Minnesota, and outfitted with a safe river canoe, preparation was made for the long journey north with supplies, gear, and a guitar. He chose to start his trip in the fall when most river paddlers are finishing theirs. He wanted to experience the fall colors and be on the river as the days got shorter and colder and the ducks and geese began their annual migration. It would mean paddling until the winter weather made him take out and wait until spring. "This added a whole new level of excitement and seriousness to the trip. To be uncomfortable and in unknown situations enticed me. Equally powerful were the miserable moments as they were also somewhat the most pleasant. One learns to take things as they come equally. Storms will forever hold magic to me."

The first mile or so entailed dragging his canoe and all his gear through a marshland with barely enough water to float the boat. On his second night out he camped with two Ojibwe Native Americans who still relied on the wild rice growing in the headwaters area. He spent the next day beating sticks over the sides of their canoe as he helped in the harvest of the wild rice. He was on river time.

Portaging was an issue in the headwaters area. Log jams, fallen trees and beaver dams had to be dealt with as well as man-made dams. "Being alone on the river and not being in a hurry or on a time schedule, one can go with the flow of whatever the river brings, on land, or off. Bliss always follows. Time doesn't exist and one lives by the sun and his own mood."

"Ask that your way be long
At many a summer dawn to enter
With what gratitude, what joy!"

Soon, the stream emerged from the Northern marshlands and opened up to a river course through the bluff country, "the Driftless Area where the glaciers didn't cut through. Massive bluffs rise on either side, and by paddling in the fall, I was moving along with the coloring of the leaves. Humble she begins, yet wildly massive she grows." Lakes were ahead, "beautiful blue water lakes that can turn into an ocean at any moment." This is the land of the great bald eagles; "they would fly off at the sound of a boat motor or an engine but would look quietly at a passing canoe with awe."

Once the river starts to grow, the lock and dam system begins. "Sometimes there would be a two or three hour wait while a barge goes through the lock. Other times the gate would be open and waiting for you and would lower you down to the next pool all by yourself. Resupply packages were shipped to these locks and lowered down to you in a rope basket, usually with a cold Snicker bar as a gift from the lockmaster."

"People on the river are happy to give"
Proud Mary, Creedence Clearwater Revival

"Some of the most magical moments I have are from meeting people and immersing myself into the culture surrounding that particular part of the river. The wilderness was breathtaking along with the wildlife, and meeting strangers along the way was one of my favorite memories. To see how each accent and culture changed from river town to river town was awesome. The spontaneous, authentic kindness people showed along the river astounded me. From simple words of encouragement, to a ride into town, shelter from a storm, or a cold beer from a passing boat, each little act of kindness and generosity will always be remembered, appreciated, and paid forward."

Had Matt not been on 'river time' it is doubtful he would have ever experienced a lot of these random acts of kindness, feelings, and sensations.

"Each day while paddling alone, a whole range of emotions course through you, from utter exhaustion to exhilaration, from absolute bliss to fright. You have to be absolutely and constantly aware of your surroundings and the river. For hours on end you must be ever extremely attentive to what is going on around you. You get into what I call a river trance: your peripheral vision widens, and a three hundred and sixty degree awareness opens the mind of the paddler. Without being aware, there is danger lurking with no backup."

Once out of the locks and dams of the upper Mississippi, and away from the quaint little river towns with beer halls on the bluffs, the Mississippi opens up to a major transportation artery as the Missouri joins her flow and then the Ohio beefs her up with its huge input of water. The river widens and barge traffic is a constant factor to deal with. Eddies, undercurrents and upheavals, dangerous swirls and flat, fast water have to be dealt with. At certain stages of the river, there may not be a sandbar to sleep on for miles, and a decision has to be made to tie up early or just hope you see sand around the next bend. The river becomes a force to be dealt with for it is no longer just a leisurely paddle downstream. Vigilance is imperative and decisions have to be made around every bend as to which side to be on and where the currents are along with the rock dikes that control the flow of the stream. Huge sandbars and islands appear with pristine backwater areas ripe for exploring. "In recalling the moments I spent on the river during those months, I can still feel my bare feet on the island sands; I can still feel the pulse of the river as I pulled myself downstream, walking with my hands for almost 2,400 miles. I can still feel and see those early morning moments and evening sunsets that produce the world's two greatest light shows, while the coffee pot boils over a driftwood fire."

"Some look at the river as masculine, as Old Man River. Yes, he will discipline you and teach you about life and survival. However, we all have our individual interpretations for aspects of this world. In my perspective, the river is feminine, a grandmother, a mother, a sister, and an intimate friend. She is a nurturer, life giver, teacher, healer, and a role model."

Matt decided not to follow the river down through Baton Rouge and New Orleans with its huge, conglomerate smoking petrochemical plants and burgeoning, towering ocean going ship traffic. He decided to take a right at the Old River Control Structure, which allows 30 percent of the total flow of the Mississippi to go down the Atchafalaya to the Gulf of Mexico. Without this structure the river, as we know it, would have changed its course by now and spilled itself into the Gulf below Morgan City. It almost did in 1973. The ports of New Orleans and Baton Rouge would possibly have silted in and dried up to navigation. The Atchafalaya River is a beautiful and pristine sanctuary with little barge traffic. It is true Cajun country and known for its swampy wilderness and lack of river industry. Alligators and nutria adorn fallen cypress trees overhung with Spanish moss. I was glad Matt chose this route to the sea.

Almost thirty miles below Morgan City is the mouth of the Atchafalaya and its opening into the Gulf of Mexico. I trailered my boat down, put in the river at Morgan City, and headed south to pick up my son and his canoe. I found him on the last island, in the last channel, where his next landfall would have been South America. His journey had ended, or maybe, it had just begun…

"Always keep ITHAKA fixed on your mind
Your arrival there is what you are destined for
But do not in the least hurry the journey
Better that it last for years
So that when you reach the island you are old
Rich with all you have gained along the way"
ITHAKA by C.P. Cavafy

Delta Artists

A Remnant of a Wall

Mortar and bricks could not hold the greatness that dwelt within these walls. Literary and artistic largesse bubbled and blossomed here among the flowers and fountains to emerge and permeate the souls and hearts of many.

There is a falling down remnant of a wall in Greenville, a dilapidated and curved portion of a walled garden, that holds the key to the literary and arts explosion in the Delta which blossomed in the 1930s and was felt throughout the country and beyond. Within these walls ideas were nurtured and thoughts bred from world travels and philosophical discussions, musical interludes, poetic dissertations, and even some drunken exhortations. William Alexander Percy's garden harbored various and quite appealing people, among them, were free thinkers, poets, writers, bohemians, Pulitzer and Nobel Prize winners, world-renowned artists and sculptors, inventors, traveling guests, and a few vagabonds. Some visited briefly, while others remained for an extended stay. Inside those brick walls passed a generation of literary and artistic greats.

William Alexander Percy was raised under the veil of several diverse personalities. His mother was a stanch Catholic New Orleanian with all the social graces and trappings that went along with that. His father, Senator Leroy Percy, was a lawyer, planter, businessman, United States Senator, and friend to extremely important and powerful men, President Theodore Roosevelt among them. His grandfather was a decorated Civil War veteran, a legendary figure in the Delta and also a planter and lawyer. He was attuned to literature and the arts and quite prominent and was known as the "Grey Eagle of the Delta." His great-grandfather, according to the book *William Alexander Percy* by Benjamin Wise, was a man who "loved beauty and looked beyond mere profit seeking for the better things in life." William was a small-framed man and more attracted to the arts, literature, poetry, and travel than his forebears who relished in the chase of wild game while pursuing business and community leadership endeavors. Will Percy once stated, "You had to be a hero or a villain or a weakling, you couldn't just be middling ordinary."

Raised in Greenville and educated by a cadre of extremely adept educators, Will Percy learned quickly and was sent to prep school at Sewanee. However, when he realized that the prep school was a military school, he enrolled in the college and was accepted at fifteen years old. He blended right in at the University of the South at Sewanee and was a founding member of the bohemian literary club called Sopnerim and became an editor of the school magazine. He was devoted to music, literature, poetry, and the arts. Upon graduation he spent a year in Paris absorbing the aura and ambiance of a cosmopolitan and worldly life. His personality evolved into one that was quietly spoken yet alluring, confident, and trustworthy.

Will Percy decided to come home and follow in his paternal footsteps and become a lawyer. He chose Harvard Law School possibly because of the proximity to an abundance of symphonies and theaters in Boston. He could be surrounded by the arts while studying law and immerse himself in philosophical and meaningful

RORY DOYLE

discussions with fellow students, professors, and friends. His life progressed into a poetic and contemplative arena as he encircled himself with like-minded souls. Upon completion of his law degree, he moved back to Greenville, taking up residency with his parents in his family home on Percy Street and practicing law with his father as they walked to and from work each day.

When World War I broke out, Will Percy joined the army earning the rank of captain. He was awarded the *Croix de Guerre* for valor on the front lines in France. During the devastating 1927 flood, he was put in charge of relief and headed up the Red Cross efforts in Greenville. Soon afterwards his mother and father passed away, and he found himself devastated and alone yet a wealthy man, having inherited the vast Trail Lake Plantation, his father's law practice, and other family resources. He went to work maintaining the plantation, practicing law, and building a private walled garden that surrounded his home. Wealth had allowed him to lead the good life of a Southern aristocrat. He was admired by many, not only for his innate abilities but for his love of the finer things in life. Percy described his garden in the book *The Percys of Mississippi* by Lewis Baker. "Water oaks and evergreens shaded the vine covered brick walls and iron and tile benches invited the visitor to pause and admire the iris, azaleas, blue Spanish scilla, and bleeding heart that bloomed around the splashing fountains. The imposing wrought iron gate at the garden's entrance reinforced the appearance of a retreat, but it was never locked, and ladies from the garden club dropped by regularly to discuss their petunias." He referred to it as "the best sort of Ivory Tower." It was a place of contemplation and solace, enclosed and quiet and peaceful, lending to reminiscence and longing. And within its borders passed untold literary and artistic personas.

In 1932, Will adopted his three nephews after their parents died and moved them into the house with him. They were raised amongst all the comings and goings, sometimes at all hours of the day and night, of a diverse plethora of people. In the book *William Alexander Percy*, Benjamin Wise stated, "Percy's Greenville home was a gathering place for artists and intellectuals. There was a constant swirl of activity. It was almost like living in a hotel. There were men who had fallen on hard times and living upstairs and there were always guests popping in and out, often world-famous writers, artists, and intellectuals..."

Local historian and educator Eugene Ham wrote, "The remnant of Mr. Will Percy's elegant brick garden wall is among the few tangible relics of what an extraordinary place the old boom and bust river town had been over time. In a town which boasted enthusiastic and serious gardeners, Mr. Percy's extensive walled garden was likely the most distinctive. Behind the walls not only did he nurture and cultivate a great range of flora but also a wide spectrum of people, many who distinguished themselves in arts and letters. His adopted son Walker, with his friends Shelby Foote and Charles Bell, were among younger writers nourished there. Sculptors Leon Koury and Malvina Hoffman, local New York educated photographer Willa Johnson and artist Elizabeth Calvert, great niece of his friend and mentor E.E. Bass, spent afternoons and evenings within those walls. Noted writers from Greenville's David Cohn to Harlem Renaissance giant Langston Hughes visited, as did William Faulkner, as a guest of his Greenville friend and literary agent, Ben Wasson. Carl Sandburg, Stephen Vincent Benet, Vachel Lindsey, Stark Young, New York portraitist William Van Dresser, and Betty and Hodding Carter, whom Mr. Percy helped 'recruit' to Greenville to start a progressive newspaper, were all frequent visitors."

Within his home and the walls of his garden, Will Percy "transitioned from artist to patron and teacher of the arts. He opened his home to writers and artists who needed an environment to create their art." For several years, David Cohn lived in Will Percy's home while he wrote *God Shakes Creation*. Once when Shelby Foote was suspended from school, Will Percy banished him to his library for a week with the instructions to read the entire time.

And those that were brought into the realm of Will Percy's intellectual sphere were somewhat changed forever. Shelby Foote stated, "He was a very good teacher, it was by example. Here was a man who was a world traveler, who was widely read, who knew about the cultural forms of life on other continents, who had experienced the company of some of the fine writers of our time, and he would talk about it in a way that made you not only know the reality of it, but appreciate the beauty of present day literature and past. I've heard Mr. Will talk about Keats in a way that made you wish the conversation would end so you could go home and read some Keats."

Sculptor Leon Koury has stated, "I can think of only one man who found a spark and tried to fan it into a flame, my friend and patron William Alexander Percy. He would not let me rest content, so I listened and learned and discovered patches of wisdom here and there and tufts of common sense that put me to shame. I was made to understand that the marvelous works of others are but the voices of artists delivering their peculiar messages to the world, to which I at any time could add my own. It was then that I understood that it is never what you say in art that is important, but how much of yourself is speaking."

Walker Percy remembered him as "a personage, a presence, one that showed exoticness and radiated that mysterious quality called charm." And Walker has stated about his uncle, "he was one of a kind; I never met anyone remotely like him. It was to encounter a complete, articulated view of the world as tragic as it was noble."

Acclaimed sculptor William Beckwith, who developed under the tutelage of Leon Koury, has stated, "He (Koury) consistently urged a bunch of searching, young bohemians to read the Harvard Classics, and many of them did. Leon wanted to expose his young friends to the same quality of art that Will Percy had exposed to him." Koury, much like Percy who had mentored him, wanted to bring the younger generation into a realm of artistic awareness and to "fan it into a flame."

In January of 1942, William Alexander Percy died from an extended illness. The city of Greenville's business closed for the day of his funeral. The editor of the *Delta Democrat Times,* Hodding Carter, described his own heartache over Percy's death: "I loved Will Percy for every reason that any of our numbered legion could have had: for the greatness of his spirit, the goodness of his heart, the courage that shone in his eyes and spurred his frail body, the honesty, the tenderness, the full catalogue of virtues that made him one of God's few saints."

From the Hands of a Master
The Delta Legacy of Auguste Rodin

The French master Auguste Rodin, 1840-1917, was known as the father of modern art. Compared to Michelangelo, he was considered by many to be the greatest artist of his era. Rodin modeled the human body with realism and physicality using intense individual character. He was able to find—through his hands in clay—"the beauty and pathos in the human animal." The Musée Rodin in Paris holds six thousand sculptures and over seven thousand drawings by Rodin, and his legacy is deeply rooted in the Mississippi Delta.

Malvina Hoffman

As a child, young Malvina Hoffman grew up in New York City amidst the art and music scene of a high social era. Her father was a concert pianist with the New York Philharmonic Orchestra, and she was constantly immersed in artistic endeavors. Daily she listened to her father practice and play on his Chickering grand piano. She began drawing at an early age, and her favorite subjects were horses and dogs, which were quite prevalent on the streets of New York in the early part of the century. When Richard Hoffman died, she and her mother went on a year's sabbatical to Europe so Malvina could study art and be a part of the creative scene. Malvina had sculpted a portrait bust of her father and one of his protégés and carried a picture of them with her to show Rodin in hopes of becoming a student of the great master.

"The Patriot" by Malvina Hoffman, was commissioned by William Alexander Percy to honor his father, Senator Leroy Percy.

After repeated attempts to gain entrance into his studio and meet him, Malvina presented two letters of introduction to the doorman from friends and arch supporters of Rodin. She was immediately brought under the aura and tutelage of the French master. He commanded her to go to the Louvre and to study the past masters and to make many drawings, not to copy them, but to develop her own technique. According to Didi Hoffman, who has written

a book called *Beautiful Bodies,* "Rodin taught Malvina Hoffman that art must come from an attempt to show the truth in nature, it must be honest, and that honesty was almost impossible to capture. Once she became master of her own art, then she could find her truth, as he continued to try to do, fearing he never would." Rodin had urged Hoffman to study human anatomy and dissection to better understand musculature and tension in clay. She took his advice, and in her works with the prima Russian ballerina Anna Pavlova, her studies of the hands, arms, legs, and torso were critically compared to the extensive studies of Michelangelo and da Vinci by the *New York Times.* She learned from Rodin to study intensively before she sculpted.

Hoffman returned to New York and worked with a frenzy, developing her own technique in her studio where she sculpted with a passion while taking courses in dissection of the human body. She learned the art of plaster casting and how to build the molds and the art of making bronze sculptures from the clay models she was expertly creating. She became very well known and was sought after for portrait and full figure busts worldwide. She accepted the monumental task for the Field Museum of Chicago to travel the world and create 103 pieces of sculpture of the different races of man. This was the largest commission in the history of bronze art, and it happened to coincide with her completion of a full-figured statue of "The Patriot" that stands in a Greenville cemetery.

William Alexander Percy

William Alexander Percy was a poet, planter, lawyer, and world traveler. He was a mentor, host, and friend to artists and intellectuals and even a few vagabonds and bohemians. William Faulkner, Ben Wasson, Carl Sandburg, Vachel Lindsey, Shelby Foote, Walker Percy, Charles Bell, David Cohn, Stephen Vincent Benet, Langston Hughes, and the Hodding Carters all were a part of Percy's close circle of friends, and they often spent time in his home and garden. Upon the death of his father, Senator Leroy Percy, William Alexander Percy commissioned Malvina Hoffman to sculpt a monument to his father. In Malvina's diary she wrote on October 22, 1930, after arriving from Chicago by train, "The Crusader now stands in the Greenville cemetery with bowed head, contemplating us and unmoved against his wall of stone." She and Percy later went to the nursery where together they selected the trees and shrubs to adorn the monument. Malvina Hoffman had become a close and personal part of the Delta scene, corresponding with and visiting with Percy on numerous occasions.

Leon Koury

Leon Koury was the son of a Syrian immigrant who grew up in a corner grocery store on Nelson Street in Greenville next door to Doe's Eat Place. Leon's father had entered a monastery before coming to America to become a monk, but he left before taking his vows. Leon grew up studying Nietzsche, Schopenhauer, and Emanuel

Swedenborg. Upon meeting William Alexander Percy, Koury found himself as a young man immersed in a world of culture, literature, and music. When he heard his first symphony in Percy's parlor, he stated, "I was in a daze for weeks. This was something that I felt I had heard thousands of years before, and it had come back home to my ears." Percy was able to instill in him the realization that "there was so much more to acquire...so much more to gain."

Showing an interest in modeling, Percy gifted Koury with fifty pounds of modeling clay. With no formal training, he began teaching himself in the back of the little grocery store. His first formal portrait bust was of Will Percy. "Somehow, I already knew." Through Percy, "I was made to understand that the marvelous works of others are but the voices of artists delivering their peculiar messages to the world, to which I could at any time add my own. Then it was that I understood that it is never what you say in art that is important, but how much of yourself is speaking."

Koury went on to be shown in the 1937 National Art Exhibit in New York, the 1939 New York World's Fair, the Whitney Museum, and in exhibits on the West Coast. Will Percy introduced Leon Koury to Malvina Hoffman in 1945, and he moved to New York to stay in Hoffman's studio and to "get some atmosphere, to absorb some of the facets and the workmanship." At that time, it wasn't a question of Hoffman instructing Koury in sculpture at all, he was long past that. He mentored under her and chauffeured her around New York as she introduced him to the "modern art scene" of the time, all the while instilling in him the depths of thought and inward seeking vision of the honesty of nature that had been so concisely implanted in her by Rodin.

Koury moved back to Greenville in 1961 and continued a series of black life and work in the South. Upon the death of his father, Leon closed the grocery store and opened a small hip bar called the Orbit Lounge. He wanted it to be a place where enlightened people could gather, much like the coffee houses and bistros of New York. In a 1962 article in the *Commercial Appeal* he said, "I wanted it to be the kind of place where creative people could come together, talk, socialize, listen to good music, and exchange ideas" (much like Will Percy's garden!). Young garage bands would come and practice late into the night at the Orbit Lounge. After listening to Dylan, Hendrix, Johnnie Winter, the Cream, and the Stones, Koury would play Tchaikovsky, Vivaldi, or some Italian opera. He became known as a "guru" to the younger crowd, enticing them to read the Harvard Classics and exposing them to the same quality of art as Will Percy had exposed to him. And he taught art lessons, opening up a whole new arena of artistic experience to talented and budding artists of the Delta.

Bill Beckwith

During one of the jam sessions at the Orbit Lounge in 1966, a young Bill Beckwith accompanied his friends Jerry and Donnie Brown, of a band called the Candy Shoestring, to the bistro on Nelson Street. Bill wanted to get into the music scene in order to "impress the girls." However, once he met Leon Koury, his attentions were turned to the art of sculpting. "From an early age, I had an affinity for the technical aspect of shaping matter. As soon as I entered Leon's studio and saw what he could do with clay and plaster, the music was forgotten, and the challenge to learn modeling was on. I was fourteen years old."

"Leon taught fine modeling, classical modeling. He stressed strong side light and working in the gray area between highlight and shadow to achieve perfect form with direction on energy from the center out, as in an egg." Bill has stated that sculpture has to be the most challenging and rewarding manipulation of materials because the artist hopes to create an object which exists with a difference of content from subject matter. "It is a poem in three dimensions where you enter the mysteries of the human condition, that area that we have no words for and you strive to build a piece that connects with a feeling and becomes a symbol of something spiritually elusive." Bill went on to excel at Ole Miss in art, garnering the Student Achievement Award for the best artist at Ole Miss. He learned the art of plaster casting and became "as hooked on casting bronze as an addict to heroin." By the end of 1974, Bill Beckwith had built a complete foundry in the back yard at Leon Koury's Nelson Street studio. "If you have ever poured molten metal or held the sun in your hand, you understand the power and the energy. I was hooked bad."

Beckwith became nationally acclaimed, with his work mainly figurative, and is best known for his portrait busts and full figure sculptures. On display in parks and museums are full figure busts of Elvis Presley, B.B. King, L.Q.C. Lamar, Chickasaw Chief Piomingo, William Faulkner, and George Merrick of Coral Gables, Florida. Renowned Mississippi artist Bill Dunlap says, "Bill Beckwith is in a class all his own. I have been a friend and an admirer since I first saw his work at Ole Miss. It's hard to make bronze look like flesh. Bill Beckwith is a master at this."

Today

Leon Koury taught many students in his studio on Nelson Street and in a studio set up in the Mississippi Levee Board building in downtown Greenville. Bill Beckwith has taught hundreds of students as a professor at Ole Miss, some who have gone on to be teachers of art themselves. And throughout the veins and artistic abilities of these many artists from the Delta and beyond flow the vision, insight, and depth of honesty and nature from some of the greatest artists of our time. Beginning with Auguste Rodin, through Malvina Hoffman, William Alexander Percy, Leon Koury, and Bill Beckwith, the masterful artistic karma continues.

For the Love of Franke

Franke Keating, lifelong photographer, world traveler, team mate and soul mate to internationally-acclaimed travel writer Bern Keating, said it was the trees that brought them to Greenville.

The young couple crossed the river from Arkansas in 1945, and riding down Washington Avenue, Franke exclaimed, "Aren't the trees pretty!" It was then they decided to move to the Delta. Twenty-seven books, hundreds of magazine articles, thousands of photographs, and millions of airline miles later, the Delta is still Franke's home, and it always will be. Even though Bern passed away in March 2004, and son John lives in Atlanta, Franke has no plans of moving anywhere. She wants to continue traveling and taking pictures. After all, she has been a photographer since she was twelve years old, when her mother gave her a Brownie box camera.

The daughter of a railroad man, Franke was reared in McGehee, Arkansas, and had never visited Mississippi. She just knew it was across the river. While attending the University of Arkansas in Fayetteville, she met and fell in love with the dashing, young Bern Keating from Quebec, Canada. Bern had been putting himself through New York University working as a transcontinental truck driver in the summer, when he chose the University of Arkansas to get his degree because he loved the Ozarks and the school was the only fully accredited school in journalism and English that had accepted him. In 1938, he graduated *summa cum laude*, the first ever from the University of Arkansas.

Bern accepted a teaching job in West Palm Beach, Florida, and began writing for the *Palm Beach Post Times*. He and Franke were soon married. They met a wealthy couple that owned a radio station in Utica, New York, and moved there while Bern worked as news director at WIBX. At the outbreak of World War II, Bern was accepted into the Navy Officers Candidate School and sent to Harvard for training. Receiving orders to report to San Francisco, the young couple moved to the soon-to-be-famous Haight-Ashbury district. Bern served as a communications officer and then as an attack officer on a destroyer in the Pacific, sinking six Japanese submarines in nine days. Franke has often stated, "World War II did two things—it got rid of Hitler and it got me out of Utica, New York!"

With the war over, Bern and Franke were anxious to start their professional careers and moved to Little Rock, Arkansas. There was not much work for Bern as a writer, so Franke persuaded him to become a photographer, concentrating on lucrative debutante and wedding photos. But the society scene in Little Rock was already covered by well-established local photographers. Once the Keatings saw the trees in Greenville, they decided to take the $900 Bern had just won in a craps game and move across the river to the Mississippi Delta.

Mrs. L. A. White, better known as "La' White," owned a dress shop in Greenville and was the preeminent designer and dress supplier for Delta debutantes and brides. She met Bern and immediately liked him. Admiring his flamboyance, courtly

KEATING FAMILY COLLECTION

Bern and Franke visiting The Shack Up Inn in Clarksdale.

manners, and exuberant wittiness, La' White took Bern under her wing, taking him to parties, debutante balls, and weddings. She often haughtily introduced him as "my New York photographer." In 1946, Franke began having babies and stayed at home. They had purchased five acres in a cotton field across cypress-studded Rattlesnake Bayou on a gravel road south of Greenville and soon built an airy, rambling, ranch style house. They began planting trees, flowers, and gardens. Caledonia Smith was hired and moved into a small house at the rear of their yard to help take care of the new babies, John and Kate. Franke once again picked up her camera, and she has yet to put it down.

Business continued to increase for Bern, and he turned his ambitions to writing while Franke took the pictures. He paired up with fellow Canadian and local Greenville photographer Dan Guravich producing a book, *Northwest Passage*. The book is about their experiences on board the first icebreaker to traverse the polar ice cap between the Atlantic and Pacific oceans. Bern began getting calls and soon he was writing for magazines such as *Town and Country, Look, Travel and Leisure, Life, National Geographic, Smithsonian,* and *Playboy.*

Travel writing opportunities took off for the Keatings. Franke accompanied Bern on many trips around the world to intriguing, far-off places. They traveled together to eighty-nine different countries, with Bern taking notes and Franke taking pictures. On one trip with a group of travel writers, the captivating couple journeyed to twenty-one countries in twenty-three days. Bern was fluent in English, Spanish, and especially French, and made Franke feel very much at home in many of the countries they visited. Yet it was Africa that leapt into Franke's heart and gave her a lifelong love of the continent. She has traveled to Kenya seventeen times and is hoping to go again. On one of her trips, she took numerous photographs for a children's book about the giraffes at Giraffe Manor. Franke is a well known and respected photographer throughout much of Africa.

In 1958, Franke entered a national contest for a single photograph depicting "the good life" while enjoying the French liqueur Dubonett. With the help of Yves Macaire, a French Air Force pilot in training at Greenville Air Force Base, and later publisher of the *Delta Review*, Franke spread a picnic blanket in her yard and picked up her camera. She won first place, a prize of $1000 and a free trip to Paris. Bern and Franke decided to take the family, John and Kate being ten and twelve years old. During that time, Yves was also visiting his hometown and located Bern a Bugatti, a French racecar built by an Italian designer. Bern bought the four-door convertible, planning to tour Europe with Franke and the kids. Ever the mechanic's dream, the Bugatti was always in need of repair. It was also evermore the envy of anyone along the way. Many times as the young family would leave a restaurant, Franke would marvel at the legs protruding from under the car and the peering eyes under the bonnet! While Bern was covering a story in Finland, Franke decided to take the kids to the coast of Italy. The Bugatti began overheating as they climbed up the steep mountains. Franke poured all the drinking water and even the case of white wine into the radiator in order to get to the top of the mountains and the border between France and Italy. From there she was able to coast downhill all the way to a seaside town and wait for the needed repairs! Bern and Franke loved the car so much they had it shipped home to Greenville. After a year or two of limping around town in need of repairs, the Bugatti was sold to a friend on the West coast in a breakeven deal. Today that very car is worth over one million dollars.

Relationships were established worldwide that evolved into lifelong friendships. Franke and Bern's home has always been a melting pot of international, artistic, and literary figures. Their close ties with the Hodding Carters, Shelby Foote, Ben Wasson, William Faulkner, Mary Virginia Watson, the Percys, and Clarke and Judy Reed allowed their home to be a vibrant and enlightened place. Kate and John's friends were always a part of the Keating household and lively social swirl. Many young Deltans grew up around some of the most literary and well-traveled minds imaginable. International visitors to the Delta were always welcome in the Keating's home and the neighbors were constantly invited over to help entertain.

Always the frugal chap, Bern would often come home from a trip abroad with excess funds in his travel allowance that needed to be spent. Returning through New York, he would stop by Tiffany and Co. and buy Franke a gold bracelet as a token of his absence from her. Franke has often been seen at parties looking like a tribal princess with scores of gold bracelets on each arm!

Franke is known throughout the Greenville community for giving an annual Christmas cookie decorating party for local children. Also, there is an annual scholarship given away to an aspiring foreign language student in memory of their beloved daughter, Kate. With the help of her mom and dad, Kate at an early age authored three books about a young American looking at France, Sweden, and Italy.

Of the twenty-seven books Bern authored, possibly the most notable and well read is *Mississippi,* a wonderful book of photographs and stories from all over our beautiful state. Franke shot all of the pictures, and Bern wrote the book. Because of their accomplishments, Bern and Franke received the award for lifetime achievement from the Mississippi Institute of Arts. This award had been presented previously only to Eudora Welty and Walker Percy.

Franke's yard emerged from a cotton field sixty years ago. Today it is covered with towering pecan and oak trees, shadowing down to the old, original levee bordering Rattlesnake Bayou. Thousands of daffodils emerge each spring as a testament to Bern's persistence in buying bulbs each year. And many a plate has been filled with Bern's organically-grown vegetables from his garden, fertilized with ample doses of horse and chicken manure. One year a friend even brought him a huge dump truck load of elephant, lion, and giraffe droppings left behind from the traveling circus!

It is in that yard that Mary Virginia's brother-in-law, Lewis Watson from Ada, Oklahoma, parachuted into a No Name Dinner Club party one weekend. He was presented with a crystal glass of Dom Pérignon champagne by Franke. And in 1980, on a brisk fall afternoon, Franke climbed aboard John Weathersby's hot air balloon, "Good Ship Faith," for a ride across the Delta as the sun set over the Mississippi River. As they ascended into the heavens above, Franke looked down at her home below and said, "Aren't the trees pretty!"

The French Canadian Duo of the Delta
*Dynamic, dapper, dashing, and debonair, Bern Keating and Dan Guravich
left their mark worldwide and called the Mississippi Delta home.*

In elite literary, scientific, and photographic circles across the globe, the names of Keating and Guravich are revered. Bern the continent-hopping travel writer and Dan the polar bear photographic genius traveled extensively writing and photographing separately and together. And it all started in Canada.

Bern was born in 1915 in Fassett, Quebec. His daddy was a heavy construction engineer and therefore traveled with his family wherever his jobs took him. Bern became fluent in French, English, and Spanish and was able to switch between languages in mid-sentence. He graduated from high school at the head of his class while caddying at the local golf course for pocket change. After moving to America, he bummed around riding freight trains and doing odd jobs. He worked on an ore carrier as a deckhand in the Great Lakes before being called to Long Island, New York, to the home of an aunt where he attended New York University and later graduated *summa cum laude* from the University of Arkansas. It was there that he met the love, soulmate, and partner of his life, Franke.

Bern and Franke were married and moved to Palm Beach, Florida. There he served as news director for a radio station before going to Utica, New York. When World War II broke out, Bern enlisted in the U.S. Navy and served as communications officer in the South Pacific on board attack destroyers. After the war, the young couple moved to Pine Bluff, Arkansas, then on to Greenville where Bern set up a photographic studio. WWII war journalist and author Quentin Reynolds soon noticed his work and helped him become a world-class photographer by showing his work to editors in New York proclaiming, "Look what some redneck from Mississippi can do!" Noticing that editors were putting captions underneath his photographs, it was not long before Bern turned the cameras over to Franke and took up his lifelong passion, writing.

Over the years Bern traveled to 105 different countries, many of them numerous times. His writing covered travel, history, biography, and his home state of Mississippi. Writing in the foreword of the well-known cookbook *Pick of the Crop*, he says, "Homeward bound from some foreign strand, I stagger into the Memphis airport, stubbled of chin and bloodshot of eye. Sour humored though I be, the Delta begins to work its magic the instant I hear those soft feminine accents spoken nowhere but between Memphis and Vicksburg. I search for the speakers and there they are—Delta women en route somewhere, cool, graceful, chic as even the Parisienne could never imagine in this climate. I am almost home."

Bern's circle of friends covered the artistic, literary, and political world extensively. William Faulkner, Shelby Foote, and Walker Percy were often weekend houseguests. Hodding and Betty Carter were the closest of friends to Bern and Franke. Republican Clarke Reed and Democrat Hodding Carter III often sat side by side on the Keating

BURDINE FAMILY COLLECTION

My wife Sallie Burdine with Dan and Bern while on our honeymoon outside Churchill, Canada, on Hudson Bay sixty miles south of the Arctic Circle.

couch sharing a devout friendship. In all the years that I spent around the Keating household, I never knew the door to be locked, the ice bucket empty, or the stove to be cold. Even when they were traveling to some far away land, the housekeeper Caledonia held the fort down with an unbelievable sense of time and place of the Keating's whereabouts.

Throughout his career, Bern contributed regularly to publications such as: *Smithsonian, Travel and Leisure, Town and Country, Look, Life, Holiday, National Geographic, Saturday Evening Post, Reader's Digest, The New Yorker,* and *Playboy,* among others. Of the more than thirty books he authored, the one of which he was most proud was the book *Mississippi* that he and Franke produced. Together, they received the Mississippi Institute of Arts and Letters Award, an award that had previously been given only to Eudora Welty and Walker Percy.

Dan was born in 1918 in Winnipeg, Manitoba, and was interested in photography and science as a child. During WWII he served as an officer in the elite Calgary Tanks in Europe. After the war, Dan received his PhD degree from the University of Wisconsin in plant genetics and landed a job at the Stoneville Experiment Station working with cotton. Joe Weilenman, Delta expatriate now living in Pago Pago, recalls, "The first time I met Dan he was living at the Experiment Station with his beautiful wife next door to my Aunt Cora Gerdes. Aunt Cora was outraged that every time she looked over at Dan's house he was walking around stark naked with the door and draperies open!"

Dan soon tired of the plant doctor job, turned in his resignation, and moved to Greenville to open a photo and hi-fi store on Washington Avenue. Joe was in the store one day when a wealthy couple from Arkansas came in and said they were building a house and wanted the best built-in stereo and sound system they could buy and what would he recommend? Dan spent about fifteen minutes describing the very best amps, mixers, turntable, stylus, and speakers along with other miscellaneous items. The husband said that's exactly what they wanted, so how much would it cost? Dan told them that the entire system would cost around $20,000. The couple said, "Cost is no problem, so we'll buy it." Dan replied, "I don't sell that stuff," and walked off.

Another curt incident occurred when Liz Workman tried to buy a set of lens filters for her husband Noel, then Information Officer at the Greenville Air Force Base. Dan refused to sell them to her claiming, "Lens filters are much too personal to pick out for somebody else."

It wasn't long until Dan decided to close the retail business and go to work as a professional photographer. He worked with large companies that sold farm chemicals. He was a master nature photographer for *National Geographic* magazine for four decades and spent more than two hundred hours in a high-wing Cessna monoplane taking photographs for Hodding Carter's *Man and the River.*

Bern and Dan were friends and often visited in the same social circles, literary clubs, and on mushroom hunts. They collaborated on two books together, *The Grand Banks,* a book about the fishermen of Newfoundland, and *Northwest Passage,* about the S.S. *Manhattan,* the first ice-breaking oil tanker to traverse the transcontinental sea route and ice pack above the Arctic Circle in order to bring oil from Alaska's Prudhoe Bay to the East Coast. It was on that trip in 1969 that Dan Guravich saw a polar bear and his life changed forever.

Dan was fifty-one years old when he dedicated the rest of his days to the study of *Ursus maritimus,* the sea bear or polar bear. He traveled to the Arctic seventy-five times. As a biologist, conservationist, and wildlife photographer, Dan was able to alert the world to our Arctic heritage. He was instrumental in stopping the wholesale slaughter of polar bears and bringing the awareness of the plight of the Arctic region and its largest inhabitants. His photographs are viewed worldwide and serve as a useful tool in scientific research throughout the Arctic world. Dan collaborated in 1978 with author Richard Davis supplying photographs for the bestselling book *Lords of the Arctic.* In 1980 Dan and Dr. Ian Sterling, a mammalogist and one of Canada's top polar bear biologists, published *Polar Bears.* This book remains the benchmark study of polar bears all over the world. Dan contributed photography to five polar bear books and numerous articles in magazines and journals along with producing a polar bear calendar for many years.

During a trip to Churchill, Canada, Dan rented a car from local businessman Len Smith to go out and see the bears on Hudson Bay. Realizing that a car was not a suitable vehicle from which to view bears, Dan suggested a polar version of the swamp buggy used in Louisiana to traverse marshes. (Dan had done extensive photographic research on the brown pelican and it's near extinction culminating in the book *Return of the Brown Pelican*.) Soon, Len had perfected the Tundra Buggy, an Arctic high rider that could move through snow drifts and over bay ice on huge agricultural tires. Able to cook and sleep inside, scientists, photographers, and tourists can spend several days at a time out on the tundra.

Dan was among the first to ever provide scientific polar bear behavior and social interaction through photographic documentation. He helped to enlighten the public's view of the world's largest carnivore. Dan once said, "Save polar bears, and you go a long way towards saving the entire habitat of the circumpolar North." Dan was instrumental in starting Polar Bears International, a non-profit organization dedicated to the conservation of the polar bear.

Bern and Dan shared a lot of interests, but one in which they were competitors was gardening. Bern was the consummate organic gardener, growing his abundant greens, squashes, tomatoes, eggplants, and tubers with natural fertilizers (sometimes the fermented manure left behind by a traveling circus.) He used a hoe to rid the garden of weeds and beautiful marigolds to keep the bugs away. Dan was the chemical gardener. Bagged fertilizers, herbicides, and insecticides kept his garden in pristine condition and overflowing with produce. Each touted their way of gardening to be the best, and there was only one way to prove whose method actually was the best. A "Battle of the Gardens, Royale" cook-off was held that ended in a dead heat with the invited dinner guests reaping the spoils of war.

Bern Keating and Dan Guravich could have lived anywhere in the world they chose, but they called our beloved Delta their home.

The Coffee House Blues of Leon Koury
William Alexander Percy molded Koury's prolific art career, yet he died destitute.
This, the life and times of Mississippi's most famous sculptor.

Small of stature, son of a Syrian immigrant, protégé of William Alexander Percy, Leon Koury was a giant among Southern artists. Born in Greenville in 1909, Leon grew up on the fringe of the black/white community helping in his father's grocery store. Koury read a poem in *Scribner's Magazine* by William Alexander Percy and wrote him a letter complimenting the poem and asking him about writing. He did not realize they were both from Greenville. An invitation was extended for the young Koury to

stop by for a visit and to bring some of his poems. Leon mustered up the courage to go and visit the acclaimed poet and author of *Lanterns on the Levee*. Looking at his small book of poems, Percy was not interested in the writing but rather the illustrations.

In an oral history recorded by Josephine Haxton on September 4, 1978, Leon recalled, "When he saw my art work, he told me to forget trying to write and to go home and draw." Before leaving the Percy mansion, Koury picked up a ball of clay from a work stand and asked what it was. "That's clay," Percy told him. "Why don't you take it home with you." Once back on Nelson Street, Koury surprised himself by molding a torso

Koury photographed in the Greenville living room of Ben Wasson with a clay bust of William Faulkner, which now sits at Faulkner's home, Rowan Oak.

out of the clay and took it back to show Percy. Soon, a gift of fifty pounds of modeling clay showed up on the doorstep of the small grocery store and the intriguing life of the budding young artist began.

As a child Leon grew up playing with the local black children and delivering groceries. Feeling that neither of his parents had any influence on him, he became somewhat of a maverick and went his own way. Before coming to America, Leon's father had entered a monastery to become a Franciscan monk but left at the age of twenty-six before taking his vows. He had taught French, Latin, and English, and Leon grew up reading and studying Nietzsche, Schopenhauer, and Emanuel Swedenborg. As a student he became awakened in the spiritualistic sense of the psychic, metaphysics, and mysticism.

Once Leon met Will Percy, he found himself in the world of culture, literature, and music. In Haxton's oral history, Leon relayed that Will Percy introduced him to those treasures. He heard his first symphony in Percy's parlor. "I was in a daze for weeks. This was something that I felt I had heard thousands of years before and it had come back home to my ears." Leon began to feel the pangs of self-pity for what he lacked in life. Percy jarred him into "realizing that there was so much more to acquire, that I hadn't lost anything. I had yet to gain..."

The first thing Leon Koury sculpted was a huge head of a Negro child, molded from memory of a little girl that came into his father's store. Through Percy, Leon had become acquainted with Ben Wasson, one of Greenville's literary figures. Wasson was living in Hollywood at the time and arranged for some of Leon's pieces to be shipped to California. The bust of the girl was sold for $500 to Lady Carnavon of England as a gift to her husband who at the time was in Egypt excavating the tomb of King Tutankhamen.

With no formal training, Koury began teaching himself in the back of the little grocery store. "Somehow, I already knew." The first formal portrait bust that Koury ever did was of Will Percy, "Portraits aren't as romantic as it sounds because many subjects interfere too much in your product. Sculpture is the art of infinite contours. Women for example, don't want sculpture, they want plastic surgery."

In a letter to Roy Bee, art professor at Ole Miss, Koury wrote about Percy, "I can think of only one man who found a spark and tried to fan it into a flame, my friend and patron William Alexander Percy. He would not let me rest content, so I listened and learned and discovered patches of wisdom here and there and tufts of common sense that put me to shame. I was made to understand that the marvelous works of others are but the voices of artists delivering their peculiar messages to the world, to which I could at any time add my own. Then it was I understood that it is never what you say in art that is important, but how much of yourself is speaking."

Koury's work was shown in the 1937 National Art Exhibit in New York and the 1939 New York World's Fair, the Whitney Museum, and galleries on the West Coast. Percy introduced Koury to Malvina Hoffman who had studied under the great French Impressionist master Rodin. She had sculpted "The Patriot" that stands in the Greenville cemetery for which Will Percy paid $13,000 at the height of the Depression as a tribute to his father. Upon Percy's insistence, Koury moved to New York in 1945 and stayed in Hoffman's studio to "get some atmosphere, to absorb some of the facets and the workmanship. It wasn't a question of her instructing me in sculpture at all, she thought I was long past that." He chauffeured for her and was taken around New York and introduced to the "modern art scene" of the time. "Naturalism was verboten then. I was what you call "square." Modern art was the thing, abstract. Even Impressionism was out." Koury found out that the world of modern art was not for him and to make a living he moved to New Jersey and began making originals of figurines for potteries to make molds and sell to hobbyists all over the country. Leon Koury was being paid minimum wage for doing original pieces.

He returned home in 1961 and continued working on a series of black life and occupation in the South. Leon ran into some difficulty when letters from the North started ridiculing him as some people thought he was portraying the Negro as a laborer. "It was never my intention to be demeaning. What I was after was the physique, nothing else. Black workers just happened to have the finest physiques in the Delta." Created in the early '50s, the full body copper and bronze sculpture of a black man called "The Compress Worker" resides in a private Percy residence in Greenville, and a copy now stands in the Brooks Memorial Gallery in Memphis.

When his father died, Koury closed the grocery store and opened a bar directly across the street from Doe's Eat Place called the Orbit Lounge. He wanted it to be a place where enlightened people gathered, much like the coffee houses and bistros he had seen in New York. In an article in the *Commercial Appeal* in 1962, Koury stated, "I wanted it to be the kind of place where creative people could come together, talk, socialize, listen to good music, and exchange ideas." It was the dawning of the Age of Aquarius and even though some of Greenville's elite ventured over after a steak at Does, the hippie generation had moved in. Local bands would play and stay late into the night talking and absorbing the aura of the funky artist Leon Koury.

Leon was a purist and not one to stray from his portraitist venue and classical loves. He had little use for the modern. According to Bill Beckwith, a pupil of Koury's at the time, "After patiently listening to Dylan, Hendrix, Johnnie Winter, Cream or the Stones, he would play Tchaikovsky, Vivaldi, or some Italian opera to the garage bands practicing at the Orbit and urge them to try adopting the music to rock 'n' roll. Most rock musicians from the Delta in the '60s got their start there."

Leon Koury became known as a "guru" to the young crowd. "They thought of themselves as outsiders, and I was also an outsider. I was 'far out' because I was a sculptor and all sculptors were supposed to be not conventional at all." The youngsters were beginning to experiment with drugs such as LSD and pot. Leon would get calls at three and four o'clock in the morning, and his young friends would come over and 'rap' with him because they wanted to know what was happening to them, and they thought he knew. They became interested in the mystic philosophies that Leon talked about, and it "took them into dimensions, they thought, where they'd rather be, than where they were. It was then they gravitated from acid to less drastic drugs like marijuana." Bill Beckwith recalled, "He consistently urged a bunch of searching, young bohemians to read the Harvard Classics, and many of them did. Leon wanted to expose his young friends to the same quality of art that Will Percy had exposed to him."

Learning at the foot of what they considered a master, the youngsters were turned on by yoga and "anything that was esoteric. If it was plain, pragmatic, practical—they had no use for it, something had to be probed and fathomed." Beckwith recalls Leon telling him, "I have come to believe that God is unlimited intelligence." Soon undesirable elements started showing up and fights began. Leon decided to close the Orbit Lounge with its black painted walls, red circular Naugahyde booths, and rotating, flashing silver disco ball. The door was padlocked, and the windows were boarded up.

Leon had to eat, so he began teaching painting and sculpting to local ladies in the old Levee Board building. The place on Nelson became a catchall for artwork, unfinished busts, and clay molds of famous people. His friend Ben Wasson was instrumental in having him commissioned to do a bust of the recently deceased William Faulkner for the University of Mississippi. Koury was charging $500 at that time to do a portrait bust. In 1964, the University paid him $750 for what today is a sculpted and bronzed piece of history that has no price. In his letter to Bill, Leon recalled his mentor Percy again, "As I modeled the bust of Faulkner, the ghost of Will intruded on my thoughts and would not be dispelled. I had no choice but to acquiesce and accept the affinity."

In 1982, Koury wanted to sell his building and move to Taylor, Mississippi, to be close to his aspiring protégé Bill Beckwith. Beckwith had built a foundry there and Koury felt the climate in Taylor to be a little more conducive to artists. According to an article in the *Jackson Daily News* in October of 1983, Koury wanted to teach sculpture and experiment with his work. "I have been characterized as a portrait sculptor. That's what I want to get away from...do more allegorical, more creative works."

But the old grocery store where he had grown up and worked his entire life did not sell. Leon Koury passed away on April 11, Easter Sunday, 1993. In a *Delta Democrat Times* article Beckwith stated, "Returning to Greenville was probably one of the worst things he could have done for his career. He died in poverty, unappreciated, and broke." Commenting on his hippie friends of thirty years before, Leon Koury once recalled, "As I said, they couldn't find the absolutes they were looking for, so they have accepted second best, which means creature comforts. Creature comforts, after all, in the long run, are winning out, really."

As His World Turned
*Anthony Herrera's illustrious career, love of Mississippi
culture, and ultimate role in the fight for his life*

To thousands, maybe even millions, he was a rascal, a scoundrel, a womanizer, and a lover. He was hated by some yet loved by all. Yes, there were those that loved to hate him.

Anthony Herrera lived a life of national and international fame. Soap opera star emeritus, Anthony played the role of James Stenbeck on *As the World Turns* off and on for almost thirty years. He was presumed dead five or six times, yet somehow managed to escape death to return another season in another episode, to ravage and rampage the silver screen during the midday hour. There were those that would arrange their work schedules to watch the soaps, and *As the World Turns* was one of the tops.

Anthony was born the oldest of six children in Wiggins, Mississippi, on January 19, 1944. He went to college at Ole Miss where he studied zoology and literature, earning a dual major while a member of the Sigma Chi Fraternity and moonlighting as a houseboy at the Tri-Delta sorority house. He visited the Delta with frat brothers and grew to love the flat land with its panoramic vistas and cultural, literary, and art heritage…and the blues. During the summer months he moved to Greenwood where he teamed up with Deltans Walter Pillow and Stewart Bridgforth checking cotton for bugs while working for Farmer's Supply. He became lifelong friends with future cotton broker Emmett Chassaniol, visiting with him on many occasions. Chassaniol has said, "Even though he was from South Mississippi, Anthony loved the Delta and its people. He would come and visit every chance he had."

Upon graduation, Anthony headed to New Orleans for the big city life, at least a little bigger than Wiggins. Soon, he was ready to tackle The Big Apple and moved to New York City. There, he studied acting for three years under the world-renowned Stella Adler. To make ends meet he waited tables in local bistros and restaurants. Anthony auditioned for and became a member of the Will Geer Shakespeare Theater. He moved to Beverly Hills and lived there for five years while he performed and fine-tuned his love for Shakespeare. And in 1980, the stars aligned, and the top-ranked daytime CBS soap opera *As the World Turns* knocked on his door. On February 1, Anthony assumed the role of the consummate, handsome, and elegant, all time super villain James Stenbeck. An international businessman and European aristocrat, James raged through the fictitious town of Oakdale creating havoc and gathering enemies galore. Over the seasons, James was shot twice, thrown out of a cargo plane, tumbled off of a lighthouse, and went down in a helicopter crash. Finally, he was given a lethal injection of a paralyzing agent causing him to have a fatal heart attack. Until then, he would always return suddenly to Oakdale and with that husky, sultry voice say to his estranged wife and lover, "Hello, Barbara." James Stenbeck's final appearance on *As the World Turns* was August 27, 2010. During his career, Anthony also played roles

FERD MOYSE COLLECTION

Herrera in 1982 at a No Name dinner club party with Gloria Virden, an unknown admirer (there were many) and Ferd Moyse III.

in *Silk Stalkings, The Young and The Restless, Loving, Emergency!, The Incredible Hulk, Search for Tomorrow, Mandrake the Magician, Helter Skelter, Mancuso, FBI* and *The Rockford Files.*

In 1984, Anthony came to Greenville and produced and directed an award-winning documentary on blues great James "Son" Thomas from Leland. All scenes were shot in Greenville, Leland, and Pantherburn. The film won five prestigious awards including the CINE Golden Eagle Award. He continued to write, direct, and produce screenplays and productions. In 1986, Anthony wrote the screenplay and directed Pulitzer Prize-winning author Eudora Welty's *The Wide Net* for the American Playhouse Series on PBS. In 1991, he co-authored *Smoke and Mirrors,* a comedy-mystery for the stage, touring Mississippi in 1992. In 1993, Anthony returned to Mississippi with *Love Letters,* a play featuring himself and Jessica Tandy. Together they played eighteen communities, putting on nineteen performances in only twenty-one days.

Anthony came to Greenville in the early '80s as a house guest of Bern and Franke Keating. He attended No Name Dinner Club parties where he wowed the ladies with his good looks and his Southern flair. When taken to Doe's Eat Place, some ladies would rush up to hug him and get his autograph while others turned away and scorned him for his villainous roles on *As the World Turns.*

But things were soon to change for Anthony. In January of 1997, he was diagnosed with mantle cell lymphoma, a rare and usually fatal cancer. Upon diagnosis, he was told he was going to die. Anthony has never been one to take anything lying down and decided to fight the cancer with all he had. He checked into the Sloan-Kettering

Cancer Center in New York City and was treated with chemotherapy and radiation. Soon he underwent an autologous bone marrow stem cell transplant. In the fall of 1998, Anthony relapsed and in April of 1999 was admitted into the MD Anderson Cancer Center in Houston. MD Anderson was pioneering a new technique in stem cell transplantation, and Anthony received a stem cell transplant from his brother John who lived in Austin. This new procedure was on the cutting edge of medical technology in treating lymphoma and was able to give Anthony hope for a cancer-free life.

Anthony had been introduced to MD Anderson board member Mrs. Desiree Lyon, and she soon discovered that Anthony was not "just one more person with cancer; he was a hurricane ready to do battle." Through their many visits, Desiree became close friends with Anthony. "I have never seen anyone fight like Anthony, and I have helped hundreds of patients. I learned from our visits that Anthony was passionate about everything he loved—poetry, medicine, movies, drama, his friends, his therapist, and the Delta. He would talk endlessly about each of his loves, but with a fresh slant so that he captivated his group of listeners, his audience…yes, audience. Anthony was an actor at heart. He was always on stage."

Once in remission, Anthony kicked into high gear and took his plight to the public. Over a three-year period, he wrote a book called *The Cancer War,* which relates to his battle and how he was able to survive not only the medical and physical setbacks but the mental anguish and turmoil of cancer. In an exclusive interview with James Pylant in 2005, Anthony attributed his success in his battle against cancer to "brilliant doctors, finding the right hospital, and a positive attitude…watching, questioning, and finding out."

Soon his plight garnered national attention as he championed stem cell research. In 2005 Anthony testified before the U.S. Congress about the importance of stem cell research on behalf of Pennsylvania Senator Arlen Specter.

Anthony began a speaking circuit and gave lectures on "The Human Spirit" at MD Anderson, Sloan-Kettering, and St. Jude. He befriended singer/songwriter Willie Nelson and was told by Willie that he should put his poetry on the internet, that the web was a very powerful medium. From that conversation, Poetry Theatre was soon founded with Steve McGraw and Tandy Cronyn. Poetry Theatre is a web-based archive of great poetry performed by actors who understand and love poetry. It is a unique and interesting way for poetry lovers to see and hear poems recited by performing artists who share a love for poetic verse. Steve McGraw stated recently, "Anthony walked the walk. If he loved it, he did it."

In a 2009 interview, Anthony described his upbeat attitude during his battle with cancer, "Art is what kept my spirit up through all the horror and pain. It's impossible to describe what a stem cell transplant is like. It was Tennessee Williams, it was Willie Nelson, and it was Louis Armstrong that kept me going."

Anthony moved to Buenos Aires, Argentina, where he continued his work with

Poetry Theatre and traveled back and forth to the states. He promoted his vision for Poetry Theatre with the Mississippi Arts Council, hoping to one day get the program into the curriculum of every school in the Magnolia State and beyond, using his home state of Mississippi as the template.

However, after ten years in remission, Anthony was diagnosed with another type of cancer, and he died on June 21, 2011, in Buenos Aires. He was sixty-seven years old, yet he had lived a life of which few only dream. A television star, playwright, producer, and director, Anthony Herrera lived the life he loved. He once stated, "The real actor works a lifetime improving his or her craft."

James Stenbeck was finally put to rest by the lethal injection, and the *As the World Turns* final episode was in September of 2010. However, Anthony Herrera's legacy is burned into the memory of many fans, and his beloved Poetry Theatre continues. Anthony worked his entire lifetime improving his art of drama and bringing the love and need for literature and poetry to millions.

Casting Call

When asked why and how he got involved in art, Bill Beckwith replied, "The why is easy, to impress girls! The how is more involved."

Bill grew up in Greenville during the '50s and '60s and began building things with his hands at an early age. His daddy subscribed to *Popular Mechanics,* and according to Bill, "that magazine was a great teacher for a young mind interested in manipulating materials in the physical world. From an early age I had an affinity for the technical aspect of shaping matter." He won the shop award in his eigth grade shop class at E.E. Bass, learning precise techniques under the expert tutelage of Owen Keeling.

"Learning to work with your hands was not considered a righteous goal. Shop class was somewhat inferior to academics. Had I not later met Leon Koury, I might have become a craftsman building utilitarian objects."

However, Bill Beckwith excelled in both art and academics. "Sculpture has to be the most challenging and rewarding manipulation of materials because you hopefully create an object that exists with a difference of content from subject matter, a poem in three dimensions. Ideally, you enter the mysteries of the human condition, that area we have no words for. You strive to build a piece that connects with a feeling and becomes a symbol of something spiritually elusive. You share the experience, capture the beauty, honor the Great Spirit...and impress the girls!"

Art teacher Bob Tompkins taught Bill during his high school years. "Bob was very influential in taking that love of drawing to a higher level. He challenged us to draw with understanding and mastery. Drawing is the basis for all the visual arts. As far back as I can remember, drawing has been very important to me."

L.Q.C. Lamar will be on display at the newly renovated and restored home of the politician and chancellor in Oxford.

The first clay Bill remembers modeling was at Carrie Stern Elementary School: "I remember shaping a head for a school project. I am sure it was awkward and primitive, and I worked on it for what I thought was a half-hour or so. I later realized two or three hours had passed. When you can lose time that way, you know you are doing something right."

Bill's friends, Jerry and Donnie Brown, had a band called The Candy Shoestring. Stopping by one day in 1966, they told Bill they had a new place to practice, at a sculptor's "pad" and would he like to come along. "What's a pad?" Bill asked, as he was taken to Nelson Street and Leon Koury's art studio. "In those days, everyone wanted to be Mick Jagger, John Lennon, or Bob Dylan. As soon as I entered Leon's studio and saw what he could do with clay and plaster, the music was forgotten, and the challenge to learn modeling was on. I was fourteen years old."

In the front of Leon Koury's studio was the Orbit Lounge. Located across the street from Doe's Eat Place, Leon's family grocery store had been turned into a coffee house/bistro. It soon became a gathering place for creative young people. According to Bill, "painters, poets, writers, musicians, and dilettante revolutionaries hung out there. It was the '60s, and several wars were being waged." He recalls modeling clay, making molds, and casting plaster as the Candy Shoestring rocked in the background. "The Shoestring was as good a band as you could find anywhere, and with Doe's right across the street, you never knew who would stop in and visit with Leon."

Recalling the days as a protégé of Koury, Bill says, "Leon taught fine modeling, classical modeling. He stressed strong side light and working in the gray area between highlight and shadow to achieve perfect form with direction of energy from the center out, as in an egg. He was a very strict disciplinarian. Seeing what Leon could do with clay was probably one of the strongest influences on me. I remember him telling me one time that to make a commitment to learn modeling, I would have to sacrifice my fishing time. This thing was getting serious!"

Bill entered the University of Mississippi in 1970 and under the guidance of Professor Charles Gross became "as hooked on casting bronze as an addict is to heroin." By the summer of 1974, Bill had built a complete foundry in the back yard at Leon's studio as his undergraduate thesis. "If you have ever poured molten metal or held the sun in your hand, you understand the power and the energy. I was hooked bad!" As a senior, Bill won the Student Achievement Award for the best artist at Ole Miss.

In 1976, Bill finished his graduate work and moved his equipment to Greenwood and set up shop with his friend and business partner Butch Mallett. The two young artists rented an empty warehouse and started casting for other sculptors in order to finance their own work. "We poured a lot of bronze. That was a time of tremendous growth for us. We worked hard, and we learned a lot."

In the meantime Bill married Jackie Shepherd from Greenville and they lived in a two-room cabin on the Yazoo River. However, the studio and cabin were broken into ten times. The police were of no help, so it was time to go. Oxford was safe; that was 1982. Greenwood is much different now.

An old store building and adjoining house, circa 1897, came up for sale in the little hamlet of Taylor, eight miles south of Oxford. The property was right next to Taylor Grocery and within the small group of dilapidated buildings that was downtown Taylor in the early 1900s. William Faulkner often rode his horse down Old Taylor Road and sat on the porches of those buildings talking with local farmers, shopkeepers, and sharecroppers. World renowned character studies of the Snopes,

Compson, and Varner families were envisioned from the old wooden benches on the porches while the fictional de Spain and Sartoris families lingered around the Square in Oxford. And it is where one local was quoted in a cover article by Willie Morris in the March 1989 issue of *National Geographic* titled "Faulkner's Mississippi," as saying, "Nicky, Snake, Al, and the boys hang around in front of Mary's General Store telling tales and lies at the very spot where Temple Drake stepped off the train and into trouble."

The quietness was noticeable, and the lifestyle was laid back and easy. Dogs roam the streets, cows bellow in the bottoms, and roosters crow at the break of day. Bill recalls, "The next thing I knew, we had bought the buildings and were living in Taylor. I moved the foundry again and started over. It turned out to be a good move."

The small town of Taylor soon became known as a mecca of sorts for creative spirits. Obie Clark, a potter, moved to Taylor as did Jane Rule Burdine, a photographer from the Delta, and Jim Dees, a writer. Obie and Bill became volunteer firemen and decided to run for city aldermen while Jane Rule ran for mayor. All won their respective seats; the bohemian spirits prevailed, and an enlightened attitude came to Taylor in an effort to keep the small town atmosphere alive in order for the arts to flourish. Other artists soon followed. Writers Barry Hannah, Larry Brown, Dean Wells, and Willie Morris would come visit and absorb the ambiance. According to Bill, "Creative spirits seem to fertilize each other here. Anomaly is the norm. Taylor has always provided some sanctuary for its working artists. Let's hope it does not lose the quiet, peaceful freedoms we have always enjoyed."

As an artist, Bill soon became nationally acclaimed. His work is mainly figurative, and he is widely known for his portrait busts and full figure sculptures. His work has been exibited in the Splashlight Studios and the Frank Marino Gallery in New York City, the Mississippi Museum of Art, the World's Fair in New Orleans, the National Museum of Art, and Smithsonian Museum in Washington, D.C. And in 2001 he and the town of Taylor were awarded The Governor's Award for Excellence in the Arts.

Of Bill's many sculptures on public display, one stands out above all others. It is of the great Chickasaw Chief Piomingo standing in front of the city hall in Tupelo. The Chickasaws were proud and fierce warriors and worthy of much respect. To this day the Chickasaw Nation is remembered as the "Unconquered and Unconquerable." Chief Piomingo was known as America's most influential Chickasaw ally and was presented the Washington Peace Medal in 1792. Bill states, "I found working on this study of Chief Piomingo very empowering. Northeast Mississippi is Chickasaw country, a special place. The energy is good. No other piece has had a similar effect on my life."

In 1996, the City of Oxford decided to have a life-size bronze sculpture of William Faulkner placed on the town square. Faulkner was a very private person, and some family members, locals, and town officials objected to this public display of a very private man. When the decision was finally made to proceed, Bill found himself with an unfortunate deadline. The foundry needed four of the six months before the unveiling date which was set for Faulkner's 100th birthday. He had only two months to model the piece and build the bench. "I worked a minumum of twelve hours a day, seven days a week, for sixty days. That all important time to step away from a piece, to let it grow cold then critique it, was not there. The small town entertainment and power struggle were at my expense. However, throughout the modeling marathon, I noticed fleeting blurs in the studio. I felt pretty sure of a known spiritual audience." The piece was finished on time, and Mr. Bill sits on a bench behind a wrought iron fence, smoking his pipe and looking across the street at the courthouse on the Square.

Once Faulkner's smoke had cleared, a commission was soon in hand to do a life-size statue of B.B. King holding his guitar, Lucille, to be placed in Indianola. Bill modeled the clay in his studio "with the King himself jukin' in the background. It took me back to Nelson Street in the '60s, walking home after a long weekend session of modeling or mold making at Leon's studio, past the open doors of the juke houses with the Delta blues and crowds spilling out and mixing with the hot, humid Delta night. All of this on a belly full of Doe's hot tamales. Those were some good times! It is hard to separate music from sculptural design and Southern literature."

In his earlier pieces, Bill incorporated turtle shells, duck's feet, and randomly found objects into his work. "Mixed media pieces involve more problem solving and engineering than straightforward modeling," says Bill. "I miss the freedom of working that way and hope to be able to find a balance. My fascination with the figure, particularly the head, grows each day. I find the challenge of imparting a little life into the clay never ending. I think God smiles when you are creative. You're happier; everything is better. I am pretty sure that when you apply to the Great Studio in the Sky, they start you out in navels and ears, maybe even toes...the head department jobs are probably filled by Carpeaux, Rodin, Koury, and Michaelangelo. You probably got to start at the bottom!"

Bill is currently building a large, well-equipped studio on forty-two acres in the rolling hills outside of Taylor. It will be large enough (9,250 square feet of studio and upstairs apartment) to hold the tons of tools and materials needed for his work. He will be able to do what his master teacher and friend, Leon Koury, was not able to accomplish in his effort to move to Taylor in 1985. "I hope to teach modeling privately here and produce those elusive pieces hiding out in the shadows. The university has finally given me the go-ahead for intensive modeling classes on the head and the un-draped figure. This is a long desired goal of mine and very exciting. I have been blessed to make a living out of a sculptor's studio in Mississippi. What an insane notion!"

Delta
Musicians

Sittin' on Top of the World

He gave dignity to the blues. Sam Chatmon, known in the blues world as the "Elder Statesman of the Blues," was born outside of Bolton, Mississippi, in 1899. He was the seventh son of thirteen children. His father, Henderson Chatmon, an ex-slave, had two other wives though and was reported to have fathered many other children by them (some accounts place his legitimate offspring at sixty or more). "But that ain't counting Charley Patton and all of them on the outside," Sam recalled one evening. However, that claim has been disputed. Henderson Chatmon died in 1934 at the age of 105 years old. He was a fiddle player during slavery times and taught most all of his children to play music of some form or other. According to Sam, he had whiskers down to his waist and reputedly tied them to the side to hold them off the fiddle as he played at square dances and parties.

Sam grew up playing music with his brothers and sisters while his daddy and mama joined in. "Corrine Corrine," "Alberta," "Sleepytime Down South," and "Sheiks of Abaree" were indicative of the many types of songs they played. The blues were being played in the Delta, while around Jackson and Vicksburg square dancing was popular, and the Chatmon family catered to whatever was wanted. In the liner to his album called *Sam Chatmon's Advice,* he stated, "Sometimes we'd play for a white man at a dance for three hours at six dollars per musician and then work fifteen hours in the field for that same man the next day for fifty cents."

"I always liked the blues, foxtrots, and one-steps the best because on a square dance you never get a chance to change chords." Calling themselves many names, the Chatmon brothers were most widely known as The Mississippi Sheiks. They were very popular during the pre-war era recording almost one hundred songs. Later on in life, Sam's musical style evolved into more of a rollicking blues rift instead of the rotgut, chant, and response of early Mississippi Delta bluesmen. It was the square dance influence that gave him this unique and particular guitar-picking technique. "The first tune I learned to pick was 'Make Me a Pallet Down on Your Floor.' Me and Lonnie put that out later as 'If You Don't Want Me, You Don't Have to Dog Me Around,' and people just thought it was a new tune that I'd got out. I'd sing a verse then holler, 'Oh, step on it', and Lonnie would get out on that fiddle."

Before Sam moved to Hollandale, he traveled to Atlanta in 1928 with three of his brothers, Lonnie, Bo, and Walter, to record music as The Mississippi Sheiks. Sam was playing bass violin, what he called a "bull fiddle," at the time but switched over to guitar when they recorded "Stop and Listen" and "Sitting on Top of the World." In Jackson all of his brothers got together and cut a record. Later he and Lonnie cut a few records as the Chatmon Brothers. In 1937 Sam lost three brothers and two sisters, and the band never played together again. Sam kept on picking his guitar though.

Sam was a farmer, working on Delta plantations and later renting land and farming with his own mules. In 1950 he quit farming and took a job as night watchman at the Hollandale Compress where ginned cotton was stored. This was a lonely job, but one where he could while away the dark hours sitting atop a cotton bale with his guitar, picking and singing the blues.

Sam retired from that job and bought a house and a half an acre of land in town. It was there that I met him one day while building the road in front of his home. He was a tall, gangly, and very dignified man, and I asked him if he played that guitar propped up on the porch of his house; "Lil' Podnah," he replied, "I been playing that guitar all my life." There began a relationship that I will forever cherish and a friendship I will never forget.

Sam began playing for parties and local festivals about 1965 and was soon known all over the country. He played at the National Folklife Festival in Washington, D.C., as well as the San Diego Folk Festival. Sam had made friends with Ken and Phyllis Swerilas in California and would travel on the bus to visit them and stay several months each year playing in coffee houses, nightclubs, and local festivals. It was there that he met Colin Linden and Jim Maclean from Canada, and together they put out an album titled *Sam Chatmon and his Bar-b-Que Boys*, with all but two of the songs written by Sam.

Sam absolutely refused to fly and would only travel by car or bus. Because of that, he never got included in the European blues tours going on in the '70s. One night while playing at my hunting camp at Willow Run and being recorded for the Carnegie Library

The Blue Front was where many blues musicians performed in Sam's hometown of Hollandale. Saturday night in Hollandale was always quite the jumping time.

in Clarksdale, Sam explained, "It ain't that I'm scared of flying, it just that if I'm up there and it's somebody else's time to go...I don't want to have to ride down wid 'em!"

Sam also played at the Mississippi Delta Blues Festival each year but was very particular about with whom he played. Eugene Powell was his favorite accompaniment. Sam was a gentleman and a gentle man. He played raucous blues in a dignified manner as in "Ashtray Taxi":

I gots me a ashtray taxi,
Yeah, I gots a ashtray taxi,
So if you'se a cigarette smokin' woman,
You can thow yo' butts over in here...

Sam always wore a cap, what some people call an "apple cap." One night I asked him why he never took his cap off. "Lil Podnah, I gots me something under there some folks wouldn't understand. I gots me a ponytail!" Sam thought that white people would not understand his having long hair, so he never showed it in public. And I never saw Sam take a drink of hard liquor, but I did keep him supplied in what he called his "doctor medicine," a half pint of Bourbon stuffed with King Leo peppermint sticks.

The last time I visited Sam, he was in and out of a coma in the South Washington County Hospital in Hollandale in February of 1983. Emphysema had set in, and he was hospitalized. My wife Sallie and I stopped by to see our dear friend. On the bedside table was his hat, and close by it lay this great old bluesman, his long grey hair, recently un-braided from a ponytail, cascaded over his cream colored shoulders. Sallie asked Sam's wife Elma if she could brush Sam's hair. Elma said yes, and for ten or fifteen minutes, I held Sam's hand as Sallie brushed and stroked his long flowing hair. Every now and then Sam would squeeze my hand and smile, making me realize he knew exactly what was going on. Shortly after we left the hospital, Sam died. I knew in my heart that he had left the Delta a better place than he found it and that he was surrounded by people who loved him when he crossed the bar.

Sam was buried in his hometown of Hollandale, and blues people from all over the country came to his funeral, including his Bar-B-Que Boys from Canada. Sam had three black and three white pallbearers. I was one of the pallbearers. The gymnasium at the Simmon's High School was packed with the overflow crowd standing out in the wet cold. The preacher told a story that followed Sam's life. He told of an old mule that stumbled and fell into a very deep pit one night and was not able to climb back out. Every day a garbage truck would come and dump a load of garbage on top of that old mule. The old mule had no choice but to just tromp that garbage down and keep on walking. Every day another load of garbage came, and that mule just kept on walking and tromping, walking and tromping that garbage down until one day he just walked right up and out of that pit. And that is where that old mule is right now, walking around on top of the world!

In the song Sam had written with his brother Bo many years ago called "Sittin' on Top of the World," he sang:

Now when I'm dead and in my grave
No more womens will my po' heart crave...
Yes, I'll be gone, but don't you worry,
Cause, I'll be sitting on top of the world.

The Gentle Giant
Blues great Howlin' Wolf was not only a big man, but a huge presence onstage, moaning and howling as he sang his blues, blues that had been deeply lashed into his soul.

Born in Aberdeen, Mississippi, in 1910, Chester Burnett grew up big and grew up hard. His daddy left when he was only one year old. His mama showed signs of mental instability even though they sang together in the choir at the Life Boat Baptist Church in nearby White Station. According to the definitive book *Moanin' at Midnight* by James Segrest and Mark Hoffman, Chester's musical talent was about the only thing he ever got from his mama. For whatever reasons, she kicked him out as a young child. "Don't come back," she said, and he walked for miles over frozen ground with his feet wrapped in burlap sacks to his great uncle Will Young's small farm. Life got harder for the young boy.

Chester was already big and had oversized feet. His maternal grandfather was a Choctaw Indian and nicknamed him Wolf, soon to become Howlin' Wolf because of the way he moaned when he sang the blues. His Uncle Will was a mean man, not only to his children but to anyone he met. According to Chester's first girlfriend, Silla Swift, "he was the meanest man between here and hell." In rural Mississippi, during the first part of the last century, kids worked. According to neighbor Annie Eggeson, "His uncle worked him like a mule, tear his ass up if he didn't work all day long. He was raised in the field, workin' cotton and pulling corn. That old man would work you 'til you fell out, you just fall down." Will Young used leather plow lines, sometimes called bullwhips, for punishment. "He was low down; he'd even whup the grown folks if they messed with him."

Wolf didn't get much schooling; he was always working. After cutting enough timber in the adjoining woods to make railroad ties for sale, Wolf bought himself a new pair of pants to impress the girls on Sunday. He was thirteen years old and dressed to go to church when his uncle ordered him into the pig pen to slop the hogs. He obeyed, but when his uncle's prize hog charged him and knocked him over in his Sunday clothes, he hit the hog on the head with the pail killing it. Knowing what he was in for, he took off running, with his uncle in hot pursuit. Annie recalled, "That man whupped that boy, runnin' behind him with a mule, whuppin' his ass with a bullwhip." Wolf hid out in the woods that night and hopped a freight train at daylight the next morning.

The Delta and Highway 10
The Southern Railway snaked out of the hills and meandered through the heart of the Delta from Greenwood to Greenville through small towns and numerous plantation whistle stops along the way. It was somewhere along that route that Wolf got off the train and moved in with an Italian family, helping them with sharecropping chores, away from the biting sting of a bullwhip. Alongside the railroad track ran a serpentine dirt road known as Highway 10, which started in Columbus and ended at the Warfield

Point Ferry Landing on the Mississippi River west of Greenville. The railroad connected the small towns in the heart of the Delta with as many plantation headquarters as it could gobble up. Every plantation had a commissary that fronted the road, and they were the hub of activity on weekends. Along this road the true Delta blues were wrought out of the dusty turnrows, blazing hot Delta sun, and the cold winter mud.

The cool porches of the plantation commissaries and the shade of cottonwood and oak trees fine-tuned the songs of Charley Patton, Son House, Robert Johnson, Eddie Taylor, Jimmy Reed, B.B. King, Sam Chatmon, Willie Foster, T-Model Ford, Muddy Waters, and many others as the blues bubbled and boiled out of places like Berclair, Matoon, Heathman, Holly Ridge, Long Switch, Dunleith, Stoneville, and Magenta. Wolf, sometimes called "Bigfoot Chester," was there, wide eyed and listening, letting it soak in. It was the blues that came from untold hours in the broiling sun, trudging behind the south end of a north-bound mule, and the chant and response of prisoner gangs laboring on nearby Parchman Farm. Mose Allison sang, "I'm putting 'dat cotton in a 'leven foot sack with a 12-gauge shotgun at my back." The Delta in those days was harsh, unforgiving, and demanding. Young Wolf had the blues all his life and didn't know what to call them until he moved to the Delta. Now, he was able to give expression to his feelings and a channel to his deep-rooted and bullwhipped emotions. He was a kind and willing boy, yet he harbored some terrible memories

Howlin' Wolf, moanin' the blues, as captured by premier blues photographer Dick Waterman at the Newport Blues Festival, 1966. The previous year, British rockers The Rolling Stones refused to play the American television show "Shindig" unless Wolf played with them. Regarding the show, Stones guitarist Keith Richards stated, "It was a very brief brush with greatness."

that would haunt him the rest of his life. Wolf would use those experiences to entertain, enrich, and enlighten blues enthusiasts for years to come.

Wolf eventually found his real daddy, "Dock" Burnett, sharecropping outside of Ruleville. Dock was a well-respected, kind, and generous man and a good father to his son. They often went hunting and fishing on the weekends. Wolf finally had a home and felt peace for the first time in his life. He sang as he plowed his mules, and the mules seemed to be at ease and would pull harder as he howled the blues.

"Three chords on a guitar and the truth."

Charley Patton lived on nearby Dockery Plantation and took a liking to the young Wolf. People came from far away on Saturday to Dockery to hear Patton play.

Whenever he performed, he was revered. According to Segrest, "He [Patton] was the best guitarist in the Delta, with a percussive drive and aggressive edge that no one could match. Snapping and bending strings with his fingers or making them sob and moan with a slide, he attacked the neck of his instrument like a hound dog shakin' a stick." Wolf watched, listened, and learned. Once his daddy got him a guitar, he picked up a few chords from Patton.

The unlikely duo played together at juke houses on Greasy Street in Ruleville. What a pair they must have been: Wolf, almost a kid, extremely dark and rich skinned, tall and weighing in at over two hundred pounds with huge hands and feet, more likened to plowing mules than playing a guitar; and Charley Patton, older and small framed, light colored, with noticeably more Indian blood, both playing their gut-rendering blues. Patton slapping his guitar, spinning it around, and playing it behind his back while Wolf threw up his head and howled at the moon.

Charley Patton moved to Holly Ridge and lived in the back of the commissary. Wolf would come down, and they would play at stores up and down Highway 10. John Collier, who grew up on a farm close by, recalled, "That little guy from Holly Ridge would come and play with a younger fellow named Bull Cow, who was a great big man that would get so excited he would cross his eyes when he played the blues." The Wolf, Bull Cow, was learning to be a presence wherever he went, wherever he played. Wolf commanded respect and got it and that was something he had never before seen. He met Sonny Boy Williamson II and learned harmonica, and they would team up with Robert Johnson and play together up and down the dusty, crooked, and blues-infused Highway 10.

Wolf's confidence was up by now, and he struck out on his own, playing juke joints like Willie Towner's in Pace, Red Boyd's in Boyle, Jap's in Rosedale, and the Coconut Grove in Cleveland. While couples juked and danced in the front room, men shot craps and played cards in the back. Drinking was heavy even in Prohibition. Moonshine, wine, and rotgut whiskey flowed freely. It was noted, "Man, they'd be whoopin' and hollerin'! Womens would be dancin' and huggin' everbody. They'd be huggin' and kissin' him [Wolf] so that they'd have to pull 'em away just so he could play his guitar." The alpha Wolf had arrived and he was on the prowl all over the Mississippi and Arkansas Deltas.

In 1941, Wolf got a summons from Uncle Sam to report for duty. Thrown into the strict discipline of military life may have been akin to being back on Uncle Will's farm, and Wolf didn't like it. He was given an honorable discharge in 1943. Yet during his time in the army, he traveled and was able to visit blues clubs in Chicago and Seattle, far different than Delta jukes. His stint in the army gave him time to think about who he really was. His mother, a street-preaching religious fanatic, had kicked him out as a child. His horribly abusive uncle that had whipped him was a deacon in the church, and Wolf was becoming a blues-playing giant, preaching what some called the devil's music.

As mechanization took over the cotton fields, the mule-driven, sharecropping days were over, and on-farm juke houses began to fade. Wolf drifted towards West Memphis and put together a band called the House Rockers, soon to be heard on WDIA radio. It wasn't long before Sam Phillips of Sun Records heard Wolf on radio and stated, "This is for me. This is where the soul of man never dies." Phillips recorded Wolf and sent the demos to his friends the Chess Brothers in Chicago. "Moanin' at Midnight" and "How Many More Years" were to be two of Wolf's most powerful songs. Like a racehorse out of the gate, Wolf was off—off to blues stardom and to Chicago to cut more records. Wolf was quoted in *Moanin' at Midnight,* "I moved to Chicago in my own car and had $3,900 in my pocket. I'm the onliest one drove out of the Delta like a gentleman."

Wolf moved in with his archrival, Muddy Waters, and Muddy helped him get work, showing him around the blues clubs until he could settle in. Wolf put together a band that included Greenwood guitarist Hubert Sumlin, who remained with him for the rest of Wolf's life. On stage, Wolf was a commanding yet terrifying presence. According to bluesman Lacy Gibson, "He'd get on the bandstand and start playing and moanin' and yellin' and goin' on, and he'd have the whole house upset. He'd get down on the floor moanin' and howlin'. He was the best there was."

Wolf respected his band members and paid them good and on time, and they repaid him with allegiance and some of the best house rocking blues ever heard. Hits like "Smokestack Lightning," "Spoonful," "Killing Floor," "Built for Comfort," "Back Door Man," "Lil' Red Rooster," "Going Down Slow," and many more climbed up and down the rhythm and blues charts for years. Billy Boy Arnold described Wolf as a "very classy, dignified man…a gentleman in every sense of the word…a man with high character… and an asset to the blues."

By 1971 stardom and prominence came with a price. The Wolf's kidneys had begun to fail, and dialysis treatments kept him alive. His heart had broken when his mama rejected him as a child and then again late in life when she rebuffed him totally for offering her money. Hubert Sumlin recalled the last time he saw her in Clarksdale, and he tried to give her money: "Turn me loose! I told you I didn't want your dirty old money! You play them dirty blues!" Wolf cried all the way to Memphis.

Wolf had just played the blues at the premiere Ann Arbor Blues Festival. *Creem* magazine wrote, "Wolf ground out music so heavy it seemed to hang over the stage like a viscous mist."

Wolf died on an operating table on January 8, 1976. At his funeral Reverend Henry Hardy ended his eulogy with, "You ain't dead, Wolf. Howl on, Wolf! Howl on!" and great, hardened bluesmen wept openly. "Wolf had taken a hard life and turned it into songs that could break your heart…he had a soft spot for folks in pain, 'cause he had been there himself…he was a good man, no matter what his mama thought."

The Wolf was eased into the frozen ground at Oak Ridge Cemetery on Chicago's West Side. As was noted by one mourner, "That evening, a full moon rose over Chicago. At the Brookfield Zoo, three miles from Wolf's grave, the captive wolves howled long, long into the night."

True Blues

Real bluesmen truly live the blues. James "Son" Thomas chopped cotton, and he picked cotton. Later he dug graves with a one-armed man. He drank rotgut whiskey, got cut up several times, and was shot by an irate live-in housewife. He played the blues in back alleys, juke houses, and at white folks parties and even at the White House. He traveled all over Europe singing the blues and was an acclaimed artist and sculptor. Yet when he played at a fundraiser for President Ronald Reagan in Jackson, he was paid a paltry $100 for his efforts.

Son Thomas was reared in Eden, Mississippi, by his maternal grandparents. He never knew his daddy. Every Saturday as a child he traveled to Leland to visit his mother and sister. Growing up and playing in the cotton fields around Eden, he would collect clay from the Yazoo River bottoms and mold animal figurines and little trucks, earning himself the nickname, "Son Ford." He used his grandmother's oven as a kiln for his trucks, frogs, pigs, and birds. Later, he would mold human skulls using real teeth given to him by local dentists. Son displayed his work in the Corcoran Gallery of Art in Washington, D.C., and on several occasions traveled with Mrs. Hodding Carter to Bowdoin College in Brunswick, Maine, as a performing guest artist, playing the blues and molding his clay.

This portrait of Son became a popular poster with a quote by Leon Bloy that read: "Man has places in his heart which do not yet exist, and into them he enters suffering in order that they may have existence."

Son's uncle, Joe Cooper, played music and taught him how to make three chords by putting pencil marks on the neck of his guitar. As a child, Son learned the changes to those chords. One day his uncle caught him playing and told him to "put my guitar down before you break it!" Son chopped cotton until he could buy a guitar from Sears and Roebuck. He started hanging out at juke houses around Yazoo City and learned under some of the most famous bluesmen of his time. Whenever Rice Miller, Tommy McClennan, and Elmore James came to town, they would let Son play along with them. This allowed him to learn firsthand from some of the greatest blues guitarists of that time. Later he was asked to play with his uncle at house parties for a dollar a night.

Son was "discovered" in Leland in 1967 by blues researcher Bill Ferris. Through the exposure that Ferris brought him, Son was soon a hit attraction at folk life festivals and blues festivals all over America. He traveled to Europe several times and was featured on five albums and a number of compilation recordings. Son Thomas has been documented in five films and was featured exclusively in native Mississippian Anthony Herrera's *Mississippi Delta Blues*. The documentary, filmed locally, won several prestigious awards including the Cine Golden Eagle Award.

However, as was the case with so many other great bluesmen of his time, Son never attained the status or financial security he was due. He lived in a dilapidated shotgun house on McGee Street in Leland. He dug graves for the white funeral home there to make ends meet. In 1981, Son's live-in wife shot him one night with a .38 Special. Some claimed it was accidental, yet when asked about it, Son would just smile. Two weeks after he was shot, he was in Washington, D.C., at the Corcoran Gallery of Art, and during that trip he played the lowdown and sometimes raunchy Mississippi Delta blues for the National Press Corps at the request of Larry Speakes. Later that day, after cleaning up his act a bit, he played at the White House for First Lady Nancy Reagan singing "Catfish Blues."

Son suffered from back pains, epilepsy, and emphysema and one night fell into a space heater at his home and was badly burned. After recovering, he was back out playing blues festivals and parties all over the Delta. In 1991 he had surgery for a brain tumor, and two years later he suffered a stroke. Son Thomas, Delta bluesman, age sixty-six, died on June 26, 1993, and was buried on the banks of the Bogue Phalia outside of Leland. He rests quietly in the clay that he molded into artwork all his life.

After the funeral service, several of Son's friends gathered around his grave on that hot day in 1993. My wife Sallie and I were reminiscing about Son with Delta expatriate Jim Dees from Taylor. We were eating fried chicken and drinking cold beer, what Jim called his "first funeral tailgate party." Jim told of a trip years back when he drove Son Thomas to Atlanta to be the opening act for the infamous blues lady Bonnie Raitt. They were all in her dressing room warming up their respective guitars and Jim recalled, "I don't think Son was convinced Bonnie Raitt was for real until she pulled out her slide. After she hit a couple of tasty rifts, he smiled to himself and looked at me as if to say, 'Now look at this little white girl play that thing.' He laughed his laugh that started modestly and ended up in a cough."

Jim continued, "Son pulled out his own guitar and metal slide. When he hit a couple of chords from outer space, Bonnie's jaw dropped. She watched Son's long slender fingers work the guitar neck unlike anything she could ever imagine. He hit chords that will never exist again...with his thumb. Her eyes bugged out. He ended his dexterous excursion by bending some notes so hard that Bonnie Raitt buckled, gasped for breath, and finally swooned, 'Oooooh, Son, I see why that woman shot you!' "

"I ain't gonna pick no cotton...

I ain't gonna drag no sack...

I ain't gonna do nothing 'til my baby get back..." – Son Thomas, *"Mississippi Delta Blues"*

White House Blues

James "Son Ford" Thomas dug graves for a living with a one-armed man in Leland, Mississippi. He was also a legendary Mississippi Delta Bluesman. He played in juke houses and back alleys and at "white folks' parties." And in January of 1982, he played the rotgut Delta blues in Washington, D.C., at the White House.

Delta native and press secretary for President Ronald Reagan, Larry Speakes, heard that Son was in town playing a festival and invited him to the Capitol. Once through the West Gate, Son played for a small group gathered to hear his music in the press office. Larry recalls how he asked Son if he was going to play the same music when they went over to the Briefing Room so the press could hear him, and Son replied, "Yeah, but it ain't gonna be like that." Son sang two versions of the "Catfish Blues." One version was cleaned up, the other was not.

I remember seeing Son when he returned from his trip to Washington. He had been shot by his live-in wife prior to the trip with a .38 caliber pistol as he ran out his front door. Someone said it was an accident. Son just winked when I asked him about it. A bullet was removed from his upper buttock, and he was soon back out playing the blues.

Stopping by his dilapidated shotgun house on McGee Street in Leland, I found Son on the front porch smoking a cigarette and having a beer. A picture of Mrs. Nancy Reagan in the Rose Garden hugging Son sat on the table beside him. I told Son that he should be mighty proud of that picture because not many people ever get to be

Son Thomas caught the attention of the national press when he played "Catfish Blues" at the White House in 1982. There he met First Lady Nancy Reagan.

hugged by the First Lady of the United States of America, much less an old Mississippi Delta bluesman. Son just shook his head as he looked at me and said, "Dat was the wors'est part of dat trip!"

I asked him why, and he replied, "When dat nice lady grabbed me for de picture, she put her hand right on da bullet hole and went to squeezing me and I felt like I'd been shot all over again!"

Years later, Son was badly burned while smoking in bed and recuperated enough to play a few more festivals. He died of a heart attack following a stroke in June of 1993.

"They calls me a Crawlin' Kingsnake,
Cause, you know I rules my den..."

Nothin' But the Blues

It has been said that the blues comes from the dirt, Delta dirt. Long hours of toiling in the sun and dust and mud and cold, breaking ground, plowing behind a mule, dragging an eleven foot sack filled with cotton gave birth to the blues and singing the blues', the chant and response even made it easier to work during those wearisome times.

Pat Thomas grew up playing in dirt and clay, digging, mixing, molding, and helping to bake it. He was brought to the Delta at a very early age from Eden, Mississippi, when his daddy, James "Son Ford" Thomas, better known as Son Thomas, moved his wife Christine and thirteen children to Leland. Son and Christine both took jobs working at the Montgomery Hotel, current site of the Highway 61 Blues Museum. However, it was not long until Son started digging graves with a one-armed man for Boone Funeral Home. Son dug graves from 1960 until 1985 when his doctor told him, "Son, you either stop digging graves, or the next one you dig will be out of a wheelchair." During this time, when Son was not digging graves, Pat would accompany his daddy to Carrollton on the edge of the hills to dig clay. Pat recalled, "There was a nice lady over in them hills would tell us to go dig all the clay we wanted. Many times that old Chevrolet Impala would be loaded to the ground with so much clay in the trunk."

Pat would play in tubs of clay, removing the rocks and sand particles so his daddy could mold the figurines he was so well known for, little Ford trucks, human skulls studded with real teeth acquired from local dentists, birds, snakes, pigs, and frogs. Pat watched his daddy deftly mold, form, and carve the primitive art work that was to soon be displayed at Bowdin College in Brunswick, Maine, the Corcoran Art Gallery in Washington, D. C., and even shown in the White House to First Lady Nancy Reagan. Yes, Pat watched, and Pat learned.

While not digging graves or molding clay, Pat's daddy played and sang the blues, the real blues, the Delta Blues, the rotgut blues. Son famously played both versions of the "Catfish Blues" while in Washington—the dirty, lowdown, and raunchy kind for Press Secretary Larry Speakes and the White House Press Corps and the cleaned-up, milder, more "lady-like" kind for the First Lady. Pat learned both versions by listening and watching his daddy's long slender fingers stroke and pluck his guitar strings and work a metal slide that one time brought tears to revered blues icon Bonnie Raitt's eyes. Son had played with and learned from Elmore James when he lived in Greenville and Sonny Boy Williamson #2, Rice Miller, when he lived outside of town on Smythe's Deadening. Again, Pat watched, and Pat learned.

Pat's great uncle Joe Cooper showed him how to make some chords and strum the guitar while keeping time by tapping his foot. Son noticed Pat taking an interest in music and began to show him some blues licks and chords that only he knew. Renowned Delta bluesman Eddie Cusic helped Pat with chord changes and techniques.

It wasn't long before Pat was playing bass while Cleveland "Broom Man" James played percussion with a handful of sand on the floor and an upturned broomstick and Son played lead with his bottleneck slide and sang vocals. Son would often say to Pat, "Boy, are you gonna play that thing? Well, you better get it and come on!" The trio played nightspots and juke joints run by local bootlegger Shelby "Papa Jazz" Brown, house parties, and even traveled to Oxford and played the venerable Hoka Theatre. Pat was coming into his own.

It wasn't long before Pat's mama Christine left, with all of the children but Pat. He stayed with his daddy helping to mold clay and play the blues. Son had several more wives and according to Pat, "street womens he associated with. One of his wives, the live-in kind, shot him in the back end with a .38 Special as he ran out the door about two weeks before he was to go to Washington, D.C. And then there was Miss Katherine, an older lady that we lived with. She was real kind to Daddy and would cook for us and take real good care of us. She was really nice." It wasn't long afterwards that Son suffered a stroke and died of a heart attack in June of 1993. His son Pat was on his own.

BILLY JOHNSON COLLECTION

Pat stayed in the old dilapidated shotgun house on McGee Street where they had lived, moping around and mourning the loss of his daddy. In the book, *Roadtrip with a Raindrop, 90 Days Along the Mississippi River,* by Gayle Harper, Pat stated, "I couldn't play for a while, I just hadda leave that guitar alone. But then, I started feeling kinda shamefaced and I knowed I hadda put my heart there for my father." Pat resumed playing his daddy's old blues songs like the "Catfish Blues," "Good Morning Little Schoolgirl," and "61 Highway." "Sometimes I'd go out to the graveyard and play, and it seem like he kinda wakes up. But then, he just gets back down in that hole o' his."

Pat never learned to read or write too well. "Cuz, you cain't learn it [playing the blues, sculpting and drawing] from no book nohow." Even though Pat may have learned about the blues himself, "Daddy always tol' me theys lotsa ways you kin have the blues. If you broke, that's the blues, if you hongry, that's the blues. If you gots a good woman and she quit ya, that ain't nothing but the blues! Sometimes, I get a happy blues feelin', and sometimes I get a sad blues feelin'. It's just something that comes in ya—ya gotta feel it."

Once Pat started playing the blues again, he also started sculpting and painting. Anything he could find to paint on he did. His favorite subject to paint is cats. Pat recalled one day at the Highway 61 Blues Museum, where he can be seen most days, "The first cat I drew, I drew on a board. The eyes was made of glass in the shape of diamonds. They kinda looked right through you." The diamond-eyed cat is now on permanent display in Germany. When asked why he picked up painting along with his sculpting and blues playing, Pat is quick to respond, "I just want to do something for Daddy. He's everything I ever had. He was so deep into the blues, that's how best I can remember him."

And then he picked up his guitar and strummed off into "Good Morning Little Schoolgirl" as I closed my eyes. When Pat screamed off in his high-pitched, wailing, and lonesome voice, tears streaked down my cheeks as I almost swore it was my friend Son, singing the song I had heard him play so many times. When he hit his last chord, he laid down his guitar and said, "I got to keep doing this for Daddy."

And do it he does, at the Sunflower River Blues and Gospel Festival, Delta Blues Festival, Highway 61 Blues Festival, Mighty Mississippi Music Festival, and the Bentonia Blues Festival. Pat has played the blues in New York City among photographs of his daddy and Eddie Cusic taken by famed blues photographer Rex Miller while they hung in professional tennis pro John McEnroe's art gallery. He was selected by the Mississippi Delta Blues Society of Indianola as the 2007 Blues Artist of the Year and went on to represent that Society in the International Blues Awards in Memphis. Pat has taught an art and a music class at Delta State playing the blues and sculpting clay and painting his catheads.

Pat's art has not gone unnoticed. Mississippi's own Cathead Vodka is named after Pat's paintings, and each bottle sports a cathead painted by Pat on its label. Cat Head Delta Blues and Art Gallery in Clarksdale is named for Pat's paintings. Owner Roger Stolle says, "As an artist and musician, I sit in awe of Pat. He puts the 'creative' on 'creativity' and is the true definition of both a folk artist and an outsider artist. His talents are certainly a part of a folk tradition handed down by his father, Son Thomas. Pat is an outsider artist working well outside of the 'trained' art world. You never know what he is going to sculpt, draw, or play next. Pat's universe is his own. We just get to visit." When Roger sends tourists south to Leland to the Highway 61 Blues Museum, he tells them, "it's the only museum in the world with a 'live' bluesman on display."

Author Gayle Harper defines Pat when she states, "It's tough to describe Pat Thomas. He is some mixture of wisdom and innocence and keen perception. When he smiles, his whole being is transformed, and when he laughs, his whole body participates—and, there is something more going on, something mysterious behind those hazel eyes."

As Gayle was preparing to leave the museum where she had met the bluesman/artist, Pat drew a diamond-eyed cat and gave it to her to keep with her for good luck. "It's got hoodoo magic," Pat said as he gave it to her with no trace of a smile. When he handed it to her, goosebumps appeared as Pat looked deep into her eyes.

Pat is one of only very few second- generation blues artists in the Delta. He is self-made and self-taught, a true folk artist. Billy Johnson, curator of the Highway 61 Blues Museum says, "Any artist, visual or performing, is a reflection of the times in which they live. They are influenced by those life forces they have experienced. Pat lives his art." When you look at one of his sculpted pieces in the museum of a man lying in a casket, you can only know where Pat's mind is. At his father's funeral, I gasped when Pat walked in behind the casket as I thought I was seeing Son's ghost in a white linen suit following his own pall.

In June of 2010, the great blues guitarist Johnny Winter from Leland was honored with a Blues Trail marker. During a break in the ceremony and the concert that followed, Winter asked if he could hear Pat Thomas play a few of the songs that he and Son would play as young bluesmen from Leland. They were placed in a room by themselves in the museum as Pat Thomas played for the esteemed Johnny Winter. When they came back out of the room, Johnny Winter said to Billy Johnson, "Son's boy is damn good. That's the real stuff there."

Walkin' in Memphis with Muriel and Marc

Webster's defines graciousness as being marked by tact and delicacy, kindness and courtesy, charm, good taste, and generosity of spirit. Muriel Wilkins was all of the above and more. She was a woman of the Lord, never missing an opportunity to grace the open doors of her beloved Pettis Memorial Christian Methodist Episcopal Church in Helena, Arkansas. Mabel Pettis, whose father-in-law founded the church, recalls Muriel as the most Christian woman she has ever known. Muriel and Mabel met in high school and were best friends for life.

Muriel was born into a preacher's family in Forrest City, Arkansas, in December of 1923. She began playing the piano and singing in Sunday School when she was three years old. She continued to practice that never-ending love of hers for sixty-four more years.

Educated in the Forrest City public schools, Muriel received her teacher's degree from AM&N College in Pine Bluff and her master's degree from the University of Arkansas at Fayetteville. She taught elementary school in Helena for thirty-three years, retiring in 1986. Muriel considered her musical ability a gift from God and played free of charge for her church, weddings, funerals, and many other community affairs. Friends recall how Muriel would pull children aside and scold them if she thought they were not attaining their full potential. "You must be ALL that you can be" was a quote I have heard several times from her friends and from Muriel herself.

In 1973, Bob Hall bought the Selden family plantation commissary/antique store/beer hall, circa 1856, and opened up the Hollywood Café. The wonderful old cypress building stood right across the railroad tracks from old Highway 61 in Hollywood, Mississippi, six miles north of Tunica. A musician and crooner himself, Bob had met a sweet black lady who was playing piano and singing at the Holiday Inn across the Mississippi River in Helena. Once his place was established, he asked her if she would consider coming over and playing at his dinner club. Thus began a relationship that would grow into a devoted friendship of almost twenty years. Bob's spiritual life was enhanced by Muriel's presence, and he sang many times in her church in Helena as an invited guest. "She was like a sister to me, and she was unshakable in her faith," Bob says. Did Hall ever record Muriel during the many times she played at the Hollywood? "No, I thought it would never end."

The original Hollywood Café burned in 1983. The Owen family bought the rights to it from Bob "Hollywood" Hall for one dollar and moved it six miles up old Highway 61 to Robinsonville. The new Hollywood Café opened up in another antiquated commissary building. The famous dill pickles were again being fried, and the catfish and steaks were heaped on the platters as Muriel continued her piano playing and singing. People resumed their trek from miles around just to hear her and to enjoy the laid back atmosphere of the dinner club. (Bob Hall said that on numerous occasions when Muriel was ready to go home and the patrons wanted her to stay a little longer,

Marc Cohn's hit song "Walking in Memphis" references his spiritual experience playing and singing with the late Muriel Wilkins at The Hollywood Café near Tunica, Mississippi.

he would whisper for one of them to ask her to play a spiritual song. Several hours later Bob would have to tell Muriel that it was indeed time to go home!)

Muriel's son, Bobby Martin, recalls his mother being very stern in her discipline but always extremely loving and jovial. Bobby would drive her when she went to play at parties and remembered her voracious appetite as she would lean back in the car and eat the heaped plates of food given to her for the ride home by the party givers. "Why, there's enough chicken bones up and down Highway 61 to fill a basketball court!" Bobby says while recalling their many travels together.

Anthony Herrera, aka James Stenbeck of the soap opera *As the World Turns,* came to the Delta to produce and direct a blues documentary. He was introduced to Muriel one evening as she played and sang at a party in Greenville. "When I heard Muriel play, I realized she had a wonderful gift of love and inspiration. Her voice and music inspired me to make the film. That moment was the beginning of *Mississippi Delta Blues.*" Anthony, from Wiggins, Mississippi, and Ole Miss educated, won five prestigious awards for the documentary including the CINE Golden Eagle Award. Muriel sings the background music to the tune of "Darkness on the Delta."

"When it's darkness on the Delta, that's the time my heart is light...
When it's darkness on the Delta, let me linger in the shelter of the night..."

As far as one can tell, that is the only time Muriel was ever recorded for the public.

I first met Muriel at the old Hollywood Café in the mid-'70s. She was one of the most awe-inspiring and wonderful ladies I had ever been around. We became very close friends, and she would often play New Year's Eve parties at my mother's house and for No Name Dinner Club parties. A certain charisma and aura surrounded her as she sang old-time big band favorites, blues numbers, and gospel songs. She seemed to sing from the depths of her soul with a beautiful and husky voice that somehow enveloped you. She always wanted to know about you. She would answer brief questions about herself, but it was you that she wanted to talk about. And it was that personality trait that enamored her to a young fledgling singer/songwriter in 1986.

Marc Cohn, originally from Cleveland, Ohio, and living in New York City, had been going through a stage of writer's block and was yet to be a recorded songwriter and singer. He had been invited by Dr. Frank Witherspoon, a long time friend of Muriel's, to come visit him in Memphis and then go down to Robinsonville to meet a sweet lady that played piano and sang. That lady would forever change Marc's life. And because of that meeting, Muriel would become known all over the world.

Marc Cohn remembers having to sit close to Muriel as she played that night in 1986 because she was unaccompanied by any amplification. During a break they began talking and she asked him to tell her about himself. He explained his life story and that his mother had died at an early age and how he seemed to be in a rut with regards to his writing. During her next set, she asked him if he would join her on stage. Muriel sang "Amazing Grace" a cappella and asked him if he would do the same. Then she asked him to sing some songs with her, whispering in his ear the lyrics that he did not know. Marc felt as if he had been transported to a place in his heart where he had never been and with a person that knew more about him than he did himself at that particular time. Marc recalls that before leaving around two a.m., Muriel "whispered things to me about my mother. Then she told me it was time for me to move on."

Returning home to New York, Marc began writing the songs he had always heard in his head. He invited Muriel to come north and play at his wedding, and she readily obliged. Later, Marc returned to the Hollywood in Robinsonville to play some of the songs he had written. One of the songs was a beautiful story about feeling in awe as he was "walking in Memphis, with my feet ten feet off of Beale" and standing at the foot of W. C. Handy's statue. And when he toured Graceland, he felt as if he were walking "with the ghost of Elvis." But is was when he traveled south on old Highway 61 and into the arms of a gospel singer that they "asked me if I would do a little number, and I played with all my might." Muriel was tickled that he would write about her, and later that same evening, she asked Marc if he would "play that little song you wrote about me one more time."

It was not long after that second visit that Marc's first CD came out to great acclaim. But Muriel had fallen and torn her ankle apart. She had also become sick while attending a church meeting in Dallas and had to be hospitalized. Complications from ankle surgery and ongoing health problems set in, and on October 6, 1990, she was dead at the age of sixty-seven. Several months after she died, Muriel became immortalized when Marc Cohn was the 1991 Grammy winner for Best New Artist. He had written a song about her and called it "Walking in Memphis." That song was the title track on his first production, one of many to follow. As Marc walked across the stage, his Grammy award in hand, he looked up towards heaven and blew a kiss. I think I know who was on the receiving end.

Muriel had lived a life of deep and devoted Christian faith. Her church door never opened that she was not sitting at the piano. The God-loving spirituality that exuded from her was ever present. Over the years, many people have been asked the proverbial question by Muriel, "Child, are you a Christian?" But no one has ever given as world-renowned an answer as Marc Cohn did that night in Robinsonville, Mississippi, when he replied, "Ma'am, I am tonight!"

Muddy Water in His Blood

Jimmy Phillips grew up in Greenville and graduated from Greenville High School in 1969. Along with friend Ralph McGee from Leland, he headed off to the University of the South at Sewanee, Tennessee, for two years. He finished up his undergraduate work at Ole Miss. With his friend at his side, Jimmy learned to play music under the expert tutelage of Ralph's daddy, "Ugg" McGee. World-renowned Leland bluesman Son Thomas often sat in on sessions playing and singing the blues late into the night. Self taught, Jimmy made music his life's ambition and work. Ralph and Jimmy worked together checking bugs for cotton planters one summer and spent a lot of time together hanging out and playing music. Ralph says, "Jimmy has a tremendous ability to write songs that are aspiring and inspiring. He has unique and great musical talents."

Jimmy wrote a song about Pantherburn Plantation that he later dedicated to "Ugg" McGee:

Pantherburn, flash me back to the place, where sandy loam is Delta Gold.

Living with the land is the nature of a man and time is just a reason to grow old.

The song tells of the four seasons on a cotton plantation. Indicative of that theme is the final verse,

Child of the river sleeps in loneliness, as the winter's desolation claims the land.

But when the springtime comes around, we drop the seeds back in the ground and life returns to fertile Pantherburn.

Graduating from Ole Miss, Jimmy hung around Oxford awhile, playing at The Gin in a local band called Cold Beer. He drifted around the South before landing in Nashville where he eventually joined fellow singer/songwriters at The Combine Music Group. Combine was a songwriting organization built by independent Nashville music publisher Bob Beckham. Describing his idea of combining great lyricists to produce a song, Beckham says, "The most important thing for a song is the lyric. I look for a lyric that is fresh, expressive, precise, simple, and original." There, Jimmy shared his writing talents while composing music and lyrics with other well-known artists including Kris Kristofferson and Tony Joe White. Jimmy composed, co-produced, and performed in his own personal album in 1988 for Dangling Carrot Records titled *They Don't Make the Blues Like They Used To.*

Jimmy's songs portray his life and those sometimes severe lessons we learn along the way. The hard living of a songwriter and musician can take some rocky roads and sharp turns. In "Temporary Insanity" he sings:

Bloody Mary, take me under this morning, I got a funny suspicion, I stripped my transmission last night.

My head is still reeling, my eyes won't focus and I'm moving uncommonly slow, so, jump me off, Mary, I believe my battery's low...

Temporary Insanity, it had to be a Saturday night, that old devil got into me and blew the pilot light

JANE RULE BURDINE

An empty bottle took the throttle and left me three sheets to the wind, Temporary Insanity, hooked on the juice again...

They tell me I was spilling wine by eleven, talking trash to the ladies, throwing cash on imported Champagne.

Well, I'm a genius when I'm rocking, everybody tells me so, and if you think I'm crazy, Baby, you just don't know!

Some revelers become legendary for their late night partying and ability to burn the candle at both ends. In "Redlight," Jimmy relates:

Woke up this morning, I was moaning and groaning, had to blow it off and phone in sick.
Went to the doctor, I said, 'Doctor, what's wrong?' He said, 'Son, you better slow down quick.'
Judging from the symptoms and the vital signs, you ran the redlight in your mind.
Your body's shaking, you got bad circulation and the blood is rushing to yo' head,
Your liver's wasted and your lungs don't function, Son, one day you gonna wake up dead.
You got the ticker working overtime, you ran the redlight in your mind.

And it is also a well-known fact that hard living has its severe drawbacks as it can sometimes take a drastic toll. In "Whiskey" the harsh reality shines through:

Whiskey, we been old friends too long, it's high time we end this honeymoon.

Lately, you been coming on too strong, you keep me up all night and let me sleep into the afternoon.

Bottle of pleasure, bottle of pain, hold me together in my hour of shame,
I can see my destination, but I can't get off the train.
Bottle of pleasure, bottle of pain.

And in a very sultry ballad, "Champagne Sensation," he croons:

The night I met you, it was spontaneous combustion, like a dream come true at a little social function...

You caught my eye, now ordinarily, I'm a little bit shy, but your smile was an invitation, all I needed was a little inspiration.

Some minor moment of truth and I'd be making my move, and then a cork hit the roof.

I may be a fool, but I'm a Champagne sensation, a creature of charm, when I'm feeling no pain and no frustration,

I'm dehydrated mojo, instant Romeo, just add Champagne…Now pour me some, Baby

In "A Good Woman is Hard to Find," Jimmy speaks the truth about relationships:

Precious gold is a treasure to hold, but all that glitters is not gold.

Fancy clothes and a painted face will make her shine, but a good woman is hard to find.

Jimmy was influenced by some of the last of the great Delta bluesmen. In his "Cooter Trilogy," he built a composite character based on Hollandale's own Sam Chatmon and Leland's Son Thomas:

Born in the Delta, back in the early days, he picked cotton down on the Paxton Place, ain't nothing down there but mosquitoes and snakes.

Favored music so he learned guitar, jungle rythym, jamming twelve to the bar, they called him Cooter cause his head was so hard.

Fry him some chicken, pour him some wine, he'll have the juke jumping by half past nine. He played mean, he played loud, he played the Devils music for a heathen crowd, washed in the water of Black Bayou, he was baptized in the blues.

In the liner notes to Jimmy's album, one of America's foremost roots music authorities Peter Guralnick wrote, "Jimmy Phillips is an original. His originality comes through in his songs... His art and his songwriting is of considerable breadth and complexity. These songs are timeless."

Down to earth, Jimmy writes songs that make us know exactly what he is talking about. In Eden Brent's award-winning CD, *Mississippi Number One*, she recorded Jimmy's song "Fried Chicken" to celebrate the best things about the Delta in her album. Recently returning from the Legendary Rhythm and Blues Cruise where "Fried Chicken" was included on their advertising sampler, Eden says, "Ain't nobody from the Delta who can write about the Delta in a song better than Jimmy. He paints the images of the Delta so that even people from Canada or Poland can relate to it. Folks request them all the time."

The opening verse to "Fried Chicken" makes you want to smack your lips:

It was high noon, Arcola, Mississippi, another Sunday feast, I popped my head into the kitchen and I heard that gurgling grease.

I said, 'Georgie, whatcha cooking?' she said, 'Jimmy, whatcha think, You better come on in the kitchen and wash yo' hands up in the sink.'

Cause we having fried chicken, wing takes a breast, leg takes a thigh, rice and gravy, black eyed peas and cornbread on the side.

It's a Southern institution, black skillet is preferred, fried chicken, a most delightful bird.

Jimmy left Nashville in 1989 and went back to Ole Miss to get his master's degree in Southern studies. He then moved to Meridian as managing editor and principal writer for *Peavey Magazine*, the quarterly magazine published by the renowned international music and sound equipment manufacturer Peavey Electronics. The magazine was distributed to 103 countries across the globe.

After living in Meridian for five years, Jimmy headed out to Austin, Texas, before moving to the Rocky Mountains and Telluride, Colorado. There he worked in hotel management and snow skied for ten years before deciding to come home.

Jimmy is now living in the small, artistic hamlet of Taylor, where he is the coordinator of the Oxford Songwriter's Association. Bi-monthly meetings of the workshop are open to the public and held at the Power House located off the Square. He plays occasionally in Jackson and Oxford and at Vince's in Leland and has re-committed himself to creating, performing, and recording music. Currently, he is working on another album with some new songs and some reconfigured old songs, tentatively titled *Strange Loop*.

Jimmy's life has taken him full circle; he's come home, as so many of us have. His enduring love of the Delta can be stated no better or more poignantly than in the closing chorus to "Muddy Water":

Any fool can see, that I long to be, back in the land of the cypress tree.

I know, some day, I'll go back to stay, I got muddy water, I got muddy water, I got muddy water in my blood.

From Hellhole, Mississippi, to Carnegie Hall
The tumultuous life of The Big Boss Man

Most of us consider Highway 61 to be the "Blues Highway." In a sense it is because that is the road that most bluesmen and displaced farm laborers took when getting outta Dodge and heading for better times. A steady migration trooped north that eventually would displace thousands of Delta families. However, there was another blues Highway known as Highway 10. And it was along this dirt road that the Delta Blues grew up, were nurtured, weaned, and finally took to their wings, flying up 61 Highway.

Highway 10 weaved its way westward from Greenwood to Indianola, Leland, and on to Greenville. Between the sporadic towns were plantation stops along the C&G Railroad where goods and supplies were dropped off and hundreds of thousands of bales of fine Delta cotton were loaded for their ride to the textile mills up east. The C&G Railroad paralleled Highway 10 wherever it could, crossing over the dirt road numerous times. My friend and majordomo John Johnson once told me, "That road was like a snake. It was so crooked you could meet yourself coming back." There were sprawling plantations with whistle stop loading ramps on the C&G and plantation commissary stores along the dusty highway. And it was under the shade of the porches of those stores on the weekends that bluesmen performed for nickels and dimes. It was there and in nearby juke houses where the blues blossomed. Many times, plantation owners and straw bosses would grab their own guitars and play right alongside the bluesmen. Young kids would scramble to get close to hear that mournful,

The Big Boss Man put his heart and soul in his music even though his body was ravaged by epilepsy and alcohol.

love forsaken, whiskey-soaked rhythm that brought one out of the funk of everyday life in order to "give my po' heart ease."

Charley Patton moved from the Dockery Plantation down to Holly Ridge playing weekends at the Holly Ridge Store. Along that winding road drifted bluesmen and women whose names would later become infamous all over the world. Robert Johnson, Tommy McClennan, Peetie Wheatstraw, Memphis Minnie, B.B. King, Big Joe Williams, Albert King, Willie Foster, Eddie Taylor, Son House, Howlin' Wolf, along with Sam Chatmon, Eugene Powell, and Pinetop Perkins, wandered in and out of the plantations working in the cotton fields and playing the blues whenever possible.

Sometimes the towns attracted bigger crowds and street corners were claimed by bluesmen with tip jars placed out to receive the pocket change thrown by the boogieing crowd. Illegal and sometimes gut-wrenching corn liquor flowed from moonshine stills while finger popping and sweet-smelling girls of the evening "shimmied they shorts." Gambling and craps shooting were widespread while gun shots peppered the night as the decadence and debauchery ran rampant. At the time, Leland was known as a "den of inequity." In a 1908 article in *Collier's Magazine,* it was referred to as the "Hellhole of the Delta."

On September 6, 1925, in the middle of John Collier's Shady Dell Plantation next to Dunlieth, Mathis James "Jimmy" Reed was born, the youngest of ten children of a hard working share cropping family. He grew up playing and then working in the cotton fields and later sang spirituals at the Pilgrim Rest Baptist Church in Meltonia. Blues harpist Willie Foster was born on a cotton sack as his mama picked cotton at Shady Dell. He was a childhood friend and playmate of Jimmy Reed. Willie, four years older, taught Jimmy how to play the blues on a twenty-cent Hohner harmonica.

Soon, Jimmy's musical talent began to come forth. His heart was torn between the "devil music" he was hearing on Saturday night and the spiritual church hymns he was singing on Sunday morning. Herstine Franklin recalled seeing ten-year-old Jimmy Reed in a gospel quartet outside of Shaw. "They were good and sang all over Bolivar County in different churches. Then Jimmy stopped singing spirituals and started singing those blues." Jimmy had begun fooling around with a guitar.

In Will Romano's book *Big Boss Man: The Life and Music of Bluesman Jimmy Reed,* Hamp Collier, second generation owner of Shady Dell recalled, "Jimmy's brother Buddy was a wonderful guitar player. Charley Patton and a great big guy named "Bull Cow" (Howlin' Wolf) would come and play. Bull Cow would get so excited he'd cross his eyes when he played the blues." It was in that atmosphere that young Jimmy Reed grew up.

Twenty miles away in Benoit, a young guitarist named Eddie Taylor was picking and singing his own style of blues. Eddie's parents split up and Eddie, a couple years older than Jimmy, was nursed by his mama's good friend Lizzie Douglas, better known as Memphis Minnie. Eddie once said, "Memphis Minnie and my mother went to school together. She used to nurse me when I was a baby… and I used to listen to her play the guitar…" Memphis Minnie introduced Eddie to Robert Johnson, Charley Patton, and Son House. "I was about seven or eight years old, and I'd see them playing at house parties. They'd play cards and shoot dice and somewhere up the front of the house, they'd have guitar playing and dancing."

Eddie Taylor would tag along with these bluesmen and Memphis Minnie as they traveled back and forth along Highway 10 to Stringtown and Dunlieth. When he got back home, he would attempt to replicate the sounds swirling in his head on a ten dollar Sears and Roebuck guitar his mother had given him. Tommy McClennan and Peetie Wheatstraw were an early influence on Eddie, but, according to him, it was Robert Johnson that had the most enduring impact on his ultimate style. And it was that style that once Eddie Taylor and Jimmy Reed got together would produce a sound that was to be recognized the world over as the classic "Jimmy Reed Shuffle."

Eddie's family moved to Stringtown, which gave him the opportunity to play with local legends such as Popcorn Jesse, Little Quick, and Boots along with the traveling bluesmen Big Joe Williams, Son House, and Howlin' Wolf. Eddie was soon playing along with sophisticated guitarists like "Honeyboy" Edwards. He began playing hillbilly and popular music as well as the blues. Sometimes white folks would stop to listen and tip him more than his usual fare.

Eddie Taylor and Jimmy Reed became friends and after a day's work in the fields would pull out their guitars and go sit under a shade tree and play music, "just fooling around, seeing what we could do." Jimmy admitted that Eddie was much better than he was, and he would go home and try to emulate that sound or add his own sound to it. And then he would grab his harmonica and blowing into a twenty-cent harp would wail off into the moonlight. Later on, that "Jimmy Reed sound" with its deep thrusting beat, the simple nasal-twanged verses, and its profound foot-shuffling boogie groove would become well known and recognizable worldwide. Bob Dylan, the Rolling Stones, Neil Young, Lou Rawls, Van Morrison, and even Elvis Presley would knit that Jimmy Reed beat into their own music. But it would take a long and rowdy ride to Chicago before that would happen.

"You gots me working Bossman, working around yo' farm, I want a little drink of water, but you won't give me none. Big Boss Man, can't you hear me when I call, well, you ain't so big, you just tall… and that's all."

Jimmy Reed was a good field hand. Good with mules and a hard worker. He barely finished the third grade in school and never learned to read or write very well, his life consumed in the cotton fields during the day and playing the blues at night. Jimmy drifted up to a farm around Duncan where he stayed with kinfolks. During his lunch break, he would sit and listen to the King Biscuit Time blues show on KFFA radio out of Helena, Arkansas. Sonny Boy Williamson II (Rice Miller) was playing along with Robert Lockwood Jr., and Jimmy would hear those songs in his head all day long walking behind a pair of mules. He seemed to have a special power over his mules; he could make them work when no one else could.

One day his manager told him, "Look, don't you stop them mules. I don't want you to stop them for nothin'." Jimmy started plowing, not giving the man another thought and stopped later to get a drink of water. The straw boss came up and cussed him for stopping the mules because he didn't think anyone could get them started again. Jimmy replied, "Man, whatcha' mean don't stop them mules? I want some water!" Jimmy turned to walk away and as he was crossing a ditch the straw boss kicked him forcing him to go back to work. Jimmy was angry, but because of his good nature kept his mouth shut. "I got the mules going and plowed them down to the other end of the field and turned 'em around to head back down the row. When the mules stopped, I just started walkin'. I ain't seen that man no more…and them mules, either." When he stopped walking, he was in Leland. Scraping together what little money he could, eighteen-year-old Jimmy Reed bought a ten-dollar ticket on the Illinois Central Railroad to Chicago and the musical world would soon become a better place for it.

"Let me tell ya Baby
I'll tell what I would do
I would rob, steal, kill somebody
Just to get back home to you!
Aint that lovin' ya Baby?"

Jimmy Reed arrived in Chicago and immediately found work as a janitor at the YMCA. It beat picking cotton and walking behind a pair of mules all day long. As soon as he got a Social Security card, he went to work at a coal company shoveling coal by the ton. His landlord sold him an acoustic guitar for seven dollars, and in the evenings he would soothe his weary mind by playing the blues and blowing on his harmonica.

Uncle Sam called, and in 1943 Jimmy joined the U.S. Navy. He never saw any action and on leave came home and married his childhood sweetheart from Lambert, Mary Lee Davis, better known as Mama Reed. She was the love of his life, and they would have eight children. After discharge, Jimmy tried farming again but soon headed back to Chicago, taking jobs in the steel mills and eventually on the killing floors of a meat packing plant. Hanging out in Club Jamboree one night, he saw his old friend Eddie Taylor, and they started playing together and being noticed around the South Side. After cutting a few demos for the fledging VeeJay Records label, the Jimmy Reed sound was soon to be heard on radios all over America, bridging the gap between urban and country blues. Whites and blacks alike heard something in the raw, simple lyrics that both could ascribe to. Coast-to-coast tours followed, and soon Jimmy Reed was riding around in a big white Cadillac convertible!

"I been here, and I been there,
Honey, I been most of everywhere,
But, I'm going to New York,
I'm going there if I have to walk!"

Mama Reed was always by his side and probably wrote most of his lyrics. She was also there to ensure he took his medicine for the epilepsy that ravaged his body. But by the '60s, alcohol had taken its toll even though he had sold hundreds of thousands of records and climbed the pop charts. By crossing over into the white world of music, he blazed trails never before seen.

In 1961, Jimmy Reed shared billing at Carnegie Hall, once reserved for classical and opera stars, with Muddy Waters and Big Maybelle. New Yorkers lined up for a two-dollar ticket to hear the Big Boss Man of the Blues, and hear him they did! But Jimmy was sick and thought staying drunk most of the time would help with his epileptic seizures. For the next decade, he traveled in and out of hospitals and up and down not only the pop but the rhythm and blues charts as well.

"Better get some insurance on me, Baby,
Take out some insurance on me. Baby
'Cause if you ever, ever say goodbye. I'm gonna haul right off and die"

Jimmy Reed, born outside of Hellhole, Mississippi, had skyrocketed to the top of the rhythm and blues world—his iconoclastic sound reverberating around the globe. He died alone in a motel room in San Francisco in 1974 of a massive seizure a week before his fifty-first birthday. If pall bearers are symbolic of one's life, then Muhamed Ali, Bobby "Blue" Bland, Eddie Taylor, James Cotton, Muddy Waters, B.B. King, John Lee Hooker, and Memphis Slim defined the prominence of Jimmy Reed, for it was those greats that introduced the Big Boss Man to the Heavenly Host.

Muddy Waters—Mannish Boy

The music of Muddy Waters evokes manhood, rash behavior, forthrightness and boldness. Yet Arkansan Levon Helm described Muddy Waters as one who "taught us to take things in context, to be respectful, and to be serious about our music, as he was. He showed us that music was a sacred thing."

Supposedly born in Rolling Fork in 1915, although very possibly born in 1913 in Issaquena County around Jug's Corner, Muddy Waters given name was McKinley Morganfield. His mother died when he was very young, and he was sent to live with his maternal grandmother on the Stovall Plantation north of Clarksdale. As a little boy he loved playing in creeks and sloughs and mud puddles, hence he was nicknamed Muddy, which later evolved into Muddy Water and finally Muddy Waters. Muddy learned to play the harmonica as a teenager and soon picked up a guitar. He had a small band that played for parties and local Delta blues clubs. His mentors were roaming Delta bluesmen Charlie Patton, Robert Johnson, and Son House. He worked the cotton fields by day and played music by night. Around 1940 Muddy traveled to St. Louis and joined the Silas Lewis Tent Show. It was the era of traveling minstrel shows, and he sang and played harmonica for about a year. Once he returned home, while living in a one-room log house on the Stovall Place, Muddy was recorded by Alan Lomax and John Work for the Library of Congress. These recordings are very instrumental and noteworthy in the annals of the early Delta blues artists.

Muddy knew he had talent and that if he was to succeed professionally as a musician, he had to leave the Delta and head north—north to the blues clubs of

DICK WATERMAN

Chicago where the urban blues was shaping a generation. He took a job at a paper mill during the day and hit the blues clubs at night. Big Bill Broonzy, one of the leading Chicago bluesmen of the time, let Muddy open for him at the raucous clubs. The noise and din in the South Side clubs was overwhelming for Muddy's acoustic guitar style, so his uncle Joe Grant gave him an electric guitar that could be amplified and heard above the noisy and boisterous crowds. Muddy was soon to change the Chicago blues scene with a driving, intense mixture of Mississippi Delta blues and the urban blues of Chicago. He commanded respect and admiration as one who grew up in the sweltering cotton fields of the Delta, while he burst upon the Chicago blues scene with a relentless drive and beat that changed the course of American music. Muddy had arrived, and melodic history was about to be made.

By 1946 he was recording for Columbia Records and eventually Aristocrat Records, run by the Chess brothers, Leonard and Phil. In the early fifties, Muddy hooked up with harmonica player Little Walter along with guitarist Jimmy Rogers and Otis Spann on piano. Songwriter and bass player Willie Dixon joined the band, and several blues classics were recorded including macho songs like, "Hoochie Coochie Man," "I Just Want to Make Love to You," and "I'm Ready" and later "Got my Mojo Working" and "Rolling Stone." Muddy was the man in charge, and in 1958 he traveled across the pond touring England. His loud, electrified, and thunderous blues style helped develop the groundwork for the birth of a blues explosion overseas. Coming home, he played the Newport Jazz Festival and recorded his first live recording, *At Newport 1960.*

Musicians from all genres were taking notice, and his remarkable influence was being fused into not only blues and rhythm and blues but rock and roll, country music, jazz, and folk music. Howling Wolf had moved to Chicago, and between the two they took the South Side clubs by storm as outlying radio stations spun blues infused whirlwinds throughout all corners of America and beyond. Rock and roll was being born and weaned with the blues as its surrogate father. As Muddy later sang, "The blues had a baby and they named it rock 'n' roll."

In Europe, British rock bands were being formed and began dominating the airwaves along with American musicians like Elvis Presley, Chuck Berry, and Bo Diddley. In 1962, a young English garage band named the Blue Boys booked a gig, but when asked what their name was, a Muddy Waters album was lying on the floor and the song "Rolling Stone" caught their attention and they claimed it. The Rolling Stones booked their first gig on July 12, 1962, and thereafter the group was instrumental in making blues an integral part of rock and roll. Today, the industry standard magazine *Rolling Stone* stands as one of the premier music publications.

During this time Muddy Waters toured extensively but never forgot his Chicago roots. Blues harpist Charlie Musselwhite recalls, "Muddy was one of the true kings of the blues. I saw him countless times in Pepper's Lounge on 43rd Street in Chicago in the early '60s. I also saw him play festivals, and the show he did at festivals was nothing like the show he might do at Pepper's. Muddy would tame it down for the festivals. He was kind and generous, and I loved being around him." His early music and amazing stage presence left an impression on young musicians. Jimmy Hendrix recalled, "The first guitar player I was aware of was Muddy Waters. I first heard him as a little boy, and it scared me to death." His music also influenced and helped shape renowned guitarist Eric Clapton and his musical career. The bands Canned Heat, The Allman Brothers, and Steppenwolf, along with Bob Dylan, all used Muddy's material and songs in their respective repertoires. Muddy was influential across a wide range of musicians.

Possibly one of the most widely known appearances of Muddy Waters was recorded in 1976 for posterity by filmmaker Martin Scorsese when Muddy appeared at the Band's farewell concert. Millions of the younger generations are aware of Muddy Waters and his influence on American music by watching, time and again, *The Last Waltz.*

Later on, Muddy teamed up with members of his earlier band, along with his friend and fellow guitarist Johnny Winters from Leland. Johnny helped him produce three of his bestselling albums, *Hard Again, I'm Ready,* and *King Bee.* Johnny Winters and Muddy Waters would travel together and perform throughout the seventies and eighties. His last performance was in June 1982 at an Eric Clapton show. Seventy-year-old Muddy Waters died of a heart attack on April 30, 1983. He was inducted into the Rock and Roll Hall of Fame in 1987 and in 1992 received a Grammy Lifetime Achievement Award. Muddy Waters, the little kid who played in Delta mud puddles and plowed, chopped, and picked cotton, went on to change the face of American music forever.

Gentle Jerry—The Killer's Softer Side

Who's gonna play this old piano after I'm not here.
Who's gonna sing those sad songs to you, cause your eyes to fill with tears...
Who's gonna keep this music going, who will carry on.
Who's gonna play this old piano after the Killer's gone?

– Jerry Lee Lewis

Seventy years ago a five-year-old little boy sat down at a piano and, by ear, pecked out "Silent Night."

That would become one of the most significant moments in the history of rock 'n' roll. Jerry Lee Lewis grew up in the Louisiana Delta in a religious household and large extended family. His folks made tremendous sacrifices to buy him a standup piano when he was eight years old, and he ain't stopped slapping those ivories yet. "I banged on that ole piano until I wore holes through the keys," said the one and only Jerry Lee Lewis, lounging in a recliner at his Nesbit ranch. "My daddy used to say, 'Son, we gonna have to go to bed.' "

Young Jerry Lee was kicked out of school one day when he and his soon to be friend got in trouble for fighting with their teachers. As the two youngsters were walking out, Cecil Harrelson turned and said, "I'll see you later, Killer." And Jerry Lee replied, "Okay, Killer, I'll meet you at the pool hall." That name has never left him.

As a teenager, Jerry Lee was sent to Southwestern Bible College in Waxahachie, Texas. After attending for several months, he was expelled from school for playing a rock 'n' roll version of a favorite gospel hymn. Coming back home to Ferriday, Louisiana, Jerry Lee played with makeshift bands and performed solo at honky tonks and county fairs. His wild, explosive piano playing wowed the crowds, and he knew then that he was meant to be a performer.

During our visit, I asked the Killer if he thought he would be a star. "I KNEW I was going to be a star," he said. "I just couldn't wait 'till I was twenty years old, and I could hit the road to Memphis and Sun Records. I wanted to see Sam Phillips; he was going to make me a star." About Sam Phillips, Jerry Lee, one of the very first performers ever to be inducted into the Rock and Roll Hall of Fame, says, "He still owes me a LOT of money. Sam don't pay, he just records, but he is a genius—pure genius."

The Killer has fond memories of the early rock 'n' rollers from the Sam Phillips/Sun Records days. "Elvis was a good friend of mine; we had some good times together," he said. "Carl Perkins was a very loyal friend. And there was Carl Smith, Eddie Arnold, Conway Twitty, and Johnny Cash. Now, they are all gone." The name of one of his recent albums, *Last Man Standing*, refers to the loss of all those original rock 'n' roll and country pioneers. Jerry Lee Lewis is the only one remaining of the old group.

We talked about his early touring days playing in Mississippi and around Memphis, and he recalled, "We used to have some good times at Hernando's

Hideaway and Bad Bob's. Hernando's Hideaway was the first nightclub in Memphis. I remember playing down in the Delta in Greenville at One Block East. It wasn't the opening of the club, but I remember playing there. We had some fun back then." When I mentioned the hectic and very fast paced lifestyle of an early rock 'n' roller, the Killer just shook his head, winked, and replied, "It wasn't easy!"

Many stories abound of the Killer and his wild and crazy times, but the Jerry Lee Lewis I met is a man of family, devotion, traditions, and certain values. One such value is that he doesn't like to play second fiddle to anyone or as a lead-on to another performer. In his living room during our visit, his son, Lee, reminded his father of one such moment. On a tour with Little Richard and Chuck Berry called the Three Kings Tour, Jerry Lee was asked to play the middle set and let Chuck Berry finish up the show. He agreed in the dressing room before the show that it would be alright. But at the end of the show, when asked to do an encore, the piano-pounding Killer came out and played "Johnny Be Good," the great Chuck Berry hit…on a guitar. Looking over his shoulder at the curtains he shouted, "Follow that, Chuck!" Needless to say, Jerry Lee finished out each show for the rest of the tour.

Now in his golden years, with many golden records adorning his walls, Jerry Lee still plays live on occasion. He had most recently performed at Memphis in May and on the calendar was a sold-out show in Philadelphia, Mississippi. Most of his traveling band lives close by in Memphis. Judith Coghlan, longtime devoted assistant from the Mississippi Delta, says, "The band is very loyal. They almost worship Jerry Lee."

Jerry Lee adds, "I have a lot of fans in Europe, never an empty seat. There is a whole new group of fans, the teenagers. They're great." He doesn't quite understand what the new rock 'n' roll is all about. "I don't really know too much about that stuff. It don't knock me out. I don't think anybody else can figure it out. Man, they are blemishing my country music."

When not touring, the Lewis Ranch is the Killer's home and hideaway. Dogs and horses roam freely, and inside there is a special tile-floored and air-conditioned room for the house dogs. Having only weeks earlier lost his companion and best friend of fourteen years, a chihuahua affectionately named Topaz, Jerry Lee remembers him with great love. Topaz's offspring run freely around the house while colorful paintings of his favorite dog are scattered about. I mentioned that it is said that in a man's life he is due one good dog and one good woman. Reflecting for a moment, the Killer turned towards me with an eyebrow lifted and said, "I've probably had more than one good woman!"

In the little town of Hernando, Mississippi, is an old time dairy bar called the Velvet Crème. It is a frequent destination of Jerry Lee and his entourage during the hot summer months for his favorite treat, a regular dipped ice cream cone. "But in this heat, sometimes it don't work. I just say baloney and throw it out the window!" And on his trips to his hometown of Ferriday, Louisiana, Jerry Lee often stops at Chamoun's Rest Haven in Clarksdale for a chili cheeseburger.

 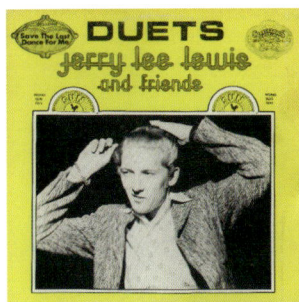 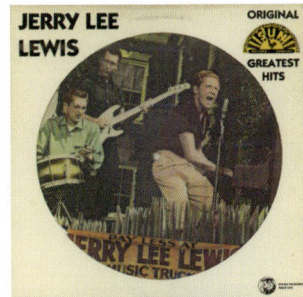

Almost seventy years of rockin' has not tarnished the Killer's love of the music or entertaining. He tours whenever he can and spends his off time at home enjoying his family, friends, and his animals. His life has been filled with ups and downs, successes and some failures, both personal and financial, and he has experienced much heartbreak. Reflecting on those events he states, "It hasn't been an easy trip, but it's been a happy trip. Friends come and go, and I've had a lot of tragedy in my life. I've buried most of my family, but God will make it work for you. He adds a special meaning to it."

At seventy-five, Jerry Lee says his next album will be "an album of gospel songs with a little rock 'n' roll in there to mix it up, while it's probably not appropriate." The name of a song and possibly the album title will be "Lord, I've Tried Every Thing but You!"

Through all the rockin' and rolling, fame and family hardships, how does he want to be remembered? After a moment of intense silence, he replied, "I just want to be remembered as Jerry Lee Lewis...and that's about a mouthful—that's a whole lifetime!"

A Bite to
Eat and Drink
in the Delta

5 O'clock in the Delta

In the early 1800s, Captain Henry Johnson bought from a disreputable fellow (a Mississippi River pirate, actually) named Bunch, the Tomahawk Indian Rights to three thousand acres of prime cotton ground along the north shore of Lake Washington. He paid fifty dollars and a keg of fine Kentucky whiskey for the land, which he later named Chatham Plantation. Such began a lifestyle that continues in the Delta today. Cocktail time, or the 5 o'clock ritual, is observed in many homes and watering holes throughout our beloved flatland. To a degree, it's a part of who we are in many instances because the harshness of the early Delta warranted, if not required, a bit of imbibement and relaxation at the end of an arduous day.

William Faulkner spent a great deal of time in the Delta, hunting and visiting with friends. He once said, "Civilization begins with distillation." Faulkner would have a nip as he wrote in the evenings, "I usually write at night. I always keep my whiskey within reach; so many ideas that I can't remember in the morning pop into my head." (Jerry Lee Lewis may have stated it more succinctly when he sang, "It takes a drink, to make me think, and live it all over again.") Although Faulkner's chosen drink was bourbon and water, the Bard of Oxford's favorite cocktail was the mint julep, prepared simply in a frosted metal cup with bourbon, one teaspoon of sugar, a sprig or two of crushed fresh mint, and ice. "There is no such thing as bad whiskey, some whiskeys just happen to be better than others."

Faulkner's niece, Dean Faulkner Wells, knew that her uncle believed in the medicinal efficacy of alcohol. "Pappy alone decided when a hot toddy was needed, and he administered it to his patient with the best bedside manner of a country doctor, bringing it upstairs on a silver tray and admonishing his patient to drink it quickly, before it cooled off. It never failed!"

Before the days of Prohibition, most Delta towns had saloons on every block. In a cistern beneath the old Weinberg Building in Greenville was found several stoneware whiskey jugs labeled, "Green Rivers Whiskey, the Whiskey without a Headache, made for the Stag Saloon." During Prohibition in order to have a drink outside of your home, you had to be discreet. My mother recalled visiting Frank's Cafe for oyster po'boys with my daddy and slipping Frank Ciolino hooch in a brown paper bag to hide behind the counter. He would then serve you your favorite libation in a coffee cup. Frank's Café was also the place where the sheriff drank his coffee, served, of course, by Frank.

The curtained cubicles of Lusco's in Greenwood were reputedly installed to allow customers to enjoy their toddies and dinner without the prying eyes of snooping neighbors. It has also been told that it was behind the beautiful façade in the present bar in the lobby of the Peabody Hotel where patrons' whiskey was kept hidden and where drinks were poured. During Prohibition, and under the tutelage of Boss Crump, guests of the famed Peabody Hotel had only to walk across the street to the alleyway, named appropriately "Whiskey Chute," buy anything they wanted from

BURDINE FAMILY COLLECTION

Author Hank Burdine's down-home, black walnut-paneled country bar, the original ticket counter to the old C&G Railroad depot in Greenville, complete with a stuffed bullfrog orchestra and Dinty Moore's cash register from the Shady Nook Café in Shaw.

street vendors, and then return to the magnificent lobby for their toddies.

Brucie McKamy Mintz recalls going to the bootleggers with her Grandmother McKamy and being told, "Don't you dare tell anyone where we've been; this is our little secret." And the next day going to the same place with her mother with the same explicit instructions! "You would simply pull up and honk your horn; Snitch knew what you wanted and would bring it out in a brown paper bag. Grandmother drank Old Crow and Mama preferred Early Times." And when traveling with her father Bill McKamy and stopping for dinner, he would always order a gin martini and from the quality of the martini would then decide if the restaurant was worth eating in.

In Cleveland, placed around one bootleggers shack, was a very low white picket fence called a Deacon's Fence. Its purpose was supposedly to keep the tee totaling churchgoers out, but low enough for the church deacons to jump over when need be. The Washington County Board of Supervisors got so tired of complaints by leading ladies of the community of the potholed existence of one particular gravel road that it was ordered paved with asphalt, right to the entrance of the bootlegger's shack.

At Vince's Package Store in Leland, Uncle Tony Giardina held court in his big chair behind the center of the room cubicle where he sat with his huge cash register at his side, greeting the locals and visiting with each one. When a lady walked in, he would point to her desired bottle of choice and instruct his attentive employee "Coondog" to deliver the package to her car. It was not proper for a lady to be seen buying liquor; she was only in the store to visit with Tony.

In Gayden Metcalfe and Charlotte Hays' book *Being Dead is No Excuse*, it is said that in the old days when someone died the first thing you did was call the bootlegger. You never wanted to run out of liquor at a funeral wake. Traditions run deep in the Delta.

During one early morning daylily party my mother hosted in her back yard in the '80s, a friend was overheard ordering a virgin mary from the bartender in the Secret Garden. My mother said, "Now, Julia, you know you shouldn't use our sweet Mother Mary's name in vain like that!" and Julia responded, "Well, Baby Jane, what should I call a bloody mary without vodka in it?" Turning to walk away, my mother replied, "Well, I would call that a bloody shame!" Baby Jane had two scotch and milks every night and lived to be eighty-seven years old. Her bones were in excellent health when she passed.

As there were speakeasies during the days of Prohibition, where gambling, entertainment and drinking were secretly hidden away, today there are private clubs, bars, and drinking rooms tucked away in towns across the Delta. Elks Clubs, country clubs, and private watering holes are cherished places of contentment where you can go and quench your thirst, maybe shuffle a deck of cards or chase the galloping dominoes. One such private club belongs to my cousin Bard Selden outside of Hollywood and is called Borneo Moon. It is a quaint cypress tenant shack tucked off the side of the highway. A story often repeated there during times of revelry is of a very prominent Delta planter whose new wife "tried to free him from the entangling tentacles of liquor." She sought the aid of the local courts but found it very difficult because she was not able to find a judge that would hear her case nor an attorney that would prosecute her erudite, well-known, and prevalent husband. Finally, she hired a prosecutor on the Gulf Coast and found a judge that would hear her cause. The farmer decided to represent himself and was called to the witness stand. When the fresh, young prosecutor asked the somber Delta planter if he drank alcohol he responded,

"Yes."

"How much do you drink?"

"I drink as much as I want to."

"Do you drink as much as a pint of whiskey a day?"

"Sir, I spill a pint of whiskey a day!"

Needless to say, he was committed to a private institution to free himself from the grasps of the evil spirits. However, after three days, the farmer called his chauffeur and instructed him to drive to Jackson where he broke out and returned to his plantation and home by the river, and the matter was never raised again.

It is widely understood that drinking is a very private affair. Some people refuse to drink alone while others look forward to the peace and consolation of a dram or two and their time of quiet reflection. One dear friend from Leland often stated, "The Delta breeds some professional drinkers." Life in the Delta is not all moonlight and magnolias. The harshness of working the land and having to do so faced with all kinds of uncertainties lends credence to the fact that sometimes a nip or two is needed to clear one's mind and garner a bit of solitude in the evening. But the reality of this can also lead to troublesome times and horrible addiction in many instances. Jimmy Phillips alludes to this fact when he sings in his song "Whiskey," "Bottle of pleasure, bottle of pain, hold me together in my hour of shame..."

When my wife Sallie and I moved to Colorado with our children, the word soon got out amongst the locals and new arrivals from California and elsewhere that, "Hank, you know, drinks that hard liquor." (They drank mostly beer and wine.) At one gathering a proper lady who had just moved into the Wet Valley from San Francisco asked me, "Do a lot of people drink where you come from?" I responded, "Madame, I come from the Mississippi Delta, and I can honestly say that I don't know many people that just don't drink. I know a lot of people that just can't drink anymore."

So what is the drink of choice of folks in the Delta? In the days of old, Old Crow bourbon was known as the Delta Bird and a proper martini was never made with vodka, only Gordon's or Beefeater's gin. My daddy drank scotch, the Dimple Pinch by Haig&Haig, and I acquired a taste for it early on in my life by jumping up in his lap and snitching an ice cube out of his silver tumbler and sucking on it, savoring the sweetness and icy bite of the fine blended whisky. Today, summertime brings out gin and tonics, mimosas, and mint juleps. The fall football and hunting seasons lean toward the heavier bourbons.

Will Gault, owner of Vince's Restaurant and Martini Bar, says that today's Deltan leans towards Jack Daniels, Crown Royal, and Maker's Mark in bourbons while Dewar's, Chivas Regal, and a host of single malts reign supreme in the scotches. Delta ladies enjoy mojitos and flavored-vodka martinis. Many times sweet brandy or bourbon laced with orange liqueur is relished on cold winter mornings in a duck blind with friends, once the shooting has stopped.

I remember as a child during Christmas season delivering nicely wrapped bottles of fine sherry to sweet little old ladies to keep in their closets for their nightcaps before retiring in the evening. There is a story of one young Delta girl visiting friends up north and when asked what she would like to drink replied, "I believe I'll have a patch," referring to what she had heard her parents say many times when they wanted another libation.

Ferd Moyse III would always have a drink on hand while he prepared for a formal affair. With his "dresser" close by, he would prim and primp until his bow tie was just right, taking a sip as he dashingly admired himself in the mirror.

There are many divergent views and feelings about liquor, ranging, according to Soggy Sweat, from the "devil's brew, the poison scourge" to the "oil of conversation, the philosophic wine." Certain church affiliations adamantly reject or respect the right to imbibe. I remember one esteemed member of St. James' Episcopal Church who would leave the Communion rail after receiving his sacraments, putting aside the remainder of the service, to go home immediately in order to prepare the martinis for his fellow parishioners who he had invited over after church.

My friend Gene Ham has written about his astute grandmother and the wife of three-time mayor of Greenville. "Grandfather was known as a 'side door Episcopalian' while Grandmother was one of the women who founded and foistered the growth of the First Baptist Church. She was a prodigious worker who not only discouraged but kept temperance pledges out of that early congregation, a rare accomplishment likely only in the Delta."

Among the early Delta Baptists, there was a secret doctrine that "salvation flows through the loins of the righteous" and "each was a church unto himself." Gene never had any doubt about his uncle C. M.'s church affiliation. On one trip across the river to deliver a piece of restored furniture, the eight-year-old boy was mannerly, listened gravely, and spoke only when spoken to. At some juncture the nice lady asked, "You are an Episcopalian, aren't you Mr. Ham?" Gene was alert when his uncle turned to him and requested, "Boy, tell the lady what your uncle's religious connection is." Gene respectfully replied, "Why, my uncle is a drinking Baptist, ma'am!"

Doe's Eat Place—A Cut Above
Dining at the most famous little steakhouse in the world

Doe's Eat Place, 502 Nelson Street, Greenville, Mississippi, is considered by Michael and Jane Stern, and many other belly-rubbing food connoisseurs, to be the "finest steakhouse in America." Anybody that is anybody, and travels through the Mississippi Delta, will eat at Doe's. No fanfare, no matching tablecloths, just the friendliest atmosphere and the best food that you will ever set your choppers into.

"Big Doe" (Dominick Signa) opened up in 1941 serving local black customers hot tamales and boot-legged beer out of the front of his store while his white friends came in the back to sit and eat in his kitchen. Today, Doe's is a bastion of equality as patrons and employees greet each other with smiles and hugs.

My mother recollected the times when you had to stop at Joe Bordelon's Gulf Station before you came to Doe's to use the rest room because the kids were asleep in the side room. That was the bedroom and entrance to the only bathroom. Miss Mamie would not let you run the risk of waking up the children. Mama said Joe Bordelon's place was always chosen because he had the only heated toilet seat in Greenville!

Doe's is a brown bag kind of place, meaning they don't serve liquor, only beer. But you can bring your own, and if you forget, or, God forbid, you run out, there is always a box of leftovers in the corner. I've shared a beer with Willie Nelson in the kitchen, supped next to sitting senators, read the *Rolling Stone* review of President Bill Clinton recorded at Doe's in Little Rock, and was horrified when Liza Minnelli was quite

GREG CAMPBELL/COURTESY OF DELTA MAGAZINE

Simply seasoned and tagged per order, the out-of-this-world hunks of meat—filets, ribeye, and porterhouse—at Doe's Eat Place await their turn on the broiler.

rude and made Aunt Mattie cry when she asked her for an autograph.

Doe's is the first place I ever took my wife Sallie. And the night we were married my majordomo John Johnson set up bar in the back room, and we held our wedding reception there. It's also the place where we gathered twenty years later and celebrated Sallie's life. Such is the cycle of life at Doe's.

I doubt the Texas Panhandle could hold all the cows it has taken to produce the "Slap yo' Mama" steaks that have been run through that blast furnace stove up front. Millions upon millions of dollars worth of towing contracts on the Mississippi River have been consummated with nothing more than a handshake and the promise of a steak at Doe's whenever the bosses met in Greenville. I even won a $1,000 bet with a local steel magnate, recorded in the guest register, as to when, or if ever, I would get married. I won that bet hands down and early on canceled the balance due when the first case of Chivas Regal showed up at my office.

Doe's has always been staffed with kinfolks. Aunt Mattie, Aunt Rosalie, Aunt Florence, and now "Sug" Signa have stood guard over the humongous wooden salad bowl with long wooden spoons as their scepters. Never have any tablecloths matched nor have the silverware and plates coincided, mainly because Robert May always supplied whatever he had left over from his dry goods store. The floors creak, and the roof leaks on occasion, but you have never had as much fun, or felt as much at home, as when you are in Doe's.

I have often seen a man from Houston that would fly his own plane in just to sit and eat a three-pound sirloin, raw, with french fried potatoes and hot tamales on the side. And you will never see local attorney Frank Thackston walk through the kitchen without grabbing a handful of uncooked potatoes, crunching on them as he looks for his table. Never have I passed the salad bowl myself without one of the ladies digging in and handing me a lettuce heart.

Many years ago, I had a standing date with Mimi Cefalu whenever she was at home in Leland from New York City. Mimi was quite a successful model on Fifth Avenue but never lost her Italian roots or her love for the Delta. We would always go to one of the three "Big O's" whenever she was in town, Lillo's, Lusco's, or Doe's. There was a note on my desk one afternoon around Christmas that simply said, "Hey, 'Running Bear,' I'm home! Let's do Doe's."

I picked up Mimi, and we headed to Nelson Street, stopping at Chillie's Package Store on the way. With expert ease, she picked the wine she liked while I grabbed a bottle of Dewar's scotch. Pulling my truck up on the curb, we headed into the awaiting arms of the extended Signa family, full of hugs and kisses and warm greetings. We walked straight to my usual table right in the middle of the kitchen as Aunt Rosalie re-arranged newspapers, coffee cups, and ashtrays. Aunt Mattie slid over to sit next to me. Mimi immediately began talking about things Italian with the ladies and telling stories of her high fashion career in the Big Apple as I got up and looked for the corkscrew. Salads were brought along with a steaming plate of hot tamales smothered in chili. Doe knows what I want, so I never have to order. He was already cutting my steak off of the side of beef hanging in the cooler.

We settled into a wonderful evening at Doe's. Soon, Stanley Sherman wheeled by and took up his station at the adjoining table. The proverbial custom of table-hopping and convivial conversations was in full force as Stanley's steak was delivered to his table before ours. Mimi's beautiful brown eyes bugged out as she smacked her lips and said, "WHAT is that?"

Judy was delivering Stanley's usual order, a "garlic steak." Doe will take an immense amount of crushed fresh garlic and completely coat both sides of a two-pound porterhouse, crystallizing the garlic as he sears the steak, which holds in all the juices. Mimi's nose was in the air following that steak like a bird dog hot on a covey of quail. She asked if she could have a bite. Stanley obliged and cut a big slug out of the filet and passed it over from his table on a fork. Mimi closed her eyes as she began to chew on that "Hunk-a-Heaven" with steak juice and bits of garlic drooling down her lovely chin. Soon she opened her eyes, wiping her mouth on her shirtsleeve, and looked at me and said, "Damn! A man that eats a garlic steak at Doe's Eat Place couldn't get a date anywhere but Leland, Mississippi!"

Bone Appetit'!

Meet Me at Mink's
Swingin' and swayin' in the dance hall days at Mink's Supper Club

Mink's Supper Club was located on Highway 82 halfway between Leland and Greenville on the banks of Black Bayou. According to Kathryn Bibb from Hollandale, a devoted regular at the club, Mink's was loaded with superb dining, fun times, great dance bands, and lots of belly-rubbing music. Mississippi was a dry state during Mink's heyday, but suffice to say that was definitely not a problem. You brought your own liquor from the bootlegger, and Mink sold you set ups. Or Mink would sell you liquor by the bottle brought over from Lake Providence, Louisiana, making as much money on the ice and set ups as he did on the liquor. Mink Mauceli saw to it that everybody had fun.

In typical dance hall style, Mink's had a large dance floor with an elevated and spotlighted bandstand. The dance floor was surrounded by dining tables. A long bar stood against the wall next to the front door. Mink's opened up early and stayed open late. Normal hours on the weekend were 4 p.m. to 1 a.m., but that could change, depending on the band and the customers' wishes.

Mink's was quite popular with the towboat captains and boat crews of the time. During their mandated days off the river, they had "money in their pockets and time on their hands." Mink's was a wonderful gathering place for the often rough-and-tumble river men. Even though Mink's was a highly respectable place, fights were numerous in the evenings as fisticuffs flew over amorous triangles and snide remarks among the locals. Once Captain George Reid of Brent Towing Company asked Mink why he didn't stop all that fighting. Mink replied, "Cap'm George, them boys will put knots on your head faster than you can rub 'em!" One night after a fight, Mink told Allen Neal, brother of Ergon towboat Captain Jackie Neal, "Allen, I can grow me some more skin, but these posts are costing me a fortune!"

Big Earl Williams from Hollandale was hired to be the bouncer. His nickname was "Tanglewood." Soon, the fights began to slow down. However, the weekend of the Arkansas-Ole Miss football game was the worst weekend of business. According to Pete "Uncle Fish" Mauceli, "All it took was one Whooee PIG, Sooie!, and the fight was on!"

Italian dishes, seafood, and steaks were splendidly prepared by head cook Minnie Lee Williams. Often, parents would bring their teenaged children out to dance and have dinner. You never knew whom you were going to see at Mink's, but everybody just about knew each other.

One of Mink's three daughters recalls that Mink's first cousin Frank "Jughead" Signa gave Mink his nickname, as he did everyone of his friends. Jughead (aptly nicknamed after he stood up into a wire containing 10,000 volts of electricity while working for a power company and had to wear a turban-style dressing for a time) said that his deep brown eyes and narrow nose reminded him of a mink! Florence Signa, Jughead's wife, remembers that even though she and Frank never spent much

Located between Leland and Greenville, Mink's Supper Club pictured in full swing back in 1958.

time out at Mink's, they were the best of friends. "Mink was such a fun person and he wanted everybody around him to have fun." Big Doe Signa, brother of Jughead and founder of Doe's Eat Place, and Mink often traveled to Hot Springs to the horse races. While visiting the extravagant clubs in the Ozarks, they were exposed to some of the big name bands traveling around the South.

The Greenville Air Force Base was in full operation during and after WWII, and many of the swing bands would swing through Greenville to perform at the Air Base, the VFW, and the American Legion. Mink would hire them to play at his supper club, and folks from all over the Delta would come to "Swing and Sway with Sammy Kaye." Glenn Miller's Band, minus Glenn Miller who had been killed in a plane crash en route to a gig, was one of the favorites. However, it was Vicksburg's own Red Tops that was the premier band at Mink's. During those days, when the Red Tops played, you weren't from Greenwood or Clarksdale or Cleveland, you were from the Delta, and you showed up wherever the Red Tops performed. You might dance with a cute planter's daughter from Tutwiler while at the country club in Rosedale one weekend and not get her name, but no matter because if the Red Tops were playing at Mink's the next weekend, she would be there! Gus Johnson of Jim's Cafe in Greenville recalls, "I was going to school at Ole Miss at the time. All I had to do when I heard the Red Tops were going to be at Mink's was call and tell him how many I was bringing. My table was always right next to the bandstand loaded with set ups. Man, did we have some fun!"

Other bands would also play at Mink's. The Burt Taggart Band from Greenville and D.D. Ferracci from Shaw often shared the limelight with a youngster from Leland. Joe Frank Carollo and the Knights were up and coming in the rhythm and blues venue. Ike and Tina Turner were Mink's close friends and played to big crowds often. Mink's son, Mike Mauceli, recalls that his daddy and Homer Luxford bought Ike his first electric guitar. And one of Mike's sisters remembers her father used to visit with Tina on some of his trips to Las Vegas.

In 1956, the Tennessee Williams screenplay *Baby Doll* was being filmed on location in Benoit, Mississippi. Director Elia Kazan and actors Karl Malden, Carroll Baker, and Eli Wallach were regulars at Mink's along with many of the film crew. Brodie Crump from Greenville and "Charlie Boy" Williams of Benoit acted out parts in the film. There is a picture of the cast in New York City at their local watering hole, personally inscribed as Mink's Supper Club, Brooklyn, New York. Needless to say, Mink's was held in very high esteem not only by locals but by many that passed through the Mississippi Delta.

Mink was a "first born in America," his parents having been Italian immigrants. He would bring his kids out to "the place" on Sunday and let them play while he cleaned up and got ready for another "night at Mink's." Cheryl Cobianchi remembers her daddy bringing her out early to hear the more popular bands and musicians warm up before the crowds came and how exciting that was to her and the other kids. Mink's other daughters, Dorothy Andrus and Becky Fitts, recall coming out and playing on the bandstand and singing in the microphones in the spotlight while their daddy cleaned up from the night before. All of the Mauceli kids were taught to shoot by setting up the empty beer bottles out back on the bank of Black Bayou and plinking at them with their daddy's .22 caliber rifle.

Sometime during the '60s Mink's changed hands, either as a gift or through a sale to Alphonse Carollo, changing the name to Al's Supper Club, and the beat went on. However, the club soon burned to the ground and was never rebuilt.

But "the place" will always be remembered as Mink's, where the Red Tops played all night. According to Howard Brent, when Rufus McKay would sing the last song of the evening, "Danny Boy," every chair in the joint was empty. No one danced, but everyone gathered close around the bandstand, swaying together as Rufus sang his heart out. The song brought tears to everyone's eyes and a hug to everyone's chest. Choking up, Howard recalled, "I could not hold my breath as long as Rufus could sing that last note."

Indeed, "Meet me at Mink's" was the word of the day back then! Oh, where have all the good times gone?

Dinty Moore's Shady Nook Café

Dinty Moore was a Delta icon. Dinty Moore loved to work hard. Dinty Moore loved beautiful women most of all!

Way back in the early 1930s, Dinty Moore opened a small one-room café in Shaw, Mississippi. He catered to farmers, railroad workers, and road builders that got up early and had breakfast before daybreak. He opened up his café by 4:30 every morning.

I remember a story told to me by one of our road superintendents, Mr. Freeman Ward. Mr. Ward was raised in Anguilla, Mississippi, and went to work at the icehouse in Shaw during the thirties for twenty-five cents an hour and all the ice he could eat. He had a hardy breakfast at the Shady Nook Café every morning.

During that time, my daddy was building Highway 61 through town and was living in the Shaw Hotel. He and Mr. Ward would have breakfast together at the Shady Nook. It was not long after they met that Mr. Ward became the payroll clerk for Burdine Construction Company. In the middle of the Depression, things were very tight, and Mr. Ward often told the story of inventory control during hard times. It seems that whenever you would order eggs and bacon, Dinty would take his apron off, don his hat, and walk across the street to the Chinese grocery store and buy his supplies and come back and cook your breakfast. He was not going to tie any of his money up in inventory in his own icebox!

The author (at far left) and friends pose with the infamous Dinty Moore at Shady Nook in the early '80s.

BURDINE FAMILY COLLECTION

Dinty continued to feed the locals all during World War II and began going to the Miss America Pageant soon thereafter. The only time he would close his café was when he was in Atlantic City. It was his only vacation each year and an outing that he loved dearly. For forty years Dinty made his annual trek to view the most beautiful women in America. And he always came home with autographed pictures, especially of Miss Mississippi, to adorn the walls of the Shady Nook!

During the '70s, Dinty met Miss Mississippi Mollie Magee, soon to become the wife of Billy Van Devender of Jackson, Mississippi. Mollie and Dinty became very close friends, and she often visited in Shaw during her many travels throughout the state. After Mollie and Billy were married, Dinty never referred to Billy by name, only to call him "that other man." Needless to say, Billy did not make many trips to Shaw with Mollie.

Mollie and Sallie Van Devender decided to take a Caribbean cruise one year and asked "Dinty Daddy" if he would accompany them as their husbands were busy with business. Dinty readily accepted and off they flew to the beautiful tropical islands.

Always the proverbial Southern gentleman, Dinty would only loosen his tie and roll up his long-sleeved shirt a couple of turns, as Mollie and Sallie sunbathed on either side of him in their respective bikinis! In his late seventies, the proprietor of the Shady Nook was very well entertained by his attendants in their twenties, and a wonderful cruise was had by all!

During the turbulent civil rights era of the sixties, a decision had to be made as to whether the Shady Nook would continue as a restaurant, open to the public, or become a private club and cater only to the customers who had supported Dinty for thirty years. The Shady Nook Key Club was formed, and all of the regulars were given keys to unlock the one-way mirrored door. You could see out, but you could not see in! This arrangement continued for over twenty years and was never contested.

During the early '80s, Dinty became ill and had to be hospitalized. We kept the Shady Nook open with the sweet black lady that cooked there continuing to run things, and everyone just put what they thought they owed in the cash register. All of Dinty's friends traveled to Greenville and visited him in the hospital.

Many nights, my wife Sallie and I would stop by the hospital late in the evening and check on Dinty. Several times we noticed a black orderly in his room holding his hand and praying with him. This man would help Dinty during the day with his personal needs and then would come back in the evening after work to pray with him. I did not think this strange at all because Dinty was a devoutly religious man.

Dinty died shortly thereafter, and a beautiful funeral was held in Shaw with his family and all of his friends attending. Several days later, I stopped by the Shady Nook and found Dinty's family going through all the memorabilia acquired from over fifty years of running a small town café. The typewriter that he used every day to type out his menus went to his son Dana. I was given the small National Cash Register along with the ominous blue sign that stated "We Reserve the Right to Refuse Service to Anyone." I saw to it that all of the Miss Mississippi and Miss America items went to Mollie and the Miss Mississippi Pageant in Vicksburg.

Behind the counter was an empty five-gallon wooden nail keg with a Naugahyde cushion attached to the top, and burned into the side of it in bold black letters was "Dinty's Prayer Stool." Dinty's knees had given out on him after so many years of standing behind his lunch counter, and he could no longer kneel down at work and say his daily prayers. His dear friend Mr. Grady Simpson, owner of the Shaw Lumber Company, made Dinty this prayer stool so he could sit down and pray.

I remembered standing at the gravesite several days before, and I thought of the kind black orderly that had held his hand and prayed with Dinty as he lay dying. We had all stood around the grave as we sang those great words...

"Amazing Grace, how sweet the sound, that saved a wretch like me...
I once was lost, but, now I'm found, I was blind, but now I see..."
Guess who received "Dinty's Prayer Stool" as a gift?

The Delta Deep Fried
Birth of a battered classic at The Hollywood Café

The girl on the couch under the pay phone was nursing a hangover when she hollered to Tait Selden, cook at The Hollywood Café in Hollywood, Mississippi, "Hey, Taterbug, fry me up a pickle!"

"How you do that?" Tait asked.

The recovering lady said, "Quarter it, and flour it, and throw it in some hot grease, and bring it to me."

Tait did just that, but it wasn't worth eating. However, the next week, Tait's brother Chad stopped by, and they worked on the recipe. Slicing the dill pickle in rounds "about the size of a bo dollar" and battering them in a thin beer batter with garlic, Tabasco, and red pepper and then dropping them in 375-degree grease would make the pickle "puff up" and cook the pickle real quick and did not leave a heavy batter that would slide off in your mouth and burn you. You just bit right through it and enjoyed. As such was born the fried dill pickle at the Hollywood Café.

Previous to the fried pickle becoming a phenomenom, The Hollywood was a beer joint started in 1969 in the old commissary, circa 1856, owned by the Selden family. Bard Selden, enrolled at Ole Miss before he went on to law school, started the joint to help make ends meet and give everyone a nice place to have a cold one. Paneled completely in beautiful pecky cypress, The Hollywood served cold beer and Stewart sandwiches heated up in a little convection oven along with a cheese and pickle plate. "Baby Gayle" Mangum bought the business from Bard and started a restaurant, renaming it The Hollywood Café.

Prior to his stint as "Chef de Taterbug," Tait was working loading pillows in a pillow truck at Tunica's Pillowtex manufacturing plant. Business began to pick up with carloads of Northwest College students converging after class and on the weekends. The fried dill pickle was an instant success. "It was the perfect machine. Eat hot pickle, drink cold beer. Eat more hot pickles, drink more cold beer!" Tait recalls.

Bob Hall bought The Hollywood Café in 1973, and Tait went on to Memphis to work as a bartender at Silky's in Overton Square. Bob improved the menu, and the Hollywood Café evolved into a dinner dance hall. Bob Hall employed Tunica's own Turnrow Cowboys as the house band, and things began to rock. One night Bob Hall, a singer himself, was crooning in the Holiday Inn lounge in Helena, Arkansas, when he met Muriel Wilkins, and each of their lives was changed forever. Muriel came over and played piano and sang, and busloads of patrons from Memphis trekked down to dine and dance the night away at The Hollywood Café.

But the old wooden commissary burned down one night in 1984, and Bob "Hollywood" Hall sold the rights and business to the Owen family for a dollar, and the Hollywood Café was moved to Robinsonville and set up in an old concrete block commissary. Muriel came along also, and one night a young singer/songwriter named Marc Cohn stopped by, and history was made when he wrote about his experience in his Grammy award-winning song "Walking in Memphis." The Hollywood Café and the fried dill pickle continue to live on with the spirit of Muriel Wilkins looking over all.

Delta Hospitality on the Mississippi Gulf Coast
*Like the Mississippi Delta, family traditions and landmarks die hard
on the Mississippi Gulf Coast. Thankfully, we still have Mary Mahoney's
to greet us with open arms in the spirit of Mary herself.*

I remember a sweet and cute Chi Omega sorority gal from Biloxi telling me during our last year at Ole Miss many moons ago, "Hank, you know there are only three regions in Mississippi: the Delta, the Coast, and the Hills—and there is not much difference between the first two!"

I never really understood exactly what she meant until years later when Burdine Construction Company was paving the approaches and parking aprons on the weigh stations of Interstate I-10 on the Coast, the last connecting link from the Atlantic to the Pacific Ocean. My fiancée Sallie was still living in Miami, and I was lonesome, missing her and missing home. Many nights I just wanted to get in my truck and drive to Greenville to Doe's Eat Place, knowing the warmth and welcome I would receive there. But Doe's was five hours away.

I had been to an old restaurant in Biloxi on Highway 90 years before that had a lovely dark bar up front, and I remembered having happy times there. So it was there at Mary Mahoney's Old French House that I would go after work during the week. I got to know Mary and her son Bob personally, and they got to know me, and what I liked to drink and eat. So when I couldn't go home to the outstretched arms of Aunt Florence at Doe's, it was Mary that would greet me at the door with a hug and Bob that would make my drink from a bottle they kept of my favorite scotch behind the bar. Sallie would come and visit on some weekends, and she was taken in by the Mahoney family with love and warmth just like I was.

Mary Mahoney's Old French House Restaurant is located in one of the earliest houses built in America, constructed sometime around 1737 during the French occupation of the Coast.

Designed and built of French architecture, the lovely home has high ceilings reminiscent of French Quarter apartments in New Orleans. Constructed of handmade bricks with huge hand hewn and wooden pegged cypress columns and roofed with slate brought over from France, the home was built to last. And last it has through almost 280 years and many gales and hurricanes, most notably Camille in 1969 and Katrina in 2005, receiving a direct hit both times.

Katrina was the most costly and destructive hurricane ever recorded in the United States. With 130 mph sustained winds and a twenty-eight-foot tidal surge, the storm wreaked havoc up and down the Coast. Mary Mahoney's received severe damage, but the old home stood the test of time and the wrath of Katrina to open her doors again within nine weeks of the water receding. Today she is resplendent in her glory and beauty, and one can only thank Mary Mahoney's forward-thinking dreams for that.

Predating American independence by almost forty years, Governor Jean Baptiste

Bienville commanded the entire Louisiana Territory from his quarters there. Other residents of the home were of Spanish, German, and English nationalities. It remained a residence until 1962 when Pennsylvania Irishman Bob and Yugoslavian descendent Mary Mahoney, and her brother Andrew Cvitanovich, bought the home.

Prior to that, Mary's husband Bob was the night auditor at a Biloxi hotel. When the opportunity arose, he insisted that Mary take over the lounge. She contended to her husband that she knew nothing about making a drink, and Bob replied, "Just bat those pretty eyes at them and ask what goes in their drink, and they will be happy to tell you." Thus began the career of one of the most respected, beloved, and successful hostesses in the South.

As a fourteen-year-old child, Mary was tutored by Father Mullen of St. Michael's Catholic Church, her priest and mentor. He introduced her to, and she read ravenously, the *New York Times Magazine* every week. According to her son Bob, by the time she went to work in her own lounge, she had a "doctorate degree in social endeavors!" Delicious food, music, and art were her specialties, and she chased those muses her entire life. Mary Mahoney was beautiful, gracious, vivacious, and voracious. She was outgoing and greeted each customer personally and made them feel at home. Those qualities allowed her to become a well-known and endeared personality, and they were instrumental to her success as a restaurateur. In 1982 Mary Mahoney was the first woman in Mississippi to be named Business Person of the Year.

In 1963, Mary lost her lease on the lounge she had been managing, and the decision was made to open Mary Mahoney's Old French House Restaurant in the family's newly acquired property. She stated, "Previously, I was not in the lounge business to make money, I just got into it to talk to people." Now, she was opening a full-scale restaurant and bar with opening night jitters. "I had no money, no knowledge, and no sense!" One patron wrote in her earliest guest book, "She has nowhere to go but up."

One evening a piano player asked her what was bothering her. Mary replied that most people that came into her lounge were artists of some sort. "I can't sing, I can't draw, I can't play any musical instrument, I can't do anything." The piano player responded, "Mary, you can go up and down this bar and talk to people and make them smile and be happy. THAT is your talent!" One artist came in that painted big and colorful portraits, but Mary did not have the resources to have one commissioned. The artist asked her if she had any cold beer and then proceeded to return to Mary Mahoney's where she drank beer and painted three beautiful portraits of Mary.

Today, Mary Mahoney's is being run by second-and third-generation family. The old home is resplendent in glamour, good taste, and exceptionally good food. Upon entering the downstairs bar, you feel a sensation and aura of hominess, warmth, and joviality. Sallie and I always spent time there first, then opted to eat in the quiet, peeling brick-walled, and somewhat romantic servant's quarters. The larger room with the big fireplace was once the kitchen, and the smaller room with the smaller fireplace was the servant's bedroom. You can choose to dine out in the personally

MARY MAHONEY FAMILY COLLECTION

Located just off the I-110 interchange with Highway 90 in Biloxi, Mary Mahoney's Old French House Restaurant has stood the test of time and hurricanes for 280 years.

designed New Orleans flavored courtyard or the front porch dining area, the floor of which is covered with four-inch thick slate brought from France as ballast on a sailing ship, or the carriage house dining area, adorned with thirty-three original oil paintings of prominent Mississippi Gulf Coast locations. The house and all dining areas are guarded by a huge live oak tree named The Patriarch. This sprawling tree is a registered live oak considered by four different certified foresters to be more than two thousand years old.

And the food, well, it is none other than superlative. The freshest of fresh seafood is only used. Flounder, seasonal lemon fish (cobia), and red snapper are stuffed with lump crabmeat, shrimp, and crawfish etouffee. Oysters, lobster, and escargot, crab claws, steaks, chicken, and pork chops share the billing with the world famous seafood gumbo. (Denzel Washington, after eating there one evening, ordered ten gallons to be shipped to three different locations.) And Yugoslavian born Chef Georgo's Veal Antonio, "succulent, tender, milk-fed veal, pan fried and enhanced with a variety of cheeses, then topped with sautéed lump crabmeat and served with pasta," is a reason to keep coming back.

Busboys become waiters, waiters become staff, and most employees stay on to serve thirty years or more. Mary Mahoney's is family, family to all who work there and to all who come through her doors. Mary's grandchildren can't wait to be old enough to become a part of the tradition.

In an epitaph to his friend Mary, John Micheal O'Keefe wrote, "There were never patrons or clients eating at Mary Mahoney's Old French House. There were only friends, new friends and old friends. A meal was an introduction to Mary and a spirited conversation about your life and her life. Of course, she wanted to know if the food was good, but more than that, she wanted to know about you."

I happened to be in Biloxi several years ago and stopped by about cocktail time. I had heard that Mary had been gone since 1985. As I walked out of the blazing sun and into the cool darkness, Mary's son Bob looked up at me from behind the bar and then walked to the far end, reaching deep under the counter. He poured a drink of my favorite scotch and slid it across the bar with a smile and an outstretched greeting hand. "Hank, I have not seen you in a very long time. How have you been? How is Sallie? We all used to have a lot of fun in here."

I told him that we had moved to Colorado and then to Florida and that my Sallie had gone to join his Mama and I had now moved our family back to the Delta. We were exchanging condolences when a couple came in the front door. As Bob walked to greet them, he turned around to me, winked, and said, "Welcome home, my friend."

The Legacy of Lillo's

Beer joint, dance hall, pizza place, or family restaurant all describe Lillo's Restaurant at one time. But "family restaurant with quality food" was what founders Jimmy and Conchetta Lillo dreamed of having when they opened the doors on Highway 82 outside of Leland in 1948. However, it didn't quite start that way.

Born in Benoit, Mississippi, young Jimmy Lillo migrated to New Jersey for a while working in a factory. It was there he was introduced to "pizza pie" and given the recipe and taught how to cook it. When he broke his leg, Jimmy Lillo returned to Leland and worked for the Ben Walker and Cameron Dean families of Tribbett. Soon he ran the commissary store later known as Cefalu's Grocery, met his wife Conchetta, and married in Leland.

Across from the store was the American Legion building that had been used for USO entertainment, complete with the maple wood floor that is still in use today. Jimmy Lillo dreamed of opening a restaurant in the big building, at that time being run as the Wise Inn Steak House. However, after leaving the store, he farmed about 1,140 acres of Delta land on Black Bayou and made a "beautiful crop" of cotton. But the worms also thought that cotton was beautiful, and they moved in and ate it up, leaving him only a quarter bale of cotton per acre. Jimmy Lillo lost everything.

But the Italian-American could not be beat. He learned of a restaurant in Greenville next to Jim's Café named the Magnolia Lounge and was able to acquire it. Learning from the cooks and waitresses, Jimmy Lillo plunged in "not knowing a thing about restaurants." And in six months' time he had lost $6,000.

While traveling back and forth from Leland each day to the Magnolia Lounge in Greenville, the Lillos would pass Mr. Wise driving to Leland. Conchetta Lillo thought it would be a good idea to trade restaurants and was able to talk Mr. Wise into the idea. By selling his equity in three houses and with the help of several Lelanders, Jimmy and Conchetta Lillo became the proud owners of the old American Legion complete with big porches, dance floor, and a full-size swimming pool! The swimming pool had no filters, pumps, or restrooms, but was soon fixed up and later leased to the City of Leland as a public pool.

Son Johnny Lillo not only worked in the restaurant but also gave swimming lessons. In a Feburary 4, 1981, article in the *Delta Democrat-Times* by Lynn Lafoe, Conchetta Lillo recalled, "I can still feel my heart fluttering when I think about the children swimming. I'd be inside the kitchen stirring up a spaghetti sauce, and I could hear the children in the pool. I was so afraid something would happen, but we never had an accident."

The majority of Lillo's business came from the Greenville Air Base with the young pilots bringing dates from the Delta to dance and enjoy the "pizza pie" that was served. Lillo's became one of the most popular dinner/dance halls in the Delta. In order to get away from the "beer hall" atmosphere of the old Wise Inn, the bootlegged beer went, and a four-dollar per couple cover charge was imposed. The cover charge mostly paid for the band with little leftover for the restaurant. After that, a minimum of one dollar per person was charged, and by ordering a sandwich and a few Cokes, customers could "eat up the dollar."

Soon, Lillo's started imposing "rules," and singles were excluded, unless they came to eat, and couples were the only patrons allowed. However, there would be no cursing and no "smooching." Coats and ties were required for the young men, and ladies could only wear dresses. One Delta belle, upon returning from Paris where the fashionable "pants suit" was in vogue and having acquired a very nice suit, was asked by Mr. Lillo to sit down because ladies were not allowed on his dance floor in pants. Not one to miss out on all the fun, she simply retired to the ladies room and removed the pants part of her outfit and continued dancing the night away! Johnny Lillo was responsible for most of the rules. "It kept out any rough ones."

The Red Tops from Vicksburg played often, and they packed the house from 1953 until the mid-70s. Joe Cary once stated, "Back in the '50s we didn't live in Greenwood or in Cleveland or in Clarksdale, we lived in the Delta. And where the Red Tops played, we went. We would take an extra suit and change at intermission because we were always wringing wet. What memories. We just danced the night away. We knew everybody from everywhere."

Jimmy Dorsey performed there occasionally sharing billings with other Delta dinner/dance halls such as Mink's Supper Club between Leland and Greenville.

Marie Lillo, the only daughter of Jimmy and Conchetta, sang with the New York based Metropolitan Opera Company. She later starred with Caesar Romero in a road production of *Welcome Home*. Marie would often send her friends from New York and Hollywood to eat at Lillo's whenever they were in the South. She toured with Milton Burle, and he and Margueritte Piazza of the Metropolitian Opera were frequent guests.

Dancing was not the only draw to Lillo's. The cook from the Magnolia Lounge, Sarah Rose, drove to Leland for many years to prepare the excellent Italian dishes such as shrimp supreme and veal scaloppini. (One night a couple from Cincinnati asked for veal scaloppini and realizing they did not have it on the menu, returned the next day and showed the cooks how to make it!) Willie Mae Reed also cooked there for over twenty-five years. Jimmy Lillo imported fresh Gulf seafood and lobsters from Maine, frog legs from Japan, and made up his own Italian sausage, which he sold by the pound. Spaghetti and meatballs and lasagna, along with succulent steaks, were accompanied by the famous Lillo's salad and the signature dressing laced with anchovies. The late Senator James O. Eastland often ate there and recommended it. "It's a very fine restaurant, run by very good people. They have a large clientele, and they deserve it!" His favorite dish was spaghetti and meatballs along with "the best salad in the world."

Soon the side screened-in porch was enclosed, and the "baby room," where Johnnie's wife Josephine would keep their eight children while she worked, was opened up and turned into a full-scale bar when prohibition ended. Quaint booths were installed adjacent to the bar, and the dancing continued on the maple floor. For

years Jimmy and Conchetta Lillo held court in big lounge chairs in the open family area always with a watchful eye on the big dance floor.

Jimmy Lillo built a small motel in 1958 on the bank of Lake Manoconoc behind the restaurant, and the family operated it before it became obsolete and was closed three years ago. The swimming pool continued to be used for public swimming until the city decided not to renew the lease, and it was filled with dirt.

Today, the family traditions continue. Upon entering, you are most likely met by owners Wesley and Debbie Lillo Keen or Johnnie's wife Josephine Labella Lillo. Doc's B's Band played for years with the Delta's own "Boogaloo" Ames on keyboard and vocals. Now, the Lillo's Legendary Band, along with Jamie Isonhood, keep the toes tapping and the shoes sliding across the maple on Sunday, Wednesday, and Thursday nights. The wonderful spaghetti, pizzas, and Italian dishes are still served— and the dancing continues much as Jimmy and Conchetta Lillo once envisioned many years ago, in a family atmosphere with quality food.

One Block East
The summer of '71 and the legend of the little bistro that could

Prohibition ended in Mississippi in the mid-'60s, and liquor by the drink became legally available in restaurants and taverns. The Downtowner Motor Inn, located at the end of Washington Avenue in Greenville, soon opened its Swinging Cellar, and the Holiday Inn opened its lounge out on the highway. Up and down 82, honky tonks and dives serving food were able to sell liquor. The Salesman's Club, Rendezvous, and Tilley's were mainstays during that time, but you could get cut or beat up pretty bad if you didn't watch out. The motel bars were small and mostly frequented by travelers. The river industry was booming, and Greenville was becoming known as the Towboat Capital of the World. What was needed was a nice upscale restaurant/lounge in the downtown area.

Stanley Sherman had been discussing that possibility with Mr. Jesse Brent of Brent Towing Company, and it was decided that if they could find a good partner, a viable business could be opened that would be a benefit to the community. Stanley contacted his friend Ken Levy, just back in town from a nine-month job in Chattanooga, about being the manager and a partner in the venture. Levy remembers, "Hell, I was unemployed, a friend of theirs,

Bonnie Jones Werbeck was a beloved bartender at One Block East along with Big Un, Robert Goodrich, Tex, Robbie Denman, Gus Hogue and many other expert gin-slingers.

and a lover of and participant in nightlife. I thought it would be a great idea! After all, Stanley and Mr. Jesse both had great financial minds, and we all knew most of the people in town." Stanley Sherman recalls, "It was selfish of us; we just wanted some place to go."

Once the decision to go ahead was made, local architect Joe Weilenman was brought in to help find a building and design a catching logo. After looking at several locations, the Washington County Savings and Loan building was chosen. Now, they needed a name. According to Levy, "The name is everything. It's your face, it's what you are all about, it's your ID, and it has to be good!" The building was one block east of the levee and Lake Ferguson. That was it! ONE BLOCK EAST!

Soon renovation began with the idea that what was needed was not a bar with a restaurant but a nice upscale restaurant with a bar. This combination could attract the working men and women by day to a nice downtown eating establishment and have a cool and inviting lounge atmosphere at night. Little did they realize the rocking monster they were about to unleash on Greenville. Levy remembers, "It was not our intention to explode immediately, but the crowd demanded it!"

To be successful, it was realized that if the ladies show up and like it, it is always a go. During renovation, the ladies room was outfitted with ten-carat gold sink fixtures and was very stylish and chic with Henri de Toulouse-Lautrec wallpaper while the men's room supplied the basics. The main sitting area was rough sawn cypress board and batten with brown carpet and a pressed tin ceiling. There was a patio out back and wrought iron stairs leading upstairs to Ken's office. The bar was custom built out of solid oak and highly varnished. Behind the bar, and underneath a huge oil painting of a sailing ship in a storm tossed sea, was a three-keg beer box. (One Block East was the largest Budweiser account in Washington County from the day they opened until they closed!)

Levy met and befriended a couple of guys coming downriver on a houseboat. After delivering the boat to New Orleans, they were hired on as bartenders for the new venture. Kitchen help and waitstaff were hired immediately from the first applicants to show up. It was assumed the help knew what they were supposed to do. This was 1971, and everyone was hippie-cool, with lots of long hair! After buying and installing a small Kmart 30-watt stereo with only two 4x6-inch speakers (mistake), One Block East was ready to open.

Levy recalls, "We had it all ready to go. We wanted a very simple, trendy, New Orleans-type bistro. We could seat eighty people. We had great sandwiches, a couple of good steaks, and salads and fries, and all the comforts of a nice place to go eat and hang out. It was perfect. What could we have forgotten?"

The doors opened on July 7, 1971, to a flood of people. "They came from everywhere. They loved it; we loved it; everybody loved it! What we didn't realize was that Greenville and the surrounding Delta was so ready for a cool little place like no other place around. The first weekend, the waiters were running into each other, the cooks were doing pretty well, and the bartenders were slinging some booze! Stanley and I were sweating bullets, yet dumfounded and very pleased!" The doors to One Block East were open and Greenville was rocking.

Jim Dees, Delta expatriate and Oxford author, remembers when One Block East opened. "It was the only place in town where an eighteen-year-old boy could comfortably go and have a beer and not have to watch his back," he says. "The place wasn't a tonk, it was a 'nice place', and it quickly caught on with the college set and young professionals."

Tommy Barnes of Woodlands, Texas, recalls having lunch one day in One Block East. A good ole boy from Arkansas asked a waitress why a technician from South

Central Bell was installing a red phone underneath the booth to the right of the front door. "That's where Jay Stein from the Stein Mart eats his lunch every day, and he has to be near a telephone. He's planning to open Stein Mart stores all over the South." Tipping his "Go Hogs" cap back, he replied, "Ain't that the place next door that sells them used clothes and stuff? Why, that's about the dumbest thing I ever heard of." Jay Stein would go on to open hundreds of Stein Mart stores all over the country. Sometimes, late night revelers had fun on the hidden red phone when they learned how to jimmy the button and have the operator pick up!

Located between the jazzy Swinging Cellar and Zolie's Disco, the One Block rocked on the weekends. Steve Azar, Kern Pratt, Charlie Ross, Gilda Jordan, Billy Haynes, and others brought the house down with local upstart rock 'n' roll bands like the Candy Shoestring performing. Headliners John Conlee, Johnny Paycheck, and Jerry Lee Lewis, along with regional bands such as Kurt Kasson and the Wheeler Sisters, made the Delta's newest club known all over Mississippi. Soon the building next door was bought for expansion. One Block East doubled in size, and a dance floor was installed, allowing two hundred seats of eating, drinking, and rocking 'n' rolling.

Julia Reed of New Orleans remembers, "The Block was revolutionary. As soon as I could pass for eighteen, honey, I was inside that door, and to this day it remains my favorite bar. In its heyday, the Block was like Greenville itself, an altogether sophisticated place with a great mix of people."

Recently attending an event at the Ogden Museum of Southern Art in New Orleans, where she is a board member, Julia was approached by a pretty twenty-something-year-old girl who had just moved to town from Dallas. "My father told me to tell you hello," she said. "He used to be a bartender at One Block East."

Julia says, "In the minds of many, it's a club that exists even today: those of us lucky enough to be members know why."

The free-spirited, longhaired attitude was alive and well in the heart of the Delta. However, that nice bistro atmosphere was not without some scraps every now and then. One afternoon a couple of heavyweight deckhands, fresh off a towboat, came in early and started drinking beer. The more they drank, the louder they got. The fourth time Levy went over to quiet them down, or ask them to leave, one of the burly sailors slammed a full beer mug against his head, spewing blood and beer all over the place. Immediately, some of the boys at the bar chased the guys out the front door and over the levee. Perry Hutchison recalls, "We caught up with 'em, but they made it to the towboat and safety before we could get 'em back to the One Block."

Recovering, Levy grabbed his pistol from behind the bar and rushed out the front door and into the path of a policewoman coming in to stop the fracas. "Mr. Levy, you go right back in there and put that pistol up, or I am going to put you in jail!"

Lewis Kilpatrick remembers rocking one night away with a winsome lass when he noticed a big guy fast approaching with a grease stained Ole Man River t-shirt on and clenched fists. "I decided very quickly to let that gal dance with the dude she came with."

Nights Not Remembered

I asked Hodding Carter III if he remembers the halcyon days of One Block East before he left Greenville to become a state department spokesman for President Jimmy Carter. "It is very easy for me to think of the nights I don't remember at the One Block East," Carter says, "but to think of the ones I do remember, well, that's the hard part!"

Harley Metcalfe from Greenville remembers the night Jerry Lee Lewis walked in the front door ready to perform wearing a full-length fur coat. "After that," he says, "my memory got very dim."

Contacted in Destin, Florida, where he recently sold an ownership position yet stays on and manages a six million dollar annual liquor budget in the famous AJ's Bar and Grill, Levy recalls, "We had it going on…everybody was having fun! I think the One Block raised us up back then. It was a learning experience for us all, the founders, customers, young and old, and our community as well. Our 'kids' are now in their fifties and sixties and most I have heard from love those old memories. 'The longest night doesn't last forever.' And that night was over in December of 1980. What a fantastic experience!"

One Block East was sold and other clubs followed in the same building: Dante, The Headless Horseman, and the Thunderbird Lounge. Finally, David Weiss re-opened as One Block East. However, the days were numbered, and the little bistro that opened in 1971 as a "nice place to go" met the wrecking ball several years ago. Stanley Sherman, original founder of One Block East, has only one thing to say, "What a shame."

Doe's Walls

In 1961, Willie Nelson made Farron Young's song "Hello Walls" a smashing country hit. And not long after, Willie sat and supped and sang that song within the very walls of Doe's Eat Place in Greenville and enjoyed his meal immensely.

Lil' Charles Signa remembers the night thirty or so years ago when a red bearded gentleman sporting sunglasses and a broad brimmed hat walked in with a friend toting a rectangular cardboard box under his arm. Given a table in the kitchen, they dined on the proverbial salad and hot tamales and huge steaks cooked in the blast furnace stove up front next to the main door.

After supper, and before anyone knew who he was, Lil' Charles recalled, "He took that big hat off and long red hair fell all the way to his ass. Willie Nelson opened up that box and took out his guitar and played a few songs right there in the middle of the kitchen. We all loved it! Willie paid with a roll of hundreds fat enough to choke a cow. We have since sent him dozens of hot tamales and steaks while he was on the road a bunch of times."

And if those greasy and smoke-stained walls of Doe's could talk, it would take multi-lingual experts from the United Nations to translate all the different languages that have been spoken and bantered about in there. On some nights the volume and pitch of laughter and conversations is so high in the back and side rooms at Doe's that you can hardly hear your neighbor ordering. But that's just Doe's, and it doesn't get any better. And so what if the table next to you speaks only German or Japanese; there are no menus anyway.

If you don't know what to order, longtime waitress Judy Saulter will bring one of each cuts of meat to your table from which to choose. A twelve-ounce filet to a bone-in rib eye, T-bone, porterhouse, and the 3- to 4-pound sirloin, all you have to do is point and smile, and then your salad is on the way. Noted author Willie Morris from Yazoo City once stated, "I prefer a table in the kitchen where I can absorb the vivid banter of the cooks and waitresses. The tamales are superlative, the french fries ineffable, and the T-bone steaks phantasmagoric. The atmosphere is so congenial that people at the other tables finish your sentences for you."

Virden Jones recalls his mother Rosemary dining one evening next to William Faulkner at Doe's. He was there with his good friends Bern and Franke Keating and literary agent Ben Wasson.

In 1956 the Burrus House in Benoit was the location and main centerpiece of the then considered steamy movie *Baby Doll* based on Tennessee Williams screenplay. The film and production crew adopted Mink's Supper Club as their local watering hole and eatery. However, director Elia Kazan and stars Caroll Baker, Eli Wallach, and Karl Malden headed on to Doe's Eat Place most nights after stopping by Jesse Brent's house for a little nip on their way back to Greenville.

Howard Brent recalls the night he and his wife Carole were eating in the side room at Doe's when Judy Garland came in and sat at the table next to them. Carole, a professional singer in her own right, wanted Garland's autograph but chose not to disturb her. Several years later, Catfish Rich and I were at the table in the kitchen where all the family sat and drank coffee, eating and talking to Aunt Rosalie and Aunt Mattie, when Liza Minnelli (Judy Garland's daughter) and her entourage walked in without a reservation. They also ate in the side room, the room that used to be the children's bedroom when the only place you could eat was in the kitchen.

One evening in 1964, Howard was summoned to the Greenville Airport to meet his daddy Jesse Brent who had hitched a ride home from Washington, D.C., aboard Texas billionaire Bunker Hunt's jet. They had met in Senator Jim Eastland's office for a cocktail after each had seen the Senator.

Captain Jesse was there on towboating and river business and Hunt on his wiretapping woes after he had caught several of his employees swindling sixty million smacks from his oil company. Howard recalled,

Big Doe Signa in the early 1950s proudly displaying the huge sirloins and T-bones that made Doe's famous along with the hot tamales. The children's bedroom is behind him. Back then you were not allowed to go to the bathroom while at Doe's for fear of waking the kids. Uncle Jug and Uncle Brock would open raw oysters in the back and pass them through the window for the customers.

"Until President Bush landed in Air Force One at the airport, Bunker Hunt's jet was the biggest thing ever to touch down out there. It was huge! We went to Doe's and had a wonderful time and meal after I found out what Mr. Hunt liked to sip on."

Texas is big and so are the portions at Doe's. Texans seem to like that. Judy recalls a gentleman that used to fly his own plane in from Dallas, catch a cab to Doe's, and order a plate of hot french fries and a raw sirloin. Raw and cold, that's how he liked it. And several times Dallas Cowboys owner Jerry Jones has stopped by Greenville in his jet and come to Doe's with his wife. "She eats a bone-in rib eye, and Jerry likes a porterhouse," says Judy.

Estelle Henderson, longtime devoted and beloved employee of Doe's, cooked french fries in the kitchen dining room for fifteen years. She took it upon herself to make sure people from out of town signed the guest register. Originating in 1978, the names and places and comments written in that dog-eared book are astounding. Egypt, France, South Africa, Germany, Australia, Argentina, Israel, Japan, England, Italy, Finland, China, and on and on and on the names and places go. Many comments are written in

211

the native languages of the far away countries. Anytime someone from out of state, or the country, visits the Delta, most often their hosts will bring them to Doe's.

Cruising through the guest book one evening, I noticed in the early part of 1979 that Dan Rather, Dolly Parton, Red Foxx, Johnny Cash, and Joe Namath had all dined there at separate times. And one evening in the '60s, Judy recalls a stretch limousine pulling up to the front door and two very attractive ladies getting out and opening the car door for Bob Hope and three to four other ladies. They were all kowtowing and hovering about Mr. Hope seeing to his every need. Of course, once inside those smoke-filled walls, the ladies from Doe's took over, and everyone had a blast!

One evening a group of movie producers showed up and at the end of their dinner told Judy, "If you will go back to Hollywood with us, we will make you a star!" Judy thanked them and said she would just as soon stay right here in the Delta at home and at Doe's. Judy has now been working at Doe's for forty-four years.

As governor of Arkansas, Bill Clinton would come to Doe's with his good friend Rodney Angel from Lake Village. The governor liked the hot tamales and big steaks. And during his run for President, Clinton had his famous *Rolling Stone Magazine* interview taken at Doe's Eat Place in Little Rock.

Republican Clarke Reed has brought many national news and political luminaries to Greenville over the years: William F. Buckley, Bob Novak, Paul Greenberg, Karl Rove, and the British Ambassador to the United States, Christopher Meyers, have all dined at Doe's. One evening Tom Brokaw flew in to Greenville to eat at Doe's, but it was closed due to a death in the family.

Clarke recalls checking into a hotel in London years ago when a man looked at his luggage and said, "Hello, mate, I see you are from Mississippi. Do you ever eat at Doe's in Greenville?"

Several years ago the film crew for the award-winning movie *Oh, Brother, Where Art Thou?* came to town, shooting scenes on the C&G Railroad tracks behind Fratesi's Store in Leland and on the Yazoo Backwater Levee in the south Delta. George Clooney and John Goodman brought their group to Doe's and had a wonderful time. When it came time to pay, Clooney pulled out his newly issued credit card only to find out embarrassingly that it had not yet been activated. His secretary came to the rescue with hers and paid the bill. The girls at Doe's recall Mr. Clooney as being very handsome and an extremely cordial, nice man.

Professional sportsmen from all over have dined at Doe's. Native Louisianan, four-time Super Bowl Champion quarterback and national sports commentator Terry Bradshaw has been to Doe's at least four times. Archie and Olivia Manning and their boys, Peyton, Eli and Cooper, have been to Doe's numerous times. During the thirty years of the Jesse Brent Memorial Golf Tournament, Archie missed only two times because of conflicts. During each tournament, Archie and many of the sports celebrities ate at Doe's on Saturday night.

So what is it that brings people from all over the world to the Delta, and specifically to the old grocery store/juke joint turned world-famous award-winning James Beard

American Classic Restaurant? Why did Jane and Michael Stern proclaim Doe's Eat Place to be America's best steak dinner in two consecutive issues of their nationally acclaimed travel guides to American eating? Bon Appétit magazine rated Doe's the third best steakhouse in America reaping Doe's national television coverage. What brought Alton Brown and Bobby Flay of the Food Network to Doe's? Why have top ranked magazines written articles and columns about the smoky little restaurant with mismatched tablecloths and uneven floors? What keeps bringing professional sports figures, politicians, national news analysts, writers, artists, musicians, and movie stars to Doe's in the heart of the Delta?

All you have to do to answer those questions is to understand the heart and soul of the Delta. We are a mixing pot of nationalities, races, and ethnic origins. There is something about the tragedies, tribulations, and triumphs we have all endured that bring us together. Doe's started out as an Italian family-owned grocery store turned jukehouse serving bootlegged beer and hot tamales out of the front room. A Syrian grocery store was next door, and a Chinese grocery store flanked each adjacent block.

A local doctor asked Big Doe to cook him a steak one night between calls, and he came back again with a lawyer friend. The black bootlegged beer-drinking bunch came in the front, and the carriage trade dining crowd began to come in the back door. Discrimination in reverse. Soon, the jukehouse was closed, and in 1941 the restaurant began serving steaks, tamales, spaghetti, chili, and salads full time. Today there are two family-owned restaurants and six franchises across the South.

Aunt Florence Signa began dating Big Doe's brother, and her future husband, in 1944 and took a job frying potatoes so she could be close to Jughead as he opened oysters. She has now worked at the kitchen table at Doe's for sixty-six years making salads. Recently we calculated that she has made over a million and a half salads. That's a lot of lettuce and loads of lemons and olive oil.

Asked about that remarkable undertaking, Aunt Florence nonchalantly comments, "Well, a lot of our guests that have eaten salads here got a hug from me as they came through the kitchen—and, when they left."

So just do the math. Hugs make hungry folks feel at home in the Delta.

A Few Places
to Go
in the Delta

The Legacy of Beaver Dam Lake

Six miles south of Tunica, in the heart of the Mississippi Flyway, rests the second oldest duck club in the United States. Founded in 1882, the legacy of Beaver Dam Lake is in its history, its bequest, and the spirit of a sporting legend.

Eons ago, the greatest of all American rivers rumbled and tumbled its way across wide parts of the North American continent. During flood years the crashing, devouring waters burst out of its banks and inundated all in its path. As each annual cycle of flood and drought repeated itself, the course of this mighty force changed with wanton abandon. Where once a great bend in the river flowed, several years later, after a neck had been broached during high water, a placid lake stood.

And it was during one of its sashays across the Mississippi/Yazoo River floodplain—that wonderful place we call "the Delta"—that a small oxbow lake called Beaver Dam was formed. A bend of the river was deserted, and what was left would over the years evolve into a pristine, almost surreal and beautiful lake. Huge bald cypress trees became the dominant cover within the confines of the standing water. Along the remaining sandbars and shallow areas, willows, bullrush, and marsh grasses grew. During drought years, the mudbanks would dry up, and a solid cover of native grasses would emerge for all types of wildlife and waterfowl to feed on and take refuge in.

Each year, as the days grew shorter and winter storms approached, a restlessness grew in the birds and waterfowl of the upper and central Canadian provinces. Baby ducks and goslings had been raised and taught to fly. When the first snowstorms of the year hit the great plains of North America and covered up the food sources, myriads of great flocks of waterfowl took flight. Greater and lesser Canada geese, tundra swans, snow geese, teal, gadwalls and widgeons, shovelers and pintails, and millions of mallards and numerous other species of waterfowl lifted off and turned on their built-in radars. Guided by a time-born sense to head south for warmer climes, the great annual migration would begin. Forty percent of all North American waterfowl follow the Mississippi River Flyway south, funneling into a narrow neck below the hills of Missouri and the Chickasaw Bluffs. To the west, the Central Flyway edges eastward until it merges with the Mississippi Flyway, and great masses of waterfowl blackened the sky as they came together and settled into the swollen river bottoms, flooded forests, and slack water swamps of the Arkansas and Mississippi Deltas. Hardwood trees had dropped tons upon tons of acorns, pecans, and hickory nuts into the water. Duck weed grew by the blanketed thousands of acres on still water. Grasses had grown profusely and stood in shallow water, dropping seeds with every wisp of wind. It was a smorgasbord that was not to be denied the hungry waterfowl.

Native Americans had settled around this small lake some forty miles south of Memphis. Wildlife abounded on its shores and high ground around its banks. Great mounds of dirt were erected by the native Tunica Indians as ceremonial grounds and as refuge from the floodwaters. Fish flourished in the still waters. In the winter the

JANE RULE BURDINE

open water of the lake and sawgrass flats would come alive as migrations of waterfowl would spool about in the sky and funnel down noisily in search of food, cover, and solitude.

On a map dating back to 1840, the horseshoe lake was called Beaver Dam. An abandoned bend in the Mississippi River, Beaver Dam is almost eight miles long with some two miles, or four hundred acres, of open water in the middle. The remaining lakebed is covered in cypress forests and water-covered flats of button willow and patches of sawgrass. Massive timbered forests enveloped the lake, and Indian trails emerged from the trees southwestward towards the present day town of Helena, Arkansas, and eastward towards the hills along which trading parties traveled.

Around 1866, Dr. R.W. Owen moved from Tennessee to the small town of Austin in Tunica County on the banks of the Mississippi River and set up practice. He was soon married and became quite successful. Dr. Owen began buying up land and after a while held extensive land holdings that bordered much of Beaver Dam Lake. Most of the open water belonged to Dr. Owen as did much of the cypress and buckbrush on the northern end of the lake. Mr. J.A. Austin, who held large land holdings around the town of Austin, invited some gentlemen friends down from Memphis by steamboat to hunt ducks, geese, swans, and deer on Beaver Dam Lake. For several years these same gentlemen returned, sleeping in camp tents and being looked after by a tenant named Mr. Knight. Soon a log clubhouse was built on the banks of the lake about midway on the open water. Drinking water came from rain caught alongside the camphouse in oaken barrels.

By 1878 the Beaver Dam Club was founded as the first and oldest of the Memphis and the Mid-South duck clubs and the second oldest in the country. Members came downriver on steamboats and then rode in mule-drawn wagons to the lake. In 1885, however, the Y&MV Railroad (Yazoo and Mississippi Valley), better known as the "Limb Dodger," snaked its way south out of Memphis and passed within a few hundred yards of the log cabin. A new clubhouse was built that stood until 1926 when a tornado came through and toppled the huge pecan tree that destroyed the old clubhouse. But it was in that old clubhouse that Beaver Dam was immortalized by the son of one of the original members of Beaver Dam Club.

Nash Buckingham was born in 1880 in Memphis and grew up in a Southern society that exposed him to a sporting way of life filled with hunting dogs, days afield, and a respect for the outdoors that stayed with him his entire life. In the introduction of the reprint of one of Buckingham's books, *De Shootinest Gent'man and Other Tales,* Jim Casada said about Nash, "...an abiding love of the South and the genteel pace that moved its people were deeply imbedded in his character." Nash was a big man, excelling in college football and boxing while attending Harvard and the University of Tennessee. It was his superb physical abilities that allowed him to perform so well afield and in the duck blind. He was a first rate wing shot and eventually became one of Winchester-Western Cartridge company's field testers for their Super-X shotshell and helped develop the principle of long-range, short shotstring loads. Through that association he was able to acquire possibly the most famous of all shotguns ever made, a Fox, 12 gauge, three-inch magnum with thirty-two-inch full choke barrels bored and built by Burt Becker, acknowledged as the world's master barrel-borer. It was nicknamed "Bo Whoop" because of its resounding "bo whoop, bo whoop," that sounded like two deep solo notes from the bass horn of an orchestra as the reports reverberated through the cypress and willow trees. Nash Buckingham and this gun were legendary on Beaver Dam Lake.

Nash became a sports writer penning many articles for the best sporting journals of the day and through the years published seven books that are arguably some of the finest writing about hunting and the out of doors to date. He began hunting at Beaver Dam Club when he was ten years old and wrote many stories about the lake and the beloved club keepers from 1902-1920, Horace and Molly Miller. Horace was a trusted tenant of Dr. Owen's and became caretaker and duck guide emeritus, and Molly was the cook without equal. Before the Millers arrived, Andrew Jackson Bounds and his wife, Victoria, looked after the club. As stated in the September 23, 1893, issue of *Forest and Stream,* "Queen Victoria's kitchen is famous there for roast duck, broiled squirrel, baked 'possum, and sweet potatoes with sop, fatty bread, fish, fresh eggs, and often venison and wild turkey. The club is another home for the members and their families." The old days at Beaver Dam come alive through Nash's pen as he and Horace paddle across the lake to the old Handwerker blind or Round Pond, and "Bo Whoop" cleanly kills ducks at distances that most hunters would not dare attempt. Through the time-honored stories, the beauty of the lake and the wildfowl are brought before your eyes as if you are in the boat with them. Nash Buckingham and Beaver Dam are synonymous the world over.

The intense conservation efforts of the Owen family and others around the lake have preserved the quality of the habitat and kept the lake from being overly exploited. The Owen, Seabrook, Hood, and Boyd families have taken it upon themselves to do all possible to maintain the integrity and serenity of the Beaver Dam Lake, and they have done an exemplary job. Because of the notoriety of the lake and the volumes that have been written about it, Beaver Dam is legendary in its own right. But it is an unequaled ecosystem and haunt of hundreds of thousands of waterfowl annually. And it almost slipped out of the hands of the current families that have controlled it for more than a hundred years. According to the January 9, 1884, minutes of the Beaver Dam Club:

"At a special meeting of the Beaver Dam Club held at the State Nation Bank, Miles S. Buckingham submitted an offer from the three landowners to sell to Beaver Dam Club the lake and surrounding acreage, up to ten thousand acres, for $2.50 an acre or $22,500. After considerable heated discussion a motion by Judge James M. Greer to purchase the land, and seconded by Miles Buckingham, was put to vote and lost 6-4."

The secretary went on record as saying he was in favor of buying, later stating, "As it turned out in a few years, a hundred acres of that timber would have paid for the entire property."

Croquet, Anyone?

We have all heard of the backyard game croquet; some of us have even played it. It's been around for a while, dating back in some form or fashion in France to the 1300s. It was called "paille-maille," which means ball-mallet.

The Scottish enjoyed the game also, and when the crowns of England and Scotland were united under King James I, he brought with him to Buckingham Palace a paille-maille set and golf clubs. King James' grandson, Charles II, enjoyed the game immensely and often played it in St. James Park. Soon a serene, tree-lined road was named Pall Mall after the game. The peaceful byway beckoned to leisurely strolls, and any road conducive to pleasant walks around the city became known as a mall. Today, any group of stores enclosed by a covered walkway is known as a mall.

Back in France, a doctor thought so much of the pleasurable and relaxing qualities of the game that he changed the rules a bit and began prescribing it to his patients. He also called the new game "croquet" after the crooked stick used to hit the balls through the wickets. The new version, and name, got back to England and spread rapidly throughout the British Empire. In 1868, an association was formed at Wimbledon, and formal rules and regulations were written. Many croquet fields were established, but they were short lived as tennis took Wimbledon by storm, and most of the croquet fields were turned into tennis courts. But croquet survived and is played today with the mere purchase of a set of balls, mallets, and wickets.

I was introduced to croquet in college, along with badminton and softball on weekends when Archie and the Rebels were not playing. Those were the halcyon

Mark Fields demonstrates the correct follow through as David Trigiani and Hillis Becker watch the play in the serene setting.

days of beer drinking and frivolity before the Age of Aquarius took over. We played backyard croquet amongst the budding flowers, instead of smoking them.

Back home in Greenville, my mother, Baby Jane, would host croquet matches in her backyard during the summer, inviting her widow friends and what few widowers were left around to play the game. They had a wonderful time, and she placed small tables around the course to hold your glass when it became your time to hit the ball.

In 1986 an invitation was extended to the ladies to join the Dooleyville Croquet and Carousal Society's Tenth Annual Fall Festival and Croquet Tournaments in Anguilla, of all places. They accepted with glee and went about formalizing their attire. Long-sleeved white shirts were ordered with the name "Wicket Widows" embroidered on the back.

I asked my mother if they won, and she replied, "I don't know. We never keep score; we just have fun getting together and playing the game."

The Dooleyville tournament series began outside of Oxford on Dooley Road in 1977 when Charles Weissinger and Joe Frasier whacked down the weeds and brush in a field to play touch football while enrolled in Ole Miss Law School. The football games never took off, but soon Joel Hunter, John Coonrod, Joe De Benvenuti, and Tom Thompson, along with Ronnie Harper, Henry Goodman, Jeff Varas, Chuck Culpepper, and others, formed the Dooleyville Croquet Society. According to Weissinger, "They were a hardy group of sports that donned their helmets and went forth into battle showing much rough and bawdy behavior."

"It was Peckerwood Croquet in the hills enhanced by many natural obstacles. In order to experience Dooleyville, you must alter your consciousness, as it is a coarse, quasi-religious experience induced by alcohol, yet, not in the least reverential."

Once most of the members finished law school, the Dooleyville Tournament moved to Bay St. Louis then on to Anguilla and the home of Henry Goodman. Located on the banks of Deer Creek and nestled against an ancient Indian mound, the series continued each year.

"It is a totally encompassing three-day experience, all day and all night, under the lights," according to Weissinger. "The originators played ruthlessly. They would hit your ball out into the middle of a cotton field or into the bottom of Deer Creek. It turned into the level of blood sport."

"Dooleyville is the only party I've ever been invited back to! It is a true test of endurance," says Henry Goodman.

In its thirty-seventh year, the tournament is a roving festival, played now anywhere from Bay St Louis to Galveston to Winchester, Illinois.

Richard Grant, a London writer who recently moved to the Delta at Gum Grove Plantation outside of Tchula, played croquet while growing up in jolly ole England. "What I remember about the class society and croquet is Pimm's Cup cocktails and braying laughter, posh women saying, 'Oh, bugger' when they missed and 'Darling, fetch me another Pimm's'," he says.

It seems to Richard that croquet and alcohol are "natural born bedfellows," and he recalls "severely inebriated midnight croquet matches by flashlight with young couples cavorting about and rutting around on the lawn." Richard thinks that it is impossible to play the game sober.

There are two croquet organizations around Jackson that meet regularly to play the international and quite formal version of Six Wicket Croquet, the Pocahontas Mallet Club and the Highland Mallet Club outside of Flora. The thirty-six members of the Highlanders meet each Sunday during the summer with practice rounds on Thursday afternoon. The "greensward," or croquet court, is immaculate, located in Mike McCree's backyard overlooking his lake. Mike has built four courts over the years, all designed and built to rival the eighteenth green on any professional golf course. Lighted, sprinkled, and sporting French drains, Mike's present greensward is overlooked by a comfortable deck and cabana complete with a well-stocked bar and wine cellar. He has called on his friends to help him build a court. "It is the only way I can get lawyers and doctors together to work and to do what I tell them to do. It takes a lot of beer, but we have built some beautiful courts."

"Croquet is a great sport for socializing, fun play, and a chance to have a cocktail with friends," Mike says. Alternating hosts bring a meal to enjoy after the matches, and the club supplies the wine. "We cut the fat hog in the ass on Sunday afternoon when we bring out the Pimm's cup." Each year, the crowning glory of the Highlands Mallet Club is the last weekend of the season. It begins with a black tie gala affair on Friday evening with matches all day Saturday and culminates with high tea on Sunday before the finals and awards ceremony that evening.

Architect, bon vivant, and devout Highland player David Trigiani states, "It is thought that croquet players consume more alcoholic beverages than any other sport."

So go out and get yourself a croquet set, stop by the local bootlegger on the way home, and then cut the grass in your backyard. Invite your friends over for an afternoon of fun. It's a great way to enjoy the wonderful spring weekends in the Delta. And while you are up, "Darling, fetch me another Pimm's!"

Navigating the Delta Mystique

I remember in the late sixties and seventies, early on many Sunday afternoons, Mr. Jere Nash's big black Cadillac pulling up with chauffeur Johnnie B at the wheel. Mr. Nash was there to collect the Wilzin and Gamwyn Park widows for a ride through the Delta. With a big picnic basket in the trunk, along with a full bar, off they would go to ride Mr. So-n-So's place, or to Tchula or Sumner or the south Delta where Mr. Nash had plantations. Returning from one trip in the winter, it was raining, and I asked how they picnicked in the rain. My mother replied, "Well, Mr. Jere built these sheds in front of all of his Delta Implement tractor dealerships so we could get out of the weather on our trips to make a patch or to picnic. (I knew those sheds were built to cover all the shiny red International tractors!) In any event, they always had fun on Delta road trips. So why can't we?

I don't know many of us that have chauffeurs today, but we can sure designate a driver or hire a limo and cruise the Delta. If, as David Cohn so aptly stated, "the Delta starts in the lobby of the Peabody Hotel and ends on Catfish Row, Vicksburg," then let's start our big road trip in Memphis.

Most of us have visited that grand lobby of The Peabody Hotel full of huge wooden brackets holding up the mezzanine and surrounding the beautiful Italian travertine marble fountain loaded with mallard ducks. And most of the time a lot of us have bellied up to the stunning bar which used to hide illegal liquor bottles that cab drivers would deliver from the alley across the street called "Whiskey Chute." According to my cousin Bard Selden, his dad once said, "You never had to leave the Peabody for anything." And so it is today, if only you didn't want to slip over to the Rendezvous for some ribs and then boogie yo' booty off down on Beale Street.

Heading south down Highway 61, slip through Clarksdale and visit the Crossroads where Robert Johnson was supposed to have sold his soul to the devil for his blues playing abilities. Then go by Red's Lounge and Ground Zero Blues Club for some sho' nuff downhome blues before checking into the Shack Up Inn. Maybe the Pinetop Perkins or the Cadillac shack is available. Founder Bill Talbot said that they "started this place because we needed a place to drink beer, listen to the blues, and play music whenever we wanted to." Don't forget to visit the Hopson Commissary next door and learn about the very first Delta farm to become totally mechanized. And for sure don't forget to pick up a bumper sticker that says "I shacked up at the Shack Up Inn!"

West of Clarksdale is the beautiful cypress lined Moon Lake where General Ulysses S. Grant dug a channel connecting the Mississippi River to the Yazoo in a failed attempt to surround Vicksburg by water. If fortunate you may witness a full-immersion baptism held on many Sundays for over a hundred years by several of the local Baptist churches.

Heading on down Highway 49 below the fearful gates of Parchman Farm ("putting that cotton in an eleven foot sack with a 12-gauge shotgun at my back"), let's pull into Ruleville and visit the gravesite and memorial garden of Fannie Lou Hamer, an American voting rights activist and civil rights leader during the 1960s. She was instrumental in the Mississippi Freedom Democratic Party while working on grass-roots Head Start programs, the Freedom Farm Cooperative, and Martin Luther King's Poor Peoples Campaign. During a trip there last year with my friend Dr. Jessica B. Harris, Professor of English at Queens College, she stated, "There is peacefulness in Ruleville, Mississippi, that can only come from the hovering presence of the soul of Fannie Lou Hamer. Her resting place in the community that nurtured her is simple and elegant as completely befits the woman who spoke so eloquently for all the folks who were 'sick and tired of being so sick and tired'."

Due west of Ruleville on Highway 8 is the Dockery Plantation started by Will Dockery in 1895. The huge plantation had its own commissary, churches, doctor, school, and post office. Hundreds of families lived and worked in harmony there. Around 1900, Charley Patton moved with his family to Dockery and along with several others, including Robert Johnson, "Son" House, "Pops" Staples, and "Honeyboy" Edwards, began playing and singing the blues. Dockery became known as the place where the blues were born. Today, the headquarters area is preserved by the Dockery Farms Foundation. Executive Director Bill Lester notes, "We have hundreds of visitors from all over the world yearly, and we always look forward to showing them the birthplace of the blues."

And what better place to learn about the blues than in Indianola where B.B. King was born (nearby) and raised. The B.B. King Museum and Delta Interpretive Center is a state-of-the-art audio and visual masterpiece that chronicles the sixty year career of the undisputed "King of the Blues." From the cotton fields of the Delta to Beale Street and WDIA Radio and on to international stardom, B.B.'s life, hardships, achievements, and music come alive before your eyes. The world icon was laid to rest in July 2015 on the museum grounds. Soon pilgrims will be able to visit the new memorial garden and pay their respects to the King on their Delta stop in Indianola.

Heading south towards Belzoni on Highway 7 are some of the oldest and biggest bald cypress trees in the world. Many of the cypress trees there are eight hundred to one thousand years old with one approaching two thousand years of age. The oldest is also the biggest tree in Sky Lake with a diameter of almost fifteen feet and a circumference of close to forty-seven feet. Sky Lake is a functioning backwater ecosystem preserved not only for its fish and wildlife significance but for its scenic, ecological, and scientific values. A 1,735-foot raised boardwalk has been built out to the biggest trees in the swamp. The Sky Lake Wildlife Management Area now encompasses 4,273 acres and is truly a Delta treasure.

Venturing over towards the Mississippi River and Greenville, you will find one of the tallest and largest Indian mound complexes in America. The Winterville Mounds cover forty-two acres and consist of twelve prehistoric Native American mounds, two large plazas, and a museum. These mounds were built between A.D. 1000 and 1450 to serve as ceremonial grounds and sacred structures. The largest stands fifty-five feet tall and artifacts collected indicate extensive contact with far away chiefdoms. The Greenville Garden Club acquired the site in 1939, and now the grounds are a part of the Mississippi Department of Archives and History.

In Greenville is the 1927 Flood Museum located in the carriage quarters of the oldest

RORY DOYLE/COURTESY OF DELTA MAGAZINE

Dockery Plantation Headquarters, the undisputed "Birthplace of the Blues."

house in town. The museum presents the history of the greatest natural disaster to befall our country until Katrina came roaring in. You can go back in time viewing actual artifacts and pictures of the impact of the flood during the four months that water covered almost half of the Delta. A documentary video explains the cause and impact of the devastation of the flood and the consequent struggle of man and livestock against the Mississippi River.

Going South on Highway 1, around Glen Allan is some of the first land to be cleared in the Delta. On the south end of Lake Washington are the ruins of St. John's Church, the first Episcopal Church in the Delta, and surrounding it is the oldest cemetery in Washington County dating back to the 1820s. During the Civil War, the leaded stained glass windows were removed so the lead could be melted down for Confederate musket balls. Open to the elements, rain and wind began to ravage the church, and in 1904 a tornado destroyed all but the bell tower and brick foundations which remain today. Each year a Greenfield Cemetery Candlelight Tour is presented depicting the lives of different people buried in the hallowed ground including Jesse Cromwell, a slave and master carpenter and builder of the church who also served as its sexton. Cromwell is buried in an unmarked grave on the church grounds.

Following the Great River Road south is The Onward Store. Stop there for a great cheeseburger and learn all about the bear hunt of President Theodore Roosevelt when bear guide Holt Collier tied a bear to a tree, and the president refused to shoot it, beginning the legend of the world famous "Teddy Bear."

Ending up within walking distance of Catfish Row in Vicksburg, you will find the Jesse Brent Lower Mississippi River Museum. It is an interactive and static display of life on the Lower Mississippi River. The river's past, present, and future significance is told in a way that all age groups can understand. A scale model of the river from Greenville to Vicksburg allows children to walk through the water and sandbars. The MV Mississippi IV gives visitors a feel of life on a towboat including a towboat simulator in the pilothouse. The museum is a great place to end a tour of the Delta, so find a weekend, designate a driver, or two, and hit the road. The Delta is waiting!

And Then
Some

Alligator Hunting in the Delta

The first week in September is always hot in the Delta, and in the south Delta, alligator season has already been open for one week and has only about three more days to go. Like wild hog hunting in February, gator hunting is a communal sport loaded with action and inherent danger. You've got to know what you are doing or you can get in big trouble real fast. Teamwork is essential, and everyone in the boat must know his or her job. Yes, gals hunt gators too, as a woman from Vicksburg holds the state record alligator measuring almost 13'8" and weighing 686 pounds.

Background

The American alligator (*Alligator mississippiensis*) is a large crocodilian reptile ranging from North Carolina all around to South Texas in brackish, swampy coastal areas living almost three hundred miles inland. The alligator prefers marshes, reservoir lakes and ponds, river drainages, and oxbow lakes. He is an opportunistic predator eating large rough fish like gar and carp, waterfowl, wading birds, snakes, turtles, muskrat, beavers, and nutria. They have even been known to prey on livestock and domestic pets.

Alligators have emerged off the Federal Endangered Species List after being hunted almost to extinction by the 1960s. However, once protected, an amazing rebound took place. By 2007, highly restricted permits were offered by the Mississippi Department of Wildlife, Fisheries, and Parks for public and private lands. In 2016 there were over eleven thousand applications submitted with 1,136 permits issued and 1,101 legal-sized alligators harvested with the majority taken on public waters.

So, how does one go about hunting and capturing a big alligator and getting him into the boat? Alligator hunting is not for the serene sportsman. But, like wild hog hunting, it is reserved for the stout of heart and those peculiar nimrods who love the sport. To feel and then softly hear the deep, reverberating guttural roar of a bull gator as he is calling for a mate, before you can see his red eyes in a spotlight, will raise the hair on the back of anyone's neck that is floating around like a fool in a small boat trying to catch a huge alligator on a fishing rod. Yes, fishing rod, because that is the only legal way to catch one in Mississippi. So come with me, and let's go gator hunting down in the south Delta around Panther Swamp. There are a lot of gators there, along with "other things that go 'bump' in the night."

The Hunt

I arrived in the early evening to meet up with my hunting friends and enjoy a lean supper and much excitement and very little libations as you have to be alert and on your toes when you are alligator hunting. Covering up with double doses of insect repellant, the gear was checked and rechecked. Three good-sized saltwater fishing rods and reels were inspected, and the big weighted treble hooks attached were sharpened with a file to ensure a quick hookup if possible.

The snare that is to be slipped over the gator's head was checked and taped open with a large loop to slip over the gator's head once he is brought to the boat. A large

Allen Moorehead, Hank Burdine, Raymond Longoria, Clint Mixon, Mark Tate, and Howard Brent.

caliber bangstick or a small caliber shotgun is safely stowed in a case to offer the dispatch when the time comes. And don't forget the duct tape to securely tape the reflexive snapping jaws of a gator once he is in the boat or tied alongside with stout coils of rope. The ice cooler, more 'skeeter spray, and bright spotlights are located, and we are ready to go.

We back off a side road through the woods and manhandle the boat into a bayou. The master of our hunt, Mark, calmly has everyone take their respective seats in the boat according to their responsibilities as he goes to the front to man the trolling motor. Evelyn and Tiffany hold the fishing rods as Raymond runs the big motor, and Allen handles the bright spotlight.

Our boat is equipped to take eight passengers, so Howard and I settle in for a night of excitement and adventure. It doesn't take long for Allen to wave his hand and Raymond to shut down the engine. Mark drops the trolling motor down into the dark and foreboding depths, and ever so quietly and stealthily we glide through the water, looking and listening.

Humming mosquitoes by the blankets have taken over the swamp, but you must be ever still and quiet. An alligator can see and hear you, and most of the time the only parts of his body out of the water are his eyes and nose. He can also feel vibrations in the water. At the sight or sense of something amiss, he just simply goes down and swims away underwater. But there is something over there by the bank, a twitch of movement, and a raccoon scurries across a fallen cypress tree. Then gator eyes—nope, those are the green eyes of a big bullfrog. While sliding under an overhanging limb of a willow tree, Allen shines the light along its length to make sure a water moccasin is not slithering across it just waiting to fall into the boat as has happened on too many occasions.

Then, I feel what seems like the water vibrating, and everyone freezes as Mark stops the quiet trolling motor. The deep guttural resonance of a bull gator forces itself into your soul as two bullfrogs begin their call and response: "juggarooooom, juggarooooom." It's sweltering hot, sticky, and dark while floating around in this slimy, snake and gator infested black water, as the moon begins a slow rise in the east. Mark motions to the paddle and nods at Raymond who slowly puts it in the water and begins to swirl it and splash around as he squeals in a high pitched replica of a small wild pig being thrashed about at the water's edge. Suddenly, two red eyes leave the bank, and cutting a V-shaped trail through the duckweed and slime of the swamp, a small alligator heads towards the boat. Mark shakes his head from side to side as he has seen the eyes and calculated it to be a small gator. The distance between the gators eyes and his nostrils in inches is roughly how long he is in feet. Yet we felt and heard the roar of a bull gator, possibly further down the bayou.

Two hours go by and the moon is almost directly overhead now when a horrendous crash of water explodes fifty yards away. We freeze as another loud splash comes from the opposite bank, and a big beaver slaps the water with his tail. Just then Allen's light stops, and he motions to the water's edge. Big red piercing eyes are looking directly into the spotlight. And they are set wide apart. Mark and Raymond reach for the rods and reels. Mark waits for the eyes to start moving downstream, and he deftly casts the big weighted three-pronged hook almost ten feet over the alligator's back and slowly begins to reel in the line.

Once the line gets a little taut and is moving with the gator, he rears back hard and sets the hook deep into the tough skin of a big gator. Raymond instinctively throws his hook over the thrashing and spinning alligator two or three times until his hook is also set. The girls, seasoned saltwater anglers, turn to the rods with outstretched arms as they are handed over, and the fight begins. Sometimes you are reeling the alligator to the boat; sometimes you are reeling the boat to the alligator; and sometimes the alligator decides to go on walkabout, and you just hold on.

This night, after about twenty minutes of swishing, splashing, swashing, and reeling, and breaking one rod in half, with the third one pressed into service, a huge twelve foot alligator surfaced next to the boat and almost bit the trolling motor off the bow next to Mark. Then, after a horrendous fight, as the girls held on, the cabled noose was slipped over his massive head, and tiring out, the alligator was overtaken, and the fight was over.

Too big to put in the boat, the twelve-foot alligator, weighing over six hundred pounds, was tied securely to the side as Raymond drove us back to our landing. Then the fun began, as we not only had to manhandle the boat onto the trailer but had to load the alligator into the back of my truck for the trip back to camp. It was 2 a.m. by then and, yes, just the right time for a cold one—or two!

Fall is Festival Time in the Delta

Back in the summer of 1988, my sister Jane Rule called and asked if I had anything planned for the fall, as her dear friends Willie Morris and Bill Allard had teamed up as writer and photographer to write a story for *National Geographic* magazine about "Faulkner's Mississippi." I told her, as a matter of fact, I was planning a dress up dove hunt to be held at my hunting compound Willow Run in November when it was cool. Everyone was going to dress in English country attire and come as proper as possible sporting knickers and plus fours, big hats, and flowing plaid skirts. We were planning a morning hunt with bloody marys served at 10 a.m. sharp and brunch to follow in the field shortly thereafter. After a light siesta, a trap shoot was to be held at the trap range next to the Larry Pryor Ladies Libation House. This, I think, blew her socks off as she loudly exclaimed, "YES, that is right down Faulkner's alley!"

The sunflowers soon wilted as the doves came in droves, and the Saturday morning of the hunt, everyone showed up at my cabin right before daybreak dressed to the nines. I don't think the Delta has ever seen such a sight. The ladies had scoured English country journals searching for the proper dress and instructed their husbands on what to wear and, by golly, how to act. After a quick sausage and biscuit and a steaming cup of Willow Run coffee, we all loaded up in the cotton wagon for the tractor ride back to the shooting fields. I led the parade on my Tennessee walking horse Guv'nor, and the hunt began.

T'was a glorious morning with the ladies sitting under the trees chattering as their men popped away at the doves, of course, missing a hell of a lot more than they dropped. By ten o'clock the whiskey wagon showed up, loaded to the brim, and all guns were cased and the frivolity began. More revelers arrived in vintage Jeeps and wood-sided antique pickup trucks, all dressed properly. A J-3 Piper Cub buzzed the field and gently set down on a turn row next to the water hole. The party had begun.

There is something about a dress-up costume party that makes people have just a little more fun, and it wasn't long before my majordomo, John Johnson, dispatched our faithful family attendant John Bogan to the liquor store in Hollandale while houseman Charlie Sykes just kept pouring drinks. Faulkner's personal physician Dr. Chester McLarty held court with my mother Baby Jane and Miss Lolly Ray, along with Aunt Pinky, regarding the old days in Oxford town. (We never had a party when we didn't invite our parents and close friends as they added SO much to the gathering.) Bill Allard just kept snapping his shutter and grinning the whole time. It was a glorious morning!

Never had I ever seen a spread laid out by the ladies under the oak trees as I saw that day. The shooting guests at the Sandringham Estate of King Edward VII would have been proud. After brunch it was snooze time, and folks were scampering for the back seats of cars and every available couch and bed in my cabin and the Ladies House to rest before the afternoon festivities began.

Soon enough, eyes were rubbed and arms stretched, and as yawns turned into smiles, hands reached for Dixie cups. The gentlemen trap shooters began to uncase their single-barrel Parkers and Ithakas, over-and-under Brownings, and double-barrel Winchesters. These were real shooters, most having won state championships; others were just good ole boys that knew the game and could shoot. Behind the trap range, folding chairs were loaded with little old ladies that knew when to "Halloo" and when to be quiet. Gentlemen shooting, ladies being ladies…it was a glorious Delta afternoon.

Later that evening, Son Thomas from Leland showed up and slapped some rotgut deep down Delta blues on the porch of the Ladies House as the whiskey flowed and the gentlemen tipped their hats and pretty girls blushed. Soon, John Bogan showed up with the great bluesman Sam Chatmon from Hollandale. Sam, of the famous Mississippi Sheiks, had given dignity to the blues and played raucous blues in a dignified manner. A good time was had by all.

Alden Farm Festival

Not long after that, I moved my family to southern Colorado and tried to continue Delta traditions in the Sangre de Christo Mountain Range. It was fun times out there but not like back down in the flatland. When my wife Sallie became ill, we moved to the Destin area of Florida to be closer to her family and to my beloved Delta. When I lost my Sallie, I moved back home and settled on the banks of Lake Washington. My friends would ask, "when are we gonna have another party?" Well, we had a few small Alden Farm Fall Festivals at my farm shop, but folks were itching for a "Big 'Un." Thanksgiving is always a big weekend in the Delta with family in from far and wide. So last year, for those not going to the annual Ole Miss/Mississippi State football game, I decided that we were going to have a party. When I say we, once the die is cast, everybody jumps in and helps put it on. Festival hostess Claire Ford, originally from Tupelo, but who grew up hunting on and around family-owned Belmont Plantation, now residing in Orange Beach, Alabama, brought ample supplies of fresh Gulf shrimp, oysters, and jumbo lump crab meat from Joe Patti's in Pensacola, and the feast was planned and prepared by Chef Stewart Robinson. One diehard Mississippi State couple decided to forego the game in person, "Honey, we can listen to it on the radio!" and stayed to help with the party. The decision was made to have everyone dress in old English country attire, very similar to the dove hunt almost thirty years before. And they did it with zest! Plus fours and knickers, woolen skirts and vests, snappy country dress with Bo Weevil even sporting a jet black top hat.

An impromptu trap shoot was held at the Sonny Rich Whiskey Shoot trap range. A Cockleburr Croquet Match was held using old wire campaign poster stands as wickets with broomsticks as mallets and beach balls as croquet balls.

As dusk approached, a sumptuous table was spread on the Peckerwood Pavilion as Chef Stewart Robinson prepared corned duck gumbo and venison shepherd's pie on an improvised outdoor range built of cinder blocks and old corrugated tin with a wire grate for an oven rack. Colorful wildflowers were jabbed into old crock pots as floral arrangements, and dogs ran rampant throughout the crowd, but mostly the old

hounds curled up next to the two big bonfires burning in old tractor rims. Eden Brent brought her little upright piano and banged away as her husband "London" Bob wailed away on his trombone. Raymond Longoria pulled out his sixty-year-old Gibson guitar, and it wasn't long before the joint was rocking. Overlooking Peckerwood Lake, I had placed multi-colored floodlights on the pavilion posts that were shining on the huge cypress trees. As the sun set beneath a blood-reddened buttermilk sky, the setting was almost surreal. Revelers were reveling, good Delta music was reverberating through the cypress and oak trees of a primeval swamp, and the bartenders were busy. The party ran well into the night and ended only when the generator that ran the lights and musical instruments ran out of gas and everything went dark. It was a fabulous Fall Festival. A Delta good time was had by all!

Forsaking Finlay

Union gunboats patrolled up and down the Mississippi River during the Siege of Vicksburg between May 18 and July 4 of 1863. One was fired upon by residents of "Old" Greenville, which was situated about three miles south of the present day city. The Yankee commander aboard the vessel ordered all buildings and homes burned to the ground. Greenville was set to the torch, and nothing remained. The residents took refuge in surrounding plantation homes and cabins.

Returning home from the war, Mississippi regiments found Greenville in a state of ruin. However, they soon decided to rebuild. A short distance upriver was some of the highest ground between Memphis and Vicksburg, with a majority of the land being owned by the Blanton family. Mrs. Harriet Blanton Theobald decided to deed enough acreage for a new town from Blantonia Plantation for schools, churches, and public buildings, and she became known for her efforts as the "Mother of Greenville." Because of its location as a cotton shipping point on the Mississippi River, Greenville soon flourished and later became known as the "Queen City of the Delta."

Confederate Major Richard O'Hea had planned the wartime defense fortifications of Vicksburg and was soon hired to lay out the new town of Greenville. Residents of Old Greenville came scrambling back to rebuild and be a part of the new town on the banks of the Mississippi. When Greenville was burned, Annie Burwell Finlay retreated with her ten children to a plantation house out in the country. The Finlays were close friends of the Blantons and instrumental in helping to lay out the plans for the new town. Believed to have been the first house built in new Greenville, a four-room house was built of heart cypress in 1865 by Mrs. Annie B. Finlay, mother of Mrs. John G. Archer, whose family would later become very prevalent in Greenville. The house was soon added onto to accommodate lodgers, eventually ending up with about 2,400 square feet of ornate living space. It has been remembered as the only Italianate-style house in the community.

Greenville was incorporated in 1870, and in 1873 Major O'Hea produced a map of Greenville with the new streets as they were laid out (including three that subsequently washed into the Mississippi River). Along the border were pictures of houses and churches built in Greenville with the Annie B. Finlay home included. In a 1954 publication of the Washington County Historical Society, W.W. Stone recalled in an address to the society in 1912 that the Annie B. Finlay home was "a long way out from the river front, on the corner of Washington Avenue and Poplar Street, now known as Brills Corner. The home was the most elastic ever built in the county. It was small in appearance, but it accommodated more people than could stand on the ground it covered. This fact was a matter of wonder at the date of which I write." The home at the time of that writing was owned by Bettie D. Finlay.

Known as the Finlay House, it began a sojourn and was moved by mules rolling along on logs in 1887 to 706 Central and in 1908 was moved again landing on 130 North Shelby Street. Turned into apartments, the house became well used as tenants

The Finlay House, considered the first house built in Greenville, was listed on the National Register of Historic Places in April of 1982.

came and went, but she never lost her character or her grace. The two-story Italianate townhouse was topped by a hipped roof with wide bracketed eaves. The three-bay façade finished in matched cypress boards was fronted by a double-tiered gallery cut under the front slope of the roof. The gallery was supported by wooden box columns, which on the second story level featured molded capitals topped by elongated brackets. On the second story, the columns were linked by a jigsaw balustrade. The windows on the façade were floor length, opening into twelve-foot ceilings. A kitchen had been attached to the rear when first built.

One evening in 1979, I was invited over to my cousin Jack Burke's apartment for an after-dinner drink. Jack lived upstairs in the old Finlay House on Shelby Street, a short walk from the One Block East. As I rolled my friend Stanley Sherman over, he began to give me a little history of the house, and it intrigued me. When I saw it, and got Stanley upstairs, I fell in love with it. It had a roominess to it that exceeded its appearance and an aura that enveloped you. Its stateliness stood out, and the feeling of grandeur and good use was eminent. One day, I thought, I would like to restore this grand old home.

Two years later, my friend and attorney Claude H. "Sandhawg" Powell informed me that the Finlay House was to be torn down by Dr. Richard Knutson to make way for a parking lot for his clinic next door. Meeting with the good doctor proved fruitful as it was learned he had a lot to the rear of the house for sale. A deal was made, and by my purchasing the lot, he would give me the house, and I would move it and turn it around to set on its new foundation. That's when the fun began.

Being in the heavy construction and road building business, I knew it could be moved, but what would it cost? The house weighed almost 150,000 pounds and it was going to be an intricate move between existing trees. Professional house movers Ed Creel and James Seard were in need of a big powerful truck with a heavy-duty winch for their business, and I just happened to have one ready for retirement. Another deal was struck, and Burdine Construction gave the truck in lieu of moving the house. In March of 1981, the Finlay House once again settled to a new location at 137 North Poplar within 150 feet from the original location where she was built.

Reconstruction soon began to return her to her original splendor. Most of the floor length windows and swirled glass panes were intact, and the doors and floors were refinished. New paint, wiring, and plumbing and a new roof were installed with an attached outbuilding built as a laundry room and guest quarters to match the original kitchen. "Sandhawg" moved into the downstairs rooms and set up his law office. The Finlay House had new air breathed into her 120-year-old bones, and she radiated in the glow. And then fate reared up when my home on Lake Ferguson burned to the ground.

Having nowhere to live, I moved into my hunting camp at Willow Run, a desolate and lonesome cabin deep in the woods of Black Bayou adjacent to Leroy Percy Park. Friends Warren Harper, Nolan Branton, Becky Wasson, and Sue Crowe took it upon themselves to finish the upstairs apartment post haste to get me out of the woods and moved into town as soon as possible. Nolan lent me period furniture to use along with an oil portrait of his great-great Uncle George, a noncommissioned officer of the Confederacy. Soon the job was complete, and I moved in one cold winter night with my two dogs.

It was a wonderful home, smelling of fresh paint and cypress and boasting new fixtures and wonderful old furniture. About three o'clock that first morning my Chesapeake Bay Retriever, Bud, started growling. As I rose up in bed, I saw the spring-loaded velvet rocking chair in my living room below Uncle George's portrait slowly rocking back and forth. The rocking lasted about five minutes and then stopped, and everything was calm, and we went back to sleep.

The next evening I was relaying that story to Nolan, and he said, "Uh, oh, Uncle George has found your house. He lives in a pier mirror out in the country in my house, and I didn't think he would follow his portrait, but he did. He won't harm you; just keep all his stuff together, and he will be fine." Uncle George had looked after the Branton Plantation and home and tried to hold the family together before and after the war according to Nolan. Many nights I could hear him walking up the outside steps and then the rocking would begin. Apple, my Aunt Pinkie's housekeeper and cook, told me to leave him a glass of whiskey by the chair, and he wouldn't bother me. So each night I did, but every now and then the chair would rock.

On April 17, 1982, the Finlay House was listed on the National Register of Historic

Places. She stood magnificent and proud and soon became the place to go for late night cocktails and revelry. During Greenville's much ballyhooed literary, cultural, and arts festival "The Time Has Come," the Finlay House became the repository for local photographers' and artists' exhibits, my sister Jane Rule Burdine and Bill Beckwith included. The guest book of attendees beams with names like Shelby Foote, Ben Wasson, Walker Percy, Hodding III, and Phillip and their mother Betty Carter, Beverly Lowry, Josephine and Kenneth Haxton, Bern and Franke Keating, Lee and Pup McCarty, among others. One could feel the house smiling, as once again she accommodated more people upon her shoulders than could possibly stand on the ground she covered.

And it was into this house that I brought my wife, Sallie Astor, in August of 1982. We lived there until we could rebuild our home on Lake Ferguson. Many quiet and splendid evenings were spent with friends on the upstairs gallery that overlooked the top of the levee as the sun slowly sank into the west. It was not long until fate struck again. Sandhawg Powell suffered an aneurism and passed away, and after Sallie and I moved into our new home on the lake, the Finlay House became vacant again.

However, it was not long before the South Delta Regional Housing Authority (SDRHA), a quasi-governmental agency funded mostly by HUD that helps provide housing for hundreds of Delta families, came knocking. Realizing this was an organization that had the capability to maintain such a house and uphold her heritage, reluctantly, I sold the Finlay House. A housing authority office was moved into the downstairs portion, and the upstairs was kept for entertaining and meetings. Repairs were made, and the outside was repainted. Her life continued.

Then, as before, fate lifted its head. An upheaval in the management of SDRHA came about, and the Finlay House was once again vacant. Several attempts were made to buy the house and move it away to a new location. All were denied. On July 13, 2009, the oldest and one of the most historic houses in Greenville was hauled away in a dump truck to a landfill. Her huge cypress beams crushed and smashed before anyone could salvage them. All this was done and directed by the hands of the executive director of SDRHA, with the knowledge of its board of directors.

A once grand home, old, yet graceful beyond her years, lives on in the hearts and minds of many that admired her, stood inside her, and enjoyed her hospitality.

Rest in peace, old Finlay House, you are missed.

Teddy's Return

Look around the Mississippi Delta; the surroundings and habitat have changed from what it used to be, but it's coming back. Where we now live in the Delta was once a swamp, possibly the most primordial, lushest, and deepest hardwood bottomland in the continental United States. The high ridges, riparian canebrakes, low willow sloughs, and cypress brakes were teeming with wild and dangerous animals. Alligators, garfish and snapping turtles, rattlesnakes and water moccasins, wildcats, panther, and bear abounded in the abundant and dense undergrowth. And beneath it all lay some of the richest land in the world.

Because of that sweet, rich, and fertile dirt, the swamp and bottomlands went the way of the ax and the crosscut saw. The logs were shipped to the screaming and steaming saw mills of Memphis, Vicksburg, Yazoo City, and Greenville. It wasn't long before the timber was gone and the land was broken with steel plows. It was then that cotton became king. The vast alluvial floodplain of the Mississippi and Yazoo Rivers was denuded. Gone were the big woods that Faulkner so often wrote about. The hardwoods had been cut and shipped to the markets of the East Coast, Chicago, and New Orleans. And along with the loss of the forests and canebrakes was the decimation of the habitat of the wild animals.

Once on the verge of extinction in the Mississippi Delta, the black bear population is on the comeback due to habitat restoration and public awareness.

Levees were built to control the annual flooding of the rivers. Drainage districts were formed to dig ditches and drain the bayous and sloughs. Bear and deer meat was plentiful to feed the hungry lumberjacks, along with the railroad and levee workers. Meat hunting and subsequently sport hunting took its toll on wildlife, especially the evasive bear. As the price of cotton went up, more and more pioneers packed up and moved into the Delta. The wildlife followed the slow yet rampant trek southward to the deepest part of the Delta, that area which annually flooded above Vicksburg. And it was in that region that the last Mississippi stronghold of the American black bear and the Louisiana black bear took its stand. By 1932 there were less than a dozen bears in the state of Mississippi. Due to continued land clearing for agriculture, 80 percent of the black bear's natural habitat of bottomland forests of the Delta had been cut, and only wide open cotton fields remained. However, today, there are certain parts of the Delta that are prime habitat for the natural re-introduction of the black bear.

As agricultural lands are reforested and protected through the Conservation Reserve Program (CRP) and Wetland Reserve Program (WRP) thousands of acres of prime bear habitat are being replenished throughout the Delta.

Black bear habitat must include a diversity of forested land types including dense escape cover, dispersal corridors between blocks of wooded areas, abundant and natural foods, water, and denning sites. Bears are known to use waterways as their travel routes within their home ranges connecting isolated blocks of forested land that are abundant in the Delta. The U.S. Fish and Wildlife Service has provided guidelines to the USDA Natural Resources Conservation Service in suggesting improved habitat on WRP/CRP tracts falling within designated black bear priority zones. One strategy is to provide a diversity of hard and soft mast trees in order to provide year round food availability. Oaks are planted along with black gum, paw paw, and persimmon trees. Overcup oak and cypress trees are planted in low-lying areas to serve as future den trees.

Black bears are extremely adaptable and historically have thrived in a variety of habitat types. A mixture of heavy and dense forest with shrub and openings located along natural water courses provide diverse natural foods and proper cover. Even though black bears are considered carnivores, they are not active predators but opportunistic feeders spending most of their time foraging and eating an abundance of plant life. In spring and summer, bears thrive on blackberries, pokeweed, wild muscadines, and paw paws. During the fall and winter, their diet consists of wild pecans, acorns, and hickory nuts along with soft mast bushes and leaves. Black bears have been observed rolling over fallen trees eating the colonial insects and beetle larvae found inside and underneath the hollow logs. Agricultural crops also play an important role in a bear's diet along with winter and spring food plots of oats, wheat, and clovers that have been planted for deer and turkey.

The availability of food and suitable habitat normally predicts travel patterns with males moving about in a much larger range for reproductive purposes. With wide and somewhat webbed feet, black bear are excellent swimmers, and even the Mississippi River is no obstacle in their travel patterns.

Black bears are hibernators, just not as deep as other hibernating creatures. Delta bears go into a period known as carnivorean lethargy or torpor. The primary purpose of this extended sleep is to survive food shortages and the extreme weather during winter months. Denning normally takes place between December and April. Dens can vary in location but mostly can be found in slash piles or logging debris, underneath fallen tree tops or in the hollow holes of standing cypress, Tupelo gum, or overcup oak trees.

Bears must den in order to give birth. After a bear gives birth in late January/early February, normally twins, the mama will keep her cubs with her throughout the following year and den with the cubs that year. During the next estrus cycle, she will run the cubs away to fend for themselves and breed for the next cycle. Little girl bears will often take up a home range close by their mother while the little boy bears will go off on their own looking for a date.

In 1976, the last documented breeding population of bears in the Mississippi Delta was in a wooded area of Issaquena County. The 4,300-acre tract was known to harbor five bears including two cubs. The land was cleared and converted to agriculture. Very possibly, this was the last reported concentration of black bears in the Delta. Occasionally, a lonesome male would be seen wandering around looking for a girlfriend dispersed from solid populations in other states.

However, because of conservation practices and habitat restoration, we now have breeding females within the Delta. Yearly sightings have occurred recently in Issaquena, Sharkey, Washington, Bolivar, and Coahoma counties. Some areas are harboring breeding bears that have established home ranges. The majority of bear sightings in Bolivar and Coahoma counties are in the proximity of the White River NWR and Big Island, a huge diverse hardwood ecosystem left mostly undisturbed on the Arkansas side of the Mississippi River. Bear sightings in Sharkey County are most common because of the proximity to the Delta National Forest and the adjoining Panther Swamp NWR. Other important bear areas in the Delta are the Dahomey NWR in Bolivar County and the Yazoo NWR in Washington County.

Today, along with the resurgence of suitable bear habitat, pertinent data being taken by skilled, professional biologists from MSU and MDWFP, and the increase in public knowledge and awareness, the historic black bears of the Mississippi Delta are on the comeback. Black bears are not aggressive and if seen, should be observed from a safe distance then reported to MDWFP. "Education has been a top priority with regard to management of black bears in Mississippi. In order for bears to make a meaningful recovery in the state, the public must be made aware of not only the existence of bears in Mississippi but also of bear biology and behavior."

In March 2015, I was allowed to go along on a bear tagging and re-collaring expedition with the MDWFP and research biologists from MSU on a large private hunting club adjoining the Mississippi River. We were to locate through radio telemetry a collared mama bear known to have had two cubs with her last year and a new set of cubs. She was located in her den and tranquilized. Her three baby cubs were then taken a short distance away for weighing, measuring and DNA sampling. Mama bear was constantly monitored and medically checked, weighed, measured and re-collared with a new battery operated device in order to be able to track her with GPS technology on a daily basis. In some instances, solar powered cameras are installed in the dens to be able to monitor in real time the bear's habits and cub-raising techniques.

We have come a long way in the Delta and are now one of the greatest fiber producing centers and bread baskets of the world, yet some areas of the Delta are being returned to the pristine and natural state that once flourished with game and wild animals. The bears are coming back!

The "Britchesless" Bachelor

In 1967 I was elected president of the Bachelor's Club. The Bachelor's Club was the group of eligible boys, a pool for the Delta Debs to draw on for dates to the assorted and sundry debutante parties scattered throughout the Delta. When Mimi Dossett's party was announced in Beulah, Tommy Barnes and I hooked up with Bland Shackleford and Kate Keating and made plans for the trip up country.

As was often the case in a family with older brothers, there was a ready supply of hand-me-down tuxedoes from which to choose. Since the one part of a tuxedo that was most readily destroyed in a fight—there were numerous bouts back then fought over winsome lasses—was the britches; they were in short supply. So when I got ready to go to the party, I had to wear my brother Jim's pants, which were about three sizes too small in the waist.

Picking up Bland and Kate, Tommy and I headed up towards Beulah. Around Scott, Mississippi, I was about to pass out because my britches were so tight; I just took off my cummerbund, undid my button, and unzipped my britches to give me a little breathing room. We had a great trip up old Highway 1.

Miss Carolyn Nye McGoy of Greenwood, Miss Kathleen Hand of Rolling Fork, Miss Anne Carrol Buntin of Greenville, Miss Sandra Stanton of Leland, Billy Hicks of Greenwood, Geren McLemore of Greenwood, Faison Smith, Jr., of Greenwood, Paul Montjoy of Greenwood, Wesley Watkins of Inverness and Otis Johnson, Jr. of Glen Allan.

Once we arrived at the Dossett Plantation, we drove down the long winding candlelight drive to the looming party with a long outdoor receiving line where we were met by eight to ten white-coated valets ready to open the car doors and help the ladies out and park the car. Bland was in a hurry, as the Budweiser had begun to take its toll on her holding tank, and she jumped out of the car before I could even stop. When the doorman opened my door, I just stood up and forgot that I had not put my too-tight britches back together, and my pants fell down to my knees! In the commotion I had also forgotten to put my car in park, and it took off down the driveway in front of the receiving line where fifteen blue-haired little ladies stood in awe as those white-coated servants chased my black two-door Pontiac Grand Prix with Tommy and Kate hanging half in and half out. I took one running step, my britches went to my ankles, and I fell flat on my face as Bland raced into the house in search of a bathroom.

Now, once the car was retrieved from the slough, and Tommy and Kate were safely extricated, we all regrouped and began our procession down the receiving line. "Yes, ma'am, how you doing? My mama is fine, thank you, so happy to see you..." and so on. We were almost at the end of the line when the band broke out in "Heard it Through the Grapevine," and Bland went to shaking and boogying. All of a sudden her left bosom shimmied out of her dress and just stood there quivering like jelly. Her sister Bebe screamed, "Bland, my Gawd," and Bland just nonchalantly reached over and tucked it right back in her top and went through the rest of the receiving line as if nothing happened.

Later, in the wee hours, Mr. Dixon Dossett invited a select few of us boys up to his gunroom where we drank good whiskey and told tall tales until dawn.

Epilogue

I met Hank Burdine through an act of journalistic subterfuge involving a dead deer. I had recently moved to a remote farm house in the Mississippi Delta, as an Englishman by way of New York City, and taken up the native custom of deer hunting. An urbane British magazine wanted to know why I had decided to become a hunter (oh, the barbarism!) and what it felt like to kill my first deer.

I wrote the story and made the case for killing your own organic meat, rather than buying the factory-farmed, hormone-injected stuff at the supermarket, especially when whitetail deer populations were so high and needed culling. I had no interest in trophy horns. I was strictly in it for the meat. The magazine accepted the story, and then the problem of photographs arose. I had killed the deer in question ten months previously. She was a big fat doe, and my girlfriend and I had just finished eating her with potatoes and gravy.

The magazine, despite its squeamish disapproval of hunting, told me to go out and kill another big fat doe, and the picture editor commissioned Jane Rule Burdine, a world-class photographer who lives in Taylor, Mississippi, to visually document the hunt, the butchering, the cooking and eating. A small, witty, thoroughly delightful and somewhat eccentric woman, Jane Rule arrived at my farm house wearing a camouflage outfit from the boys' section at Walmart with a red bandanna around her forehead and a blue one in her back pocket.

The following morning at first light, we had eight hunters on eight different deer stands, scattered across Pluto Plantation and nearby Stonewall, near the tiny hamlet of Thornton in Holmes County close to the hills. The hunters were all under instructions to kill a big fat doe and then call me, so I could come over there with Jane Rule and pose with the dead deer, as if I'd killed it. While we waited for the call, Jane Rule took photographs of me with a deer rifle pretending to hunt. Don't believe anyone who says the camera never lies. In my experience, the camera is far better at lying than revealing the truth.

Luck was not on our side that morning. None of the hunters saw a big fat doe, nor did they kill any deer. Jane Rule said she had a brother named Hank over by Lake Washington who was good at solving problems, and a mad keen hunter with a bunch of deer stands on his farm. She called him up and explained the situation, "We need a dead doe lying on the ground, and Richard here from London, 'Angland,' needs to pretend that he killed it." Just thirty minutes later Hank called back. I could hear his thick, raspy drawl through Jane Rule's phone, "Alright Sistah Baby, I've got your doe. You want me to drag it out in the field or leave in the woods?"

"In the field, I guess," she said. "That's where Richard killed his." We jumped into Jane Rule's vehicle and drove across the Delta. We counted hawks as we crossed the monochromatic winter landscape and had reached the number thirty-seven by the time we arrived at a little down-home restaurant on Highway 1 almost to the Big River, where Brother Hank was waiting for us. White-haired and white-bearded, with a ruddy complexion and that big raspy voice, he bought us lunch and started telling stories about the Mississippi Delta, and he soon had me weeping with astonished laughter over my fried chicken and stewed okra.

One of the things I love most about the Mississippi Delta is the culture of storytelling, and here was a true master of the art, with a treasure trove of material gathered and memorized over a lifetime. I remember one he told that day about a Chevrolet dealer who had a circus elephant named Susi and rode it into the Delta National Forest to go squirrel-hunting, and another about a black man who claimed to be so poor, all the while chomping on a two-dollar Duke of York cigar, that he didn't have eye-water to cry with. (Actually, John Johnson was his majordomo and dear friend, who stood beside Hank during his wedding.) That was the first of many times I should have just set down a recording device.

After lunch, we drove up to the house that Hank had built for himself by Lake Washington. It was the manliest house I had ever seen with a huge slab of cypress for a kitchen counter and a saucepan rack hanging from the ceiling on oversized heavy-duty black iron chains; the ticket counter from the old C&G Railway station was his bar, and he'd built his own bed out of 8x8 cypress beams, which struck me as the very mark of manliness. Then we got on a four-wheeler and roared off through the mud to the dead doe he had killed. I posed next to it and tried to summon that mixed feeling of pride and sadness I had felt, while Jane Rule lined me up in her camera sights. We hefted the deer on the back of the four-wheeler and butchered it at Hank's farm shop. I got far more of the meat than I deserved, and an additional four pounds of duck breasts because Hank Burdine is steeped in the Delta code of extreme generosity and militant hospitality. Then it was time for some drinks and more storytelling.

Hank and I became good friends. He taught me how to hunt ducks and took me hog-hunting, and passed along the lore and history of the Delta through his stories and his extensive library of books, sometimes leaning against the old C&G bar. He introduced me to Doe's Eat Place in Greenville, America's most idiosyncratic steakhouse. He became a regular fixture at the big, international, three-day parties that we would throw at our farmhouse near Pluto, with Brits, Germans, New Yorkers, Arizonans, New Englanders, Cajuns, and Mississippians, black and white all folded into the mix, all drinking and dancing together to live music and 33 rpm turntable sessions. Hank would always cook something—smoked Boston butts, duck poppers, Hoover duck, bullfrog legs marinated in champagne—and introduce the outsiders to the Mississippi Delta by telling wild crazy stories late into the night, of the sort that could never possibly happen anywhere else.

Hank Burdine is best appreciated live and direct with a Styrofoam cup full of ice and Scotch whiskey in his hand, salting his stories with oaths and accents, country slang and uproarious bursts of his infectious laughter. But he can also tell a wonderful story on the written page, and I'm glad that you got to spend some time with him and let him show you around the Delta that he loves so hard. There's no better guide to this twisted amalgamation of heaven and hell, this heat-blasted floodplain and open-air lunatic asylum, this proud and damaged crucible for so many great American artforms, than its native son and *raconteur par excellence*, Hank Burdine.

– Richard Grant